D0953556

Encounters with the Future:

Encounters with the Future:
A Forecast of Life into the 21ST Century

MARVIN CETRON
THOMAS O'TOOLE

McGRAW-HILL BOOK COMPANY

New York   San Francisco   Mexico
St. Louis   Toronto   Hamburg

1 2 3 4 5 6 7 8 9 D O D O 8 7 6 5 4 3 2

ISBN 0-07-010347-X

LIBRARY OF CONGRESS CATALOGING IN PUBLICATION DATA

Cetron, Marvin J.
    Encounters with the future.
    1. Twenty-first century—Forecasts.
I. O'Toole, Thomas, 1941–   . II. Title.
CB161.C4   303.4'82   81–20938
ISBN 0–07–010347–X   AACR2

Book design by Jerry Wilke

This book is dedicated to my future—my sons, Ed and Adam, and with love to Glor "14."
—Marv

This book is dedicated to Tommy, Owen, Ellen, and Peter, to whom the future belongs—and to my wife, Vitaline.
—Tom

CONTENTS

Introduction: The Next 20 Years *1*

1 Social Shock *19*

2 What If People Lived as Long as Trees? *45*

3 Energy Sources for Tomorrow *77*

4 The Crystal Globe—Which Nations Will Survive? *103*

5 Will There Be War or Peace? *137*

6 Religions of the Future *161*

7 There's Profit in Prophecy *185*

8 The Telecommunications Revolution *209*

9 Robotics—The Next Wave *231*

10 Jobs for Tomorrow *253*

11 The Space Program: Will It Fly? *273*

Epilogue: Telescoping the Future *293*

Index *301*

ACKNOWLEDGMENTS

▼▼▼▼▼▼

▲▲▲▲▲▲▲

*T*his book was written to offer to the general reader a picture of the future. It derives from forecasts previously available only to the government, the executives of a handful of large corporations, and other highly specialized organizations. The authors wish to acknowledge a large debt of gratitude to the present and former members of the Forecasting International staff. The following engineers, scientists, physicists, economists, anthropologists, historians, business majors, social psychologists and humanists all contributed greatly through their prior endeavors:

William Allen
Dr. Robert Anthony
Jay Arvai
Bonnie Ayres
Miriam Balaban
Eva Barkman
Dr. Charles Bartfeld
Leonard Bianchi
Ethelyn Bishop
Sandra Brown
Carol Burket
Edward Cetron
Roger Charin
Audrey Clayton
Sue Clayton
Lawrence Connor

James Duda
Monica Ecklof
Margaret Fisher
Dr. George Foster
Sue Gardner
Howard Gobstein
Bob Godec
Dr. Joel Goldhar
Mary Jo Guilda
James Hendry
Eric Huggare
Katheryn Humes
Dr. Jean Johnson
Michael Johnson
William Keasbey
Doris Lam

Carol Lane
David Lee
Amit Matri
Charles McFadden
Doreen McGirr
Dr. Anne Nelsen
Norman Nisenoff
Dr. Bruce Peters
Sue Richmond
Lew Roepcke
Marge Sorber
Sharon Sugarek
John Tipton
Arthur Weinberg

Other individuals also must not be overlooked, in particular those who assisted in gathering data and offering ideas for certain chapters: specifically, Rabbi Arnold Fink, Temple Beth El; Dr. David Scott, the Episcopal Church's Virginia Theological Seminary; Professor Philip J. Hitti, Princeton University; Dr. Charles Curran, Catholic University of America; Dr. John LaRosa and Marilyn Basford, both with the Coronary Prevention Clinic at George Washington Hospital; Dr. Karen Shanor, a psychologist and author working with WRC of NBC radio and television in Washington, D.C.; Dr. John Ellison, the National Defense University; Betty Lodewick and Gordon Smith from Miller and Smith Builders; Bill Lynch, a stockbroker with Dean Witter; Clyde Helms, president of Occupational Forecasting, Inc.; Al Hibbs, Jet Propulsion Lab; Frank Cotter, Westinghouse Electric; Congressman Tony Cuelho of California; Geoffrey Raisman, Oxford University, England; Solomon Snyder, Johns Hopkins University School of Medicine; Dr. Joshua Menkes and Dr. Patrick Johnson of the National Science Foundation; and Col. Larry Lodewick, U.S. Army.

We would especially like to thank Ann Buchwald for her encouragement and for keeping our respective noses to the grindstone during the preparation of this book. Last, but certainly not least, we particularly want to thank Gladys Justin Carr, editor-in-chief and chairman of the editorial board of McGraw-Hill, for her major editorial contributions, as well as Leslie Meredith, assistant editor.

This book was a joint venture between the president of a forecasting firm and a national reporter for the *Washington Post*. The first and final manuscripts were prepared by Susan McGuirk and Colleen Duffy of the Forecasting International staff. Proofreading and editorial comment were provided by Cathryn Acton, director of administration for Forecasting International.

For the encouragement and many contributions of these people we would like to express our sincere gratitude. Naturally, the authors accept responsibility for any errors of fact or logic that might appear.

INTRODUCTION: THE NEXT 20 YEARS

▼▼▼▼▼▼

*"The trouble with
our time is that the
future is not what it used to be."*

—Paul Valery

▲▲▲▲▲▲▲

*T*ime was when we grew up to do what our parents did, live where they lived, worship where they worshipped and think what they thought. Life was pedestrian but predictable. The accumulated wisdom of the present was adequate groundwork for the future, the past indeed was prologue to whatever lay ahead. *Que sera, sera.* What will be, will be.

That time is gone forever. To many of us today, the past seems immaterial and the present obsolete. Technology has so accelerated the pace of change that the future arrives faster every day, bringing with it the gnawing fear that the routine of daily living is no longer routine and may even be getting dangerously out of hand. We live in a time of such endless change that "anxiety attack" has become part of our everyday speech. More and more, we suffer a strong fear of what's next and an even stronger wish to know what it is. Put simply, we want to be in a position where we can at least start to forecast our own future.

There are still no workable crystal balls on our planet but we can do a lot more than cross the *t*'s and dot the *i*'s on the trends that shape the future. There are no mysteries involved. Psychics and astrologers need not apply. Part of the process is knowing what to look for. Still another part of the process is knowing what it is when we find it.

A striking example of dependable forecasting comes from one of the authors of this book, who grew up in Lebanon, Pennsylvania, not far from the chocolate factory in Hershey. Every morning, his next-door neighbor would

3

forecast the weather before the neighborhood kids went to school. "Better bring your boots." Nine times out of ten, it would snow if he said so. Everybody wondered how he did it. Even the weatherman on the local radio station never batted better than .500 predicting Pennsylvania's weather. "I can feel it in my bones," the neighbor used to answer when he was asked. Years later, his secret came out and it had nothing to do with his bones. He would wait until eight o'clock, when the morning train from Pittsburgh passed by on its way to Philadelphia. If the train's cars were wet, he'd predict rain. If the cars had snow on them, he'd forecast snow. Since the train always beat the prevailing winds blowing the weather eastward from Pittsburgh, our man in Lebanon wasn't taking too many chances with his forecasts.

An open mind helps in forecasting. "Minds are like parachutes," somebody once said. "They only work when they're open." Closed minds can never hope to forecast anything with accuracy, even if they stumble onto the truth. Many people who call themselves futurists work with closed minds or minds that are not fully open. Futurists predict we'll colonize space in 50 years even though the people in the space business know it would cost too much money and there's no need to do it. Futurists predict that solar energy will be the wave of the 21st century even though it's priced at almost twice what oil costs today. Their favorite prediction is that the billions of people on earth will someday unite under one government, one flag and one language. If anything, true forecasters will tell you, the world will be more divided in the years ahead as populations increase, resources dwindle and frictions rise. There is no way on earth that the world will unite in the foreseeable future.

Professional forecasting is not a game of chance. Nowadays, it involves the collection, analysis and synthesis of data, and extensive use of computers. It involves the

4

computer analysis of trends and "indicators," which are often obscure nuggets of information that tell you which way a trend is headed. An extraordinary example of an offbeat indicator and how it could have been used was the growing disparity between rich and poor in Iran during the shah's last years on the throne. By the time the revolution toppled the shah, the richest tenth of Iran's population was earning 38 times what the poorest tenth was making. The income gap between the highest and lowest tenth percentiles is an indicator of a nation's stability. Certainly, it should have told anybody in the forecasting business what to expect of Iran's future as far back as 1974, when the shah was still in power. It also proved Winston Churchill's point: "Men occasionally stumble over the truth but most of them pick themselves up and hurry off as if nothing happened."

The professional forecasting business is not brand new but it has matured dramatically since its infant beginnings at the start of World War II. As far as any forecasting historian can tell, it goes back to 1940 when the late Theodore von Karman was asked by the National Academy of Sciences to predict the future of jet and rocket engines. Von Karman predicted they had no future because there were no materials tough enough to stand up under their high combustion temperatures. Five years later, von Karman did another forecast for the United States Army and the fledging Jet Propulsion Laboratory and predicted 90 percent of what actually happened in the ensuing 20 years that it took to develop today's jet and rocket engines. In 1955, von Karman was asked what he did wrong in his 1940 forecast. "What I did wrong was I wrote it down." Forecasting grew as the Pentagon grew in the Cold War years of the 1950s and 1960s. It evolved in these years, as each military service told itself: Here's what our scientists say we know, here's what our engineers say they can build from what we know. What kinds of weapons can I make?

The huge C5-A transport plane was predicted as far back as 1961, when the air force got into the forecasting business in a big way. Two years later, the navy conducted a $2.7 million project code-named Project Forecast that is still the biggest forecast ever done in the U.S. Out of it came MIRVs (Multiple Independent Re-Entry Vehicles), laser weapon systems, and the Trident submarine. The air force followed up with a project called Over-the-Horizon that led to STEALTH and pulsed-beam weapons. At the same time, private industry was being drawn into the forecasting business. More and more, business leaders planning for the future were asking themselves: "Is it technically feasible? Is it economically feasible? If it doesn't cost too much, will the consuming public want it and will the government let me sell it?" Even today, these are the three basic concepts that guide professional forecasters. *Is it technically feasible?* Forecast whether I can make it or not. *Is it economically feasible?* Predict what it will cost to make and whether those costs are prohibitive. *Is it socially and politically acceptable?* Tell me if the government will let me sell it and if the consumer will buy it.

Today, there are more than half a dozen organizations in the United States that do professional forecasting. Data Resources, Inc. (a subsidiary of McGraw-Hill) and Chase Econometrics (owned by Chase Manhattan Bank) are both in New York. The Futures Group is in Glastonbury, Connecticut. The Stanford Research Institute and the Center for Futures Research of the University of California are in northern California. The Wharton School is a part of the University of Pennsylvania and Herman Kahn's Hudson Institute is located along the Hudson River 40 miles north of New York City.

Another is Forecasting International, a consulting firm in Arlington, Virginia, headed by one of the authors (Marvin J. Cetron) of this book. Its clients are a measure of how the forecasting business has grown. They include General Motors, Xerox, Volvo, Citibank, General Telephone & Electronics, Westinghouse, Occidental Petroleum, the Defense Department, the Department of Energy, and the National Aeronautics and Space Administration, as well as the governments of Israel, Yugoslavia, Sweden, Kenya and Brazil.

Does forecasting work? Six years ago we told business clients of Forecasting International to reduce their investments in Iran. Why? We saw that Iran was growing dangerously unstable. Matching 3,500 different trends and indicators against one another in hundreds of different combinations, our computer was cranking out the warnings. The Iranian rich were getting richer and the poor were getting poorer. Inflation was rampant and housing nonexistent. Unemployment was growing, especially among the newly educated young males. Just as important, the shah was losing contact with his people. We were being told that the shah had stopped payments to the mullahs (the clergy), who then began to cut themselves in for a share of receipts in the bazaars to make up their losses. The mullahs' loss was the shah's wife's gain. She began cutting herself in for a share of the government contracts the shah was letting to beef up his military machine. As proof that the shah had lost contact, the shah doubled the salaries of his military officers to buy their loyalty. All of these events were indicators of Iran's raging instability. Eleven of our clients listened and lowered their holdings in Iran, saving themselves as much as $500 million when the revolution came. Nine clients failed to heed the warnings and lost at least as much as the others saved.

Following the trends and the indicators, we predicted the unrest and instability in Poland, the coup d'etat in Turkey, the political changes in India and the warlike position of Iraq in the Persian Gulf a year before it happened. We forecast the Arab oil embargo of 1973 and the gasoline queues that followed the embargo. Long before they became realities, we predicted no-fault divorce, the graying of America, new living arrangements between the sexes and the rise of conservatism in America. We advised a cigarette client to manufacture a cigarette low in tar and nicotine before it caught on and urged one of Detroit's Big Three to build a small car before Toyota became a household word. How did we pick up on these trends? By watching the same trends develop years earlier in Sweden, the precursor nation, the bellwether of the rest of the world. For most of the 20th century, social change has come first to Sweden, then swept through the rest of Scandinavia before coming to America. Once here, social change most often starts in New York City, moves west to California, then on to Oregon, back across the country to the northeast corridor (the area from Boston to Washington), westward to Minnesota and Wisconsin, in all directions to the rest of the country and finally comes to the most conservative states, Alabama, Mississippi and Utah, the last three to effect social change.

The "new" American attitudes about sex and toward women have come from Sweden, where a feminist movement began back in 1932 when women started moving out of their traditional jobs as teachers and nurses into the rest of the workplace. Sweden had a social security program before we did; it had a paid-for health-care plan before Medicare. Sweden was first to outlaw the death penalty, first to insist on occupational safety, first with seat belts and padded dashboards in cars and first to consider consumerism as a legitimate social movement. Products listed their contents in Sweden long before they did in the United States. That's why we foresaw the day of the low-tar, low-nicotine cigarette in America. Sweden long ago ordered the tar and nicotine contents of cigarettes marked on cigarette packages, which led in Sweden to the production and consumption of lower tar and nicotine cigarettes. Their acceptance in Sweden convinced us they would be accepted in America.

In the next 10 years, Sweden will pass on to us things like paternity leave for new fathers, government-paid catastrophic medical insurance and free university education on a scholarship performance basis. Sweden's welfare system will be adopted here, which is welfare only for the disabled and the handicapped. Free universal day care for children will require that every able-bodied person work. Expect tougher laws on drunken driving. They were tested in Sweden and found effective. Sweden's emphasis on the rights of children is beginning to catch on here. A five-year-old Swede can decide which divorced parent he wants to live with. Older Swedish children (teenagers) can divorce parents they find inadequate, meaning they can get permission from the state to move away from their parents and in with relatives or friends who will welcome them. Some states will experiment with coed prison cells in the years ahead. Men and women in minimum security jails in Sweden share cells, if they both request it, where the practice has been found to raise morale and reduce tension and homosexuality among prisoners. Do you know what Sweden's answer has been to its problems with alien workers? Sweden decided to let aliens vote in local elections, a move that we think will be adopted in the United States. Alien voting rights make the alien workers feel more at home and make them more acceptable to resident citizens.

You have to go back to the end of World War II to know why we predicted the unrest in Poland. Like most European countries, Poland lost its heavy industry to the war. Unlike the rest, Poland did not modernize its factories and shipyards when it rebuilt. Poland stepped out from the postwar period on the wrong foot, using brand new 30-year-old machinery to compete with its thoroughly modernized neighbors. Poland quickly fell into debt, and to bail itself out, now owes Western banks almost $27 billion in hard currency. What's more, Poland wasn't built for communism, being far too headstrong and independent to follow an ideology as ironbound and centralized as communism. In Poland, local party leaders made decisions central party leaders should have made and vice versa. Local leaders decided they would make automobiles, ignoring the fact that they couldn't compete with Russian and European cars. Who approved workers' leaves? The Central Committee in Warsaw, not the local leaders.

There are intangibles in Poland's case. Most Poles have American relatives, who write them constantly telling them how good life is in the United States. Why are you still working six days a week? Americans only work five days and soon will be working four days a week. By the way, we're glad you're eating so well. The Polish hams you export are the best we've ever tasted. What? You only export those hams, you don't get to eat them yourselves? Meanwhile, the government raises food prices but doesn't raise wages and tightens the reins on the Catholic Church without knowing the world is about to get its first Polish pope. The election of Pope John Paul II is the straw that breaks the camel's back. Once again, the Poles are proud enough of their Catholicism that they want to show the world they're not afraid to strike out against what they perceive to be tyranny and oppression. Poles went to church again in droves to pray with a Polish pope and listen to their priests talk about God, not communism. Something else was happening in Poland. After years of controlling and censoring its press, the Polish government succumbed to pressure from the people and decided to let water seek its own level in the Polish press. The result was a flood of criticism of communism, the regime, high food prices, low wages and long work weeks. When our experts cranked the Polish pope and a free Polish press into their computer, the machine tilted and said "unstable" and "strike." Which is just what Solidarity, the world's largest organized labor force, did.

Forecasting the military takeover in Turkey did not come all that hard. Some of the same signs of instability showed up in Turkey that had cropped up in Iran. The Moslems were restless because of the inroads made by Western ways, there was no settlement with Greece over

Cyprus and the separation of rich and poor grew to where
the rich were earning as much as 35 times what the poor
earned. The key to the coup was political. The split between left and right grew wider, with no faction taking up
the slack in between. Leftists would kill rightists and
rightists would kill leftists on the streets of Ankara. The
strong Turkish army could take a widening gap between
rich and poor, it could take Western ways, it could even take
the lack of a victory in Cyprus but it could not take
political murder on the streets. The time came for the
army, which considers itself the repository of national
honor, to take over, which it did.

The rapid political changes in India that saw Madame
Gandhi in power, then out, then in prison and then back in
power again were not hard to foresee. India has no resources, too many people and not enough food. Only two
things about Indira Gandhi stand out today. She tried to
force sterilization on her people and she gave them an
atomic bomb, an act of her will that led the Export-Import
Bank and the German Bundesbank to withdraw their promise of $1 billion in loans that would have brought at least
some stability to her impoverished country.

The growing warlike stance of Iraq was not hard to
foresee either. New to oil wealth, Iraq began to wax strong
just as Iran was weakening in the last days of the shah, a
ruler who had staked Iran's claim to the Shatt-al-Arab
waterway at the end of the Persian Gulf. As soon as the
Ayatollah fired and executed the shah's generals, Iraq
moved into Iran in force and started a war it may never win.
Iraq's insistence on going ahead with its nuclear research
reactor outside Baghdad was easy game for our computer,
which knew all along that Israel would take a bellicose
view of its plutonium potential. We look for more trouble
from Iraq in the future. If the Iraqis don't win in Iran, they
may attempt a takeover of Kuwait on the western shore of
the Persian Gulf.

As difficult as it looks to Western eyes, the Middle East

is not all that impossible to figure out. In 1971, we were asked by the Common Market to look over the situation in the Middle East and come up with some predictions. The Arabs had just floated an abortive peace plan that the Israelis rejected, in part because they were still feeling like supermen after their lightning six-day defeat of the Arabs in the 1967 war. We looked at the Israeli rejection of the peace package, at growing Arab strength from its oil riches and growing European dependence on Middle East oil and sounded the warning fully 18 months before it happened. Beware of an interruption of oil deliveries by the Arab bloc, we said, and if there is an interruption it will not be just Western Europe that suffers. The outright support of Israel by the United States has never sat well with the Arab world, who this time around have taken notice of how much Arab oil is being pumped through American refineries. We came out and told anybody who would listen (there were not many) that there would be gasoline lines in the United States if there was another war in the Middle East. One veteran and important United States senator looked us in the eye and said: "Don't you understand that you can't deal with a crisis until it becomes a crisis."

One of the things we try to do in this book is forecast a crisis before it becomes a crisis. We also forecast trends and developments in fields as diverse as medicine and religion. We haven't taken our own computer's word for anything. We've checked its forecasts and spoken with experts as far apart (and as close together) as Jewish rabbis and Catholic priests. Before we sat down to write this book, we tried to ask ourselves as many questions as we could about what people want to know about the future. Will there be more Vietnams for the United States? More Afghanistans for the Soviet Union? How many countries will possess nuclear weapons? What will be the value of the world's currencies? What will a new car look like in the year 1990? Will I live longer than my parents? What are the chances of my being divorced? Will the energy crisis ever end? Will Reagan win a second term as president? How long will the Republicans control the Senate? Will interest rates ever come down? Is my job safe? Will we ever go back to the moon?

We don't pretend to know all the answers but the answers we think we know are here in black and white on the pages of this book. We're not futurists. We will not tell you what we would *like* to happen. We make predictions in this book that might not be pleasant to read but are based on solid fact. We're not astrologers either. There are no predictions in this book based on the way the tea leaves are arranged or the way the planets are positioned. We try our best to be rational and reasoning in our forecasts. Where we felt we didn't know the answers, we consulted others. We've tried to come up with an accurate forecast of the future. We think people want to know what it will bring.

Why is it important to be able to predict the future? Because times are changing so fast we can no longer prosper by ad-libbing responses to future events. A look at gasoline prices, dwindling bank accounts and soaring interest rates should be enough to convince anybody that we need better information about tomorrow and more help with tomorrow. Imagine for a moment that in 1970 you had known that small cars would soon be a must, that the average home would cost $75,000 and that the country's mobile population would soon be moving to the Sun Belt. Are there a few things you might have done differently if you had known these things? At the least, you might have saved yourself some free-floating anxiety. At the most, you might have made a start on your personal fortune.

Aren't there a few hundred things about the next 20 years you'd like to know? Money, for instance. Having enough money will continue to be a major preoccupation of most Americans until 1995 or 2000 when the successful demonstration of fusion begins to drive energy prices down. Gasoline will double in price in the next 10 years but there won't be rationing in the United States unless Middle East oil is interrupted again the way it was in 1973. Cars will be made of plastic, weigh half what they do today and get twice the mileage they do today. How do we know that? The substitution rule. That's the rule that says that one thing will replace another if it's cheaper, safer or does the job better. Cars are already almost half plastic and once a substitute material reaches the halfway mark it almost always goes to 90 percent or better. It happened that way with margarine and butter, water-based paints and lead-based paints, coal and wood, oil and coal, artificial sweeteners and sugar. In cars, the first thing we substituted was the synthetic rubber for tires, then we put plastics inside the car and took out the cotton and wool upholstery, then we put in vinyl dashboards. Next were the bumpers, then engine parts made of heat-resistant and high-impact plastic. Next will be the body and the frame and finally the engine itself. By 1990, cars will be 92 percent plastic.

In this book, we forecast events and trends right across the board. We forecast social trends, political trends, even sexual trends. We predict what the price of oil will be in the year 2000. We tell you what to expect from nuclear power, solar power, wind power and fusion power. We even tell you where the United States will bury its radioactive waste. We talk about the new drugs you can expect to treat disease, the new vaccines you can expect to prevent disease. We discuss gene splicing, the need for coronary bypass surgery and the chances for artificial blood and the artificial heart. We talk about the inflation rate out to the year 2000 and what Congress might do about extending President Reagan's new tax-free policy on all-savers certificates. Should people change their stock market strategy in light of Reagan's new tax plan? We tell you whether they should.

Beyond Reaganomics, we go into the workings of the world's two fastest growing religions. We tell you whether Catholic priests will ever marry or whether women will ever become Catholic priests. We discuss the future of homosexual priests, ministers and rabbis. We talk about the future for women rabbis. We bring up Confucianism, one of the world's oldest and most interesting religions. We talk about how the Pentagon will use cameras in space and how the space agency will use a camera in space called the Large Space Telescope that will see 14 billion years back through time and more than halfway to the edge of the universe.

Will there be war or peace in the next 20 years? There will be war *and* peace. Unhappily, there have always been wars. Happily, we do not believe there will be an all-out nuclear war in the next 20 years. We talk about the office of the future where talking machines do some of the work and listening machines do some of the work and stenographers and typists are almost a relic of the past. We talk about jobs of the future where new job titles like laser technician and robot technician replace titles like tool and die maker and machinist. We discuss the new and somewhat eerie era of the robot when machines that have eyes and ears and arms and hands take over entire assembly lines. The robots are coming because they don't take coffee breaks, don't ask for raises and don't go on strike. Don't be frightened by these robots. They don't mate—at least not yet.

Though much of what lies ahead may appear to be downbeat, we look at the future through upbeat eyes. There will be fewer people living in poverty once welfare practices are reformed and new social reforms are made late in this decade. We think the richest Americans will be entertainers and professional athletes, whose incomes will grow ever larger through the medium of cable television. We think that artists who can create something original will be more richly rewarded. So will writers, and garbagemen who can recycle goods in a world slowly losing its natural resources. There will be shorter workweeks, 32 hours a week by 1990 and 25 hours a week by 2000. Flexible schedules will be the rule, with two or three people sharing a job and arranging their shifts. Robots will take over the hardest, most stifling tasks in the factory. Unions will become less important to blue-collar workers and more important to white-collar workers. People will retire later as they live longer, taking an active role in the workplace to ages 70 and 75.

Harder to predict are the social and political changes of the next 20 years. America is definitely in the grip of a new conservatism that will probably last until 1988. The social changes of the last 10 years will not be reversed but neither will there be much new change. In a sense, the pendulum is swinging back but it is a Hegelian swing. It will not swing *all* the way back. The United States of the next seven years will be a lot like Sweden of the last seven when the Swedes called a halt to social change and made new commitments to nuclear power and the gross national product instead of gross national happiness. There will be a new approach to welfare. Americans are sick of welfare waste and welfare fraud.

The baby boom is over and will stay that way for the foreseeable future as the ranks of young single people continue to rise and defer marriage or don't even choose it. Even those who choose marriage are limiting the size of their families to one and two children and will continue to do so. People will continue to want a more convenient life-style, women will continue to want more freedom and, let's face it, very few can afford large families anymore. At the same time, the nation's senior citizens will live longer as they continue to get better health care. Gray power is what you can expect to see more of in the future. The elderly are a mounting political force. At the turn of the century, there will be more than 30 million old folks in the United States.

There will be more divorce because people will no longer regard a first marriage as their only marriage. Many states will have no-fault divorce. More Americans will take three spouses in life, the first for romance, the second for children and the third for companionship. More women will initiate divorce just as they will initiate more premarital and extramarital sex. More people will live together in trial marriages. More elderly men and women will move in together without making the legal move of getting married.

There will be a morning-after birth-control pill for women and a birth-control pill for men. More single women will elect to have children and more women will act as surrogate mothers for women who cannot have children. Sex will never be the bugaboo it was for our parents and grandparents. Liberal attitudes about sex are here to stay.

In this book we make no moral judgments. If we say that divorce is on the rise and that men and women may take as many as three wives and husbands during their lives we're not saying that because we'd like that to happen. We're saying it because the trends of the times are predicting it will happen.

Despite the problems and perils of the human condition, our book forecasts that most of the world's people will go right on improving their lot. The blind will get technological help to see and the deaf to hear. Paraplegics will walk away from their wheelchairs as research begins to prove that spinal cord injuries are reparable. Tendons and ligaments will be regenerated, there will be vaccines against dental decay, hepatitis, gonorrhea and some cancers. Lasers will perform brain surgery now considered impossible, there will be cures for drug addiction and the creation of nonaddictive painkillers more powerful than morphine. There will be medicines that cure phobias. Fear of heights, crowds, strangers, elevators, closed-in places, even fear of flying will be phobias of the past. There will be drugs to improve learning and even memory. Our forecasts in health and medicine will be aided by close observation of pharmaceutical research around the world. Foreign drug firms are often three years ahead of American firms because they don't have to answer to a Food and Drug Administration that enforces strict regulations on the development and testing of new drugs. In the pages that follow, we predict that we shall all be feeling better in the years ahead. Children born in 1982 will have life spans of eighty-three years. The time is not far off when people will live as long as trees.

1
▲▲▲▲▲▲▲

SOCIAL SHOCK

▼▼▼▼▼▼▼

"Only the supremely wise
and abysmally ignorant
do not change."

—*Confucius*

▲▲▲▲▲▲▲

*N*o matter how old you
are in the year 2000, profound change will have been
written into your life by the time you start the 21st
century. Today's children, teenagers, young adults, the
middle-aged, men and women in their fifties and sixties—it
doesn't matter who you are today. None of us will be the
same when the century turns. If the dramatic change of the
sixties is not in the air these days, do not for one minute
think that change is not on its way. It may not be sudden, it
may not seem deep, it may not even look like change when
it comes but change is as sure a part of our future as death
and taxes.

Think back to the sixties. Who could have predicted
the Beatles? Could anyone have forecast the sixties, the
decade that gave us hair, hippies, communes and drugs?
The decade when college students burned their draft cards
and their universities, the decade of Lyndon Johnson and
America in Vietnam, when tear gas was used in American
cities, when there were police riots and Kent State and
"Beat the Press" made the headlines from a political
convention in Chicago and when the Pentagon was trashed
and priests spilled their own blood on draft records in towns
like Catonsville.

The sixties were when nuns took off their habits, when
a lot of other women took off their lipstick and brassieres,
when a magazine named *Playboy* spawned dozens just like
it in an age of nudity and sexual freedom spawned by the

21

Pill. The feminist movement took hold and so did the civil rights movement that began with marches in places like Selma and fires in places like Watts. There was a price to pay for such progress. Martin Luther King was martyred for his cause and a president and his brother were assassinated. There is no question about it. Whatever else they were, the sixties were symbols of change unlike any other decade in our history.

If it can be said that we marched through the sixties, then it must be said that we sneaked through the seventies. The Vietnam war ended, which was about all there was to remember. Outside of men landing on the moon, there was little to be proud of. Ours was a country mired in Vietnam and wallowing in Watergate. The pendulum had swung a little too far in the sixties, and it was time for it to swing back in a more Hegelian fashion as successive swings brought it back a little more toward center. People were tired of change, they were sick of protest. It was time to take a national rest, to take inventory of where we had been and where we were going. A conservative mood gripped the nation, peaking in Ronald Reagan's landslide defeat of Jimmy Carter. It was not an accident that the Equal Rights Amendment, the Voting Rights Act and the Fair Housing Bill stalled in the seventies. People were not ready for them.

By the time Ronald Reagan became president, the country had already swung through a change of image. Country clothes and blue jeans were out. Three-piece suits, white shirts and rep ties had returned. The preppie look was back. Bumper stickers appeared: "Save an Alligator. Kill a Preppie." Lipstick was back on women's mouths about the same time that blondes returned, not all of them original. College fraternities reappeared, in part because individuals were beginning to reassert themselves. The mass movements, social actions and larger causes that had occupied college students in the sixties and part of the seventies had lost their meaning to the students of the eighties.

So quickly did the country want to forget Watergate

that it was once again fashionable to be Republican. Clearly, America was in the grip of a new conservatism that appeared to have a lasting power of its own. Today's high-schoolers are closer politically to their parents than they are to their older brothers and sisters. They think it's cool to have a job, chic to make money and boss to drive a fast car. They're backing away from hard drugs and liquor and using softer drugs, like marijuana, and softer drinks, like beer. Trouble is, from a look at beer sales around the country, they're drinking too much beer. In a way, things are much as they were in their parents' teenage years. Students are swelling the ranks of the engineering schools, just as their fathers did a quarter of a century ago. If any prediction can safely be made about the next six or seven years, it is that the United States will stay conservative out to 1988 when Ronald Reagan must vacate his office. While it is safe to say that the social change of the last 10 years will not be reversed, it is just as safe to say there will not be too many new changes in the years just ahead. Once again, the pendulum will swing back and forth but it will swing in the Hegelian way that slows the swing down from time to time.

SWEDEN,
THE BELLWETHER NATION

Sweden underwent in the fifties some of the same social changes the United States took on in the sixties. Unmarried men and women routinely lived with each other in Sweden long before they did in the United States. My "sambo," the Swedes call their live-in lovers. Some Swedish social change is slower than other change to reach the United States. Swedish women have been paid the same as Swedish men for years. American women are still not paid the same as American men. Sweden is now in the midst of a conservatism that began in

1975 when the Swedes made new commitments to nuclear power at the same time the United States was turning its back on atomic energy. While there are signs that Sweden may be about to break out again in change, the Swedes have more or less called a halt to social change for the last five or six years. Don't forget, Sweden is the bellwether nation. Sweden has no rich and no poor and suffers almost no unemployment. It has no rich because it taxes up to 87 percent of one's income, driving its talented and highly paid entrepreneur filmmakers and film stars and athletes to seek tax havens elsewhere. At the same time, Sweden is a remarkably stable country. It does not export arms, it exports money. Its industrial products are coveted the world over. Expect the United States to look more and more like Sweden in the next seven years.

We can expect further Swedish social change to make it across the seas to the United States in the next 10 years. Sweden's emphasis on the rights of children is one example. A five-year-old can already decide with which divorced Swedish parent he wants to live. Older Swedish children can divorce parents they do not want to live with. A new Swedish law prohibits parents from spanking their children. Why is Sweden so far ahead of the times? Swedes say it's not that they're so far ahead, it's just that we're so far behind. They say we have too many lawyers, who do not contribute to progress and whose inclinations force them to delay endlessly and debate change when it appears. The Swedes practice what they preach. While there are lawyers and judges in Sweden, they are far fewer per capita than they are in the United States. No-fault auto insurance, no-fault divorce and compulsory arbitration in business lessen the need for lawyers in Sweden. In the Swedish parliament, there is only one attorney and he is the consumer ombudsman for the Swedish people. Swedish lawyers do not make Swedish laws. Their laws are made by the representatives of parliament, who come from almost every walk of life but the law.

In the years just ahead, Americans can expect such Swedish exports of social change as paternity leave for fathers, government funding for college scholarships on a performance basis and the start of a federal program to pay for catastrophic medical insurance. The reason for paternity leave is simple. There will be a continued blurring of the roles of marriage partners, with more fathers taking care of children while the mothers work. Free college education is further away but the soaring costs of university tuitions make it almost impossible for most Americans to afford college for more than one child. This almost certainly means that the United States will follow Sweden's example and pick up more of the tab. The backbone of the United States is its upwardly mobile and overachieving middle class. The federal government must do something to strengthen that backbone.

Catastrophic medical insurance is an idea whose time may have come. Even the Chinese recognized the importance of paid medical insurance, paying their doctors only if their assigned patients are well. Called prophylactic medicine, it's like putting the doctors on retainers. Not only is catastrophic medical insurance already in place in Sweden, it is on the books in Norway, Denmark and Finland, accepted as one of life's expectations through all of Scandinavia. One way to watch for Swedish change in the United States is to see how it does in the rest of Scandinavia. If it does well in the rest of Norseland, it will almost surely be accepted in the United States. What do we mean by catastrophic medical insurance? We mean the kind of insurance that saves you from financial ruin in the case of a single serious illness or injury, so that a heart attack will not put you in the poor house nor a car accident leave you hopelessly in debt.

We find that Americans are sick of welfare cheaters and welfare waste and fraud. In Sweden, only the disabled and the handicapped are on welfare; everybody else works; they even baby-sit or aid teachers at a day-care center when mothers and fathers are at their job. Welfare mothers, women who bear more children to collect more welfare, do not exist in Sweden. The time is coming when they won't exist in America.

Every study on welfare states has drawn the same conclusions. The first generation to take welfare feels bad about it—they're embarrassed to be on welfare. The second generation is no longer embarrassed by their status; they saw their parents get welfare and they expect it themselves. The third generation is the permanent welfare generation. Not only do they expect it, they want more. These are the recipients who have lost their self-esteem, who feel needed only if they have more children, if all they are raising is another generation of people on welfare. Our studies show that the U.S. will break the welfare habit. There will be major changes in the distribution of welfare in the United States.

THE GRAYING OF AMERICA

One change will come in the way Uncle Sam takes care of the elderly, one of the fastest-growing age groups in the country. The baby boom is over and the ranks of young single people are on the rise as more of them defer marriage or simply don't choose it. Even those who choose it limit the size of their families to one and two children. They want a more convenient life-style, the women want more freedom and many simply can no longer afford larger families. There was a time when there was a need for larger families: People needed the extra income that working children brought in, many lived on farms and needed the help and parents looked on children as financial security for their old age. No longer. Large families are anachronisms these days. They don't fit in.

At the same time that family size is shrinking, the

nation's senior citizens have begun to live longer. Gray power is what you can expect to see more of in the future. The elderly are a wise and sophisticated political force. The rising number of elderly in the United States is no longer a social prediction, it's fact. From fewer than 21 million in 1972, the ranks of people over 65 grew to 23 million in 1978 and will stand at 25 million by 1983. Their numbers will continue to rise. By 1995, the elderly will number almost 29 million and at the turn of the century there will be more than 30 million old folks living in the United States. The graying of America is something you can see in labor unions. The average union member is 51, in part because the youngsters aren't joining unions and in part because so many workers are aging. Memberships of unions will decline dramatically to the point where major political parties will be able to ignore their impact at the voting booth.

One reason senior citizens are living longer is because they're getting better health care. The trouble is, their social security checks aren't enough to pay for health care any more. What savings they've managed to keep are crunched by inflation. What's the answer to this new dilemma? The government can't help the country to kick its welfare habit by cracking down on young people drawing welfare if it turns around and creates a new class of old people on welfare. Neither can it afford to turn its back on this powerful new group of needy people. The elderly represent a strong voting bloc that will only get stronger in the years ahead. You've heard of the Black Panthers? Get ready for the Gray Panthers. Something must be done to provide reasonably priced health care to senior citizens.

MORE CONSERVATIVE VICTORIES IN 1982

We are forecasting at least six more years of conservatism in America. Gray power will be squarely behind the conservative movement. Ronald Reagan is more than just a symbol to our senior citizens—he's a hero. Older people want to be part of a constituency, they don't want to be pushed aside. And they want special treatment like geriatric foods and drugs and geriatric entertainment. They want to be treated like real people, have sex together and even live together without benefit of marriage as their grandchildren do today. Reagan is a symbol to the elderly, and their support will be an important element of Reagan's continuing success.

Count on another conservative victory in the congressional elections of 1982. The Democratic majority in the House could fall from the 51-seat edge the Democrats have now to as little as 40 in 1982. The Republicans will at least maintain their six-seat edge in the Senate, could even improve it to eight. Barring an unexpected breakdown of his health, Reagan will be back in the White House for four more years in 1984. His conservative politics will continue to stifle change in America but there will be growing resistance to his cutbacks in social programs. Angered by the fact that the Equal Rights Amendment did not pass before the 1982 deadline, the feminists will become a revitalized political force. So will civil rights activists, disillusioned with the slow passage of the Voting Rights Act and the Fair Housing Bill and angry over the way Reagan downgrades racial quotas and busing to achieve school balance as he upgrades the importance of the death penalty and tougher legislation on crime.

DEMOCRATIC CONTROL BY 1988

Slowly but surely, however, the pendulum will begin to swing away from conservatism. Barely surviving a Republican challenge in 1984 to control the House, the Democrats will make enough gains in 1986 to regain decisive control and narrow the Republican margin of control in the Senate. By 1988, the Democrats once more will hold the balance of power in the House and Senate and will elect their own president. The forces of change will be back in power. That's the way things work in America.

One force that will bring back the Democrats in 1988 will be one of the same forces that turned them out of office in 1980. Gradually, the elderly will grow disillusioned with Republican welfare policies, especially the refusal to put more money into public housing so older people can live near available transportation services, and the refusal to support public cable television. Cable television will become extremely important to older people. Its services will include at-home shopping and medical diagnoses essential to older people too ill or otherwise unable to get to stores and clinics because the weather is bad. The cable will be a social lifesaver for the elderly, providing necessary services and specialized entertainment. Programs about shopping, health, diet, exercise, how to live on a fixed budget and what to expect from aging will be universally available by 1990. The Democrats' offer of public support for the cable will help bring them back in 1988.

The extremes of conservatism will also help to turn the Republicans out of office by 1988. The abortion issue will no longer be so important because of the extreme attempts to defeat it by the right wing. The Moral Majority will no longer be a household word for the same reason. The right-to-lifers will be banished by the right-to-selfers. Most people will reach a conclusion that goes something like this: "Look, we've worked too hard for our personal freedoms. People have a right to liberal attitudes about their own bodies and their own happiness. If you want to turn your personal clock back, go right ahead but leave me alone and leave me out of it."

CABLE CONNECTIONS

Cable television will be a major social force out to the turn of the century. By 1986, the cable will be in more than half of America's households, where as many as 80 subscription channels will offer about 30 different round-the-clock programs. By 1990, the cable will touch all parts of human life: It will allow students to attend school three days a week, letting them learn at home on the other days over two-way television. Programs for young school children will be like "Sesame Street" and "The Electric Company," except that teachers and students will be able to interrupt the programs. Over-the-air broadcasters will have settled their copyright disputes with cable operators, who will end up paying small copyright fees for over-the-air programs. The winners will be the viewers, who will get clearer color reception and limitless program variety. At-home viewers will be participants in live television quiz shows as more than half of America's households subscribe to two-way cable by 1990. At-home banking over the cable will make its appearance. So will computer-assisted instruction and personal bookkeeping. The cost of watching movies, live entertainment and sports events over the cable will continue to decline, forcing down attendance at theaters and stadiums.

Satellite interconnection of regional cables will make it economical to offer nationwide programs of limited appeal, like a Shakespeare festival played by university drama groups. After 1990, personal selection of plays and movies will be possible. When a prescribed number of requests for a program is received, the program will be transmitted during off hours, recorded on a home video machine priced below $200 and played back by an individual viewer at his or her convenience. People who want them will get their X-rated movies this way so that people who don't want them won't have to watch them.

Money will be more important than ever in the years

ahead. Having enough money will continue to be one of the highest priorities of most Americans until the successful demonstration of fusion power begins to drive energy prices down. Cars will cost almost twice what they do today even though they'll be made mostly of plastic and weigh half what they do now. There will be a luxury tax on these new plastic cars, whose lifetimes will double in the next 20 years as more people value durability. Expect no more than an eight percent per year inflation rate starting at the end of 1982 out to the year 2000, with interest rates stabilizing at no more than 11 percent. Variable rates will catch on, where the interest on mortgages stays the same for three years before moving up again with the consumer-price index. Tight money will create a pent-up demand for housing that won't be relieved until 1990 when technology will force major changes in prefabricated housing techniques that will lower housing costs. Homes will be built at the factory in modules, one for the bathroom, a second for the dining room, a third for the family room and so forth. The modules will be erected on site in a matter of weeks. The rage in the suburbs, especially in the South and West, will be efficiency houses with no garage, no basement to heat and maintain.

Before 1990 arrives, housing will be so expensive that college-age children will opt to study near home so they can live at home and have their own cars. Divorced single parents will have to move themselves and their children right in with *their* parents, simply to save money. By 1990, we expect that as many as nine percent of American households will be made up of families that include three generations. Parents won't be deliriously happy about that, thinking perhaps: "Look, we raised you once, do we have to do it again?" Group housing will be a substitute for moving back in with the parents, with divorced friends sharing a home with two sets of children. Fully four percent of American households will be "unattached" households by 1990. These are households where people live who are unrelated by blood, marriage or even love interest. The other alternative will be to let the children move in with friends and pay the friends' parents for their room and board. This might become the American alternative to the Swedish idea of having children choose which divorced parent they'd like to live with.

TAX REFORMS

We shall soon enter a checkless, cashless society. Only diehards will use cash, paying a penalty for the privilege because cash will require special handling, a cash register, a safe and all the worry and concern those things entail. Funds will be transferred by voiceprint. Nobody with a voiceprint identification card or number will have to shop in person. Dial a store through your two-way television at home or in the office, check prices on your screen and order by credit card or checking account number. The merchant will push a button that lights up green if you have the funds in your account, red if you don't and yellow if you're in the process of transferring funds to your account.

There will be fewer millionaires as tax reforms are finally made; there will also be fewer people living in poverty as new kinds of jobs open up and hiring reforms are made when the Democrats return to power in 1988. The richest people in America will be entertainers and professional athletes, who will be in such demand because of cable television that their incomes will be three times what they are today.

Salaries will begin to equalize, as they have in Sweden, where nobody makes more than two and one half times what anybody else makes. By 1990, the percentage of Americans making less than $10,000 a year will drop from the 34 percent it is today to 29 percent. The lowest-paid semi-professional and professional Americans will continue to be policemen, firemen and schoolteachers. There will be 32-hour workweeks by 1990 and 25-hour workweeks by 2000. Work schedules will become flexible, with people sharing the same jobs and arranging their shifts among themselves. Unions will shrink in size and become less important to blue-collar workers as corporations become more benevolent and arrange new fringe benefits like group auto and home insurance for their employees. Once again, the pattern for such change began in Sweden where Volvo, Saab and SKF instituted these changes.

THE FUTURE LOOKS SOUTH

People will retire later as they live longer, taking an active role in the workplace until age 70 and 75. This will rescue the nation's social security plan because more people will be putting money into Social Security. People will also phase into retirement instead of doing it abruptly. The emotional savings of gradual retirement will be enormous. Taxes will go down for most people and the prices of most stocks will rise as America reindustrializes and increases productivity mainly by moving into robotics. The energy crisis will be a cause of social concern until 1995, when breeders start to generate large amounts of nuclear electricity and fusion power is demonstrated for the first time. Solar energy will be a sun-sized social disappointment. Solar-powered buildings will be looked on as the windmills of the 21st century. Most energy sources, except for automobile engines, will continue to pollute the air. More cars will be electric and those that are not won't pollute as much because they'll be so much smaller than today's cars. Cars will be safer because they will *all* be smaller. According to the National Transportation Safety Board, the worst accidents are between big cars and little cars.

A major social force out to the year 2000 will be the stepped-up migration to the Sun Belt. More and more Americans of all ages will follow the sun and go where the jobs will be going. American business is no longer interested in expanding to places like upstate New York and Minnesota. The future looks south. The only thing that will restrict mass migrations to the Sun Belt is a shortage of resources, especially water. A massive shortage of water will be one of the major social and political issues of the 1990s. Population growth in Colorado, Arizona, New Mexico, California, Utah and Nevada could screech to a halt because of water shortages, which will become so severe in the 1990s there could be "water wars" between the western states. Look for much of the world to suffer water shortages. Look for Saudi Arabia to build nuclear power plants just to remove the salt from the waters of the Persian Gulf. Look for Israel and Jordan to build a canal from the Mediterranean to the Dead Sea to help solve their water shortages and look for the United States to recycle as much as 35 percent of its water and begin the practice of towing glaciers out of the Arctic to East and West Coast ports where they'll be tapped for their water.

The glaciers will serve a second purpose. They'll be used as floating islands where the country can locate breeder power reactors, using the melting glacial ice to cool down the reactors while they produce enough electricity to light up entire coastal regions. The melting ice will have a third use. The uncontaminated thousand-year-old water condensing out of the glacier will be more sought after than Perrier water, which after all comes out of the ground and not a virgin mountain of Arctic ice.

There are potential water disasters looming ahead. As more underground rivers dry up in states like Colorado and California, more land will collapse unexpectedly to fill in the voids. Sinkholes like those in Florida that swallowed buildings and streets will become more commonplace until communities find ways to detect and prevent them before they happen. There is a major water catastrophe ahead for the city of New York, one whose precursor took place last year for the city of Newark in New Jersey. Vandalism caused the collapse of an old aqueduct that carried water from five major reservoirs to the 350,000 people of Newark. It won't necessarily be vandalism in New York that causes a far worse catastrophe. The aging viaducts that have transported New York's water for the last 75 years have never been shut down for maintenance and repair. They are all in disrepair and if even one of them should fail, New York City would face a water shortage unlike anything the arid West might run up against. New Yorkers would have to start collecting rainwater. The National Guard would have to be called out to run water into the city the way the Allies flew in food during the Berlin airlift.

Because it has enough water and because it is more adaptable to change, Texas will be the only Sun Belt state to enjoy relatively unrestricted growth in the years ahead. Texas is also more acceptable to business, which is attracted by the friendly attitudes toward business in Dallas and Houston. South Carolina, Georgia, Alabama and Mississippi will never be full beneficiaries of migration to the Sun Belt because they are too slow to change and the jobs won't move there in the droves needed to attract the new migrants. In contrast to the other Sun Belt states, Florida will undergo still another boom-and-bust, mostly because the elderly will continue to choose Florida for their retirement homes and discover they can't afford it because their savings and Social Security checks won't be enough to cover inflation. Again, the elderly will have to delay their retirements so they can support themselves against inflation. "Late" retirement is already happening in Japan, where Datsun and Toyota are asking their workers to delay retirement until they're 70 years old. The Japanese have a special worry in this regard. Between 20 and 25 percent of Japan's work force will be retiring at 80 percent of their salaries between 1985 and 1990. Toyota no longer gives pay increases to people over 40 on grounds that it would not be able to afford their retirement. Japan will be hard pressed to afford so many retirements when they come.

There will be another trend at work here. Americans who retired in their fifties because it was a popular and trendy thing to do have discovered they don't like it. The idle pensioners were just that, people who collected early pensions and became quickly bored by their new idleness. Elderly people will no longer mind working past 65. Their friends will be doing it and they will be doing it to keep busy and stay mentally healthy.

CITIES THAT ARE
TOO OLD

Even as the Sun Belt swells with people, the nation's oldest cities will be emptying out. Suburbs continue to grow because people will not return to the cities, whose older buildings are too expensive to heat and, even worse, whose older mass transit systems will not run on time. New York City is the classic case of the city becoming a dinosaur, no longer able to care for itself. New York City lost more than 10 percent of its population in the last 10 years and could lose another 10 percent in the next 10 years, leaving Gotham with less than 6.5 million residents. Never again will there be 8 million stories in the Naked City.

New York City is nearing a crossroads. We think that because federal policy will look with favor on cities for their energy-saving ways of life, New York will struggle through to the end of the century. We think New York's rate of population loss will slow down at the same time its unemployment rate declines, thereby saving the city. But if anything, life in the city will be harder than it is today. Crime will continue to grow. We expect constant conflict among ethnic groups and between the city and its unions.

Demands for pay raises will trigger a new rash of municipal strikes. Parks will deteriorate and museums close down or curtail their hours. Parochial schools will become schools for minorities, especially Hispanics. The New York Stock Exchange will move to New Jersey, but enough corporations will stay behind to ensure the city's viability. National attitudes toward the city will remain essentially neutral, meaning they will be neither hostile nor eager to help it in time of need. By 1995, the city will be diminished in size and influence but will still have much to offer. The future of the city of New York will continue to depend on the willingness of its private and corporate residents to make sacrifices in its behalf.

More cities than New York will lose people. Chicago, Detroit, Cleveland, St. Louis, Philadelphia—they're all examples of cities that are too old. Young people won't move there because they cost too much. The middle-aged move out because there's too much crime, squalor and congestion. The elderly won't move back because they can't get around on the ancient mass transit systems. Nothing these cities try to do seems able to reverse the trend. If they raise the income tax, the employers move elsewhere. Pass a commuter tax and the commuters change to jobs closer to home. The cities need to rebuild themselves but cannot raise the money to do it. More and more, the older cities are for the rich who can afford a second home and the poor who cannot afford anything else. Almost nobody in between lives in the older cities anymore.

THE NEW LABOR
FORCE

The older regions, the cities and suburbs outside the Sun Belt, will survive only through ingenuity and adaptability to change. They will have to retool and reindustrialize to attract industry by increasing productivity through the use of robotics. No matter what part of the country we're talking about, the wave of the future is robotics. Not only will it raise productivity, robotics will take the drudgery out of factory work. Japan already sees the factory run by robots as its industrial savior and is going robotic in shipbuilding, textiles, steel, automobiles and appliances. So sold are the Japanese on robotics they hope to be robot exporters to the world. Imagine! Push a button in Tokyo and start a computer tape rolling that starts a factory in California to work. A rapid rise in the minority labor force will be a social development of the next 20 years. Minorities, most notably Hispanics, now make up 22 percent of the new entrants into the labor force. By 1990, we expect that minorities will be 30 percent of the new labor force. Expect a growing pressure on corporations to hire more Hispanics and to use Spanish as a second language in everyday life.

Expect more working women in the next 20 years, too. We anticipate that more than 70 percent of the women between 25 and 44 years old will be working by 1990, many of them at home using the same cable television for work that their children use for learning. We also expect that almost 60 percent of all adult women will have jobs by 1990.

PERSONAL SOCIAL
CHANGES

So far, we've talked largely about new trends, new social changes that are either just taking hold or that are on their way and have not reached our shores as yet. There are some trends of the sixties and seventies that will run unchecked through the eighties and nineties. We're thinking about more personal social changes started up by the sexual revolution and the feminist movement of the last decade and a half. Take divorce. There will be more divorce because people will no longer regard a first marriage as their only marriage, in part because they'll be living longer and won't be satisfied with the same spouse for 40 or 50 years. By 1990, the *average* American will have been through divorce. Many states will have no-fault divorce, pioneered in Sweden. Others will pass laws that require a wait of no more than six weeks for divorce to become legal. More Americans will take three mates through life, the first for romance and excitement, the second to raise children and the third for mature companionship. Years ago, anthropologist Margaret Mead predicted that would happen.

More women will initiate more premarital sex and more married women will have sex outside their marriage, seeking companionship they cannot find inside their homes. More single women will have children, not just women living with men they do not marry. More women living alone will choose a man to become a father to a child the man may never see or acknowledge as his child. This is a trend that has already begun. More single women will become surrogate mothers for women who cannot have children. These women will be surrogate mothers for the money they are paid and for the experience of pregnancy and childbirth, just to get a share of one of life's rare trips without the responsibility that goes with it. More women will initiate divorce, a trend that began in the seventies. Census takers in 1980 found that more and more professional women sought divorce as their incomes rose, they achieved economic independence and could afford to break their ties with their husbands. The census takers in 1990 will discover that all levels of working women, not just professionals, will be divorcing their mates for the same reason. One of the most remarkable studies we ever made was a study of what kinds of women were best suited for factory work and what these women wanted most from jobs on the assembly line. The women best suited for factory work were those who fit the stereotyped image of housewife and PTA mother. One of the main reasons these women wanted assembly-line jobs was the financial independence it afforded them so they could divorce their mates. True story. We did this study five years ago for a major industrial client.

More and more people will live together in trial marriages, in part because it will continue to be cheaper to do so. More elderly men and women will move in together without making a legal move to get married. Priests, ministers and rabbis are already seeing the start of this trend. One rabbi told us that he has had to turn down a growing number of men and women over 65 who want to be married in the eyes of the syngogue without being married legally. Of course, he can't perform a synagogue wedding without making it legal.

There will be a morning-after birth control pill for women and a birth control pill for men, more of whom will seek vasectomies as their answer to the problem of conceiving unwanted children. A device now being sold in Great Britain for $45 will soon reach the United States and become a new method of birth control for people who refuse to practice birth control. On insertion into the vagina, this device lights up red if the women is fertile and green if she isn't. Supposedly super-reliable, the device works by measuring to a fraction of a degree the vaginal temperature that indicates that it's a fertile time of the month.

The birth rate will continue to fall as people place more stress on self. Call it fallout from the "me generation." By the year 2000, American women of childbearing years will average half the pregnancies (1.3 per fertile woman) today's women do. There will be other reasons for a new drop in the birth rate. More and more working women will not tolerate the confinement and lack of freedom that pregnancy and maternity bring. The state will make it more expensive to have children, in part to crack down on welfare mothers and in part to ease the overpopulation burden. By the year 2000, there could be laws allowing a $1,000 deduction for the first child, $500 for the second, none for the third and a $500 penalty for a fourth child. Believe it. China already has a similar law on the books.

The ongoing sexual revolution will continue through the end of the century. Never again will sex be the bugaboo it was for our parents and grandparents. Like it or not, liberal attitudes about sex are here to stay. What's behind the sexual revolution? In part, it's the rootlessness of late 20th-century society. Religion no longer plays a major role in keeping married couples together and single couples apart. No longer do people live all their lives in the same communities, where families often ostracized people for aberrant sexual behavior. People have more leisure time and meet more different people than they did before in the course of a lifetime. In a sense, the sexes are mixing in so many new ways they're bound to trigger sexual fallout. Finally, people are simply becoming more sexually active because they are no longer afraid of being found out, of becoming infected with a social disease, or of becoming pregnant through carelessness.

The emphasis on self is also producing a new tolerance for sexual openness, freedom and change. This is what's behind the general acceptance of nudity and pornography in films and magazines. It's also behind the growing acceptance of homosexuality, now so far removed from the closet that admitted homosexuals have begun to win security clearances for the first time. We predict that even the Central Intelligence Agency will give security clearances to homosexuals.

Whatever the reason for it, the sexual revolution will continue to proceed apace. Fully 17 percent of all births in 1981 were out of wedlock, a trend that will continue to grow in the years ahead. Sodomy, which is still illegal in 25 states, will no longer be a crime anywhere in America by the turn of the century. The rule of thumb will be that *anything* that is agreed between consenting adults will be permissible. Acts of sexual intercourse will be experienced

41

by more younger people. Boys and girls both have sex these days in their preteen years, when they turn 11 and 12. They're no longer afraid. Fear of the unknown, fear of being caught, are no longer factors when boys and girls decide to experience sex for themselves.

This new sexual freedom will catch many young people unaware and ill-prepared. There will be pre-teen pregnancies, preteen abortions and epidemics of preteen gonorrhea. Alcoholism will go right on being a serious social problem for young people, in part because more young people will turn to alcohol to ease the strain of their new-found social lives. The good news is that there will be drugs that remove the addiction to alcohol. More and more states will also enact alcoholic rehabilitation legislation, taking their cues from Sweden, which substituted the public health approach for the penal approach to alcoholism as long ago as 1969.

At the same time, expect tougher laws on drunk driving in the 1990s. Once again, these will be laws that were tested in Sweden and found to be effective. The first time a drunken driver is arrested in Sweden, he loses his license for 90 days and goes to jail for 30 days. The second time, his license is suspended for one year and he gets 90 days in jail. He's also given a stiff fine, half of which is paid by whoever it was who served him. Some of these laws have been tried to no avail in parts of the U.S., partly because American policemen and judges have been lenient on drunken driving. This will change when new generations of policemen and judges replace the older generations.

ANSWERS TO VIOLENT CRIME

Violent crime will continue to be the most worrisome form of crime in America for years to come. Judges in the mid-eighties will begin to raise bail and hand out longer sentences for violent crimes. During this same period, more prisons will be opened, many of them abandoned schools, closed military bases, and hospitals that will be taken over by the state and barred over. At the same time new prisons are being opened, the prisons of the past will be closed down. In the years ahead, prisoners will be segregated by the crimes they've committed. Lesser criminals will be jailed in low-security prisons, where they'll even be integrated sexually. Once again, the example was set by Sweden, which found that mingling the sexes in co-habitational cells in low-security prisons motivated the prisoners to behave and cut down dramatically on homosexuality in the jails.

There are solutions to the problem of violent crime, some of which will begin to be applied by 1985. One reason for violent crime is the high unemployment rate among blacks, poor whites and Chicanos. Look for Congress to pass double-minimum wage laws whereby teenagers will be paid $1 an hour less than the minimum wage. Say the legal minimum wage is $3.50 an hour. The new law will authorize a second minimum wage of $2.50 an hour for people under 18 years of age. The big fear of a double minimum is that it will put older people out of work by giving their jobs at lower wages to the people falling under the scale of the minimum wage. The Europeans have already found that a double minimum doesn't take jobs away from older people, it creates jobs for younger people who wouldn't have jobs otherwise. They also found it dramatically reduces crime rates in the slum regions of large cities.

RAISING THE ARMY
STANDARD

There's another answer to violent crime. Raise the educational opportunities of the volunteer army to where they're competitive with civilian

43

life. Take the brightest volunteers, put them in jobs they will sustain in civilian life when they're discharged and double their salaries so they don't feel so economically deprived. Watch the inner-city blacks, poor whites and Chicanos who might choose a life of street crime change their minds about joining the army. Not only will this cut down on violent crime and raise the standards of the army, it will eliminate any need for renewing the draft. No matter how you look at it, the draft will be as unpopular a means of strengthening the military in the eighties as it was to beef up our forces in Vietnam during the seventies.

White-collar crime is a different matter. There are no ready answers to bribery, political corruption and embezzlement by computer, which are now among the fastest-growing crimes in America. Tougher laws are one solution, more vigilance another, new technology that uses the computer to make it harder to steal a third. No matter. The growth of white-collar crime will outstrip any attempts to slow it down. White-collar crime will be a major social sickness of the eighties and nineties. New methods of combatting white-collar crime will be one way we measure the way that times will change out to the end of the century.

We will really know that times are changing when all 50 states ratify the Equal Rights Amendment. Expect it in 1989, when the fiftieth state to do so moves to ratify an amendment to the constitution that is a lot like the Equal Rights Amendment. The fiftieth state to do so? Why, it will be Utah, whose overwhelming Mormon majority often makes it the last state to adopt radical social change of any kind. No matter. By the end of the decade, American women will achieve the same kind of power and freedom long ago won by the women of Finland, where one-fourth of Finnish parliament is female.

2
▲▲▲▲▲▲▲

WHAT IF
PEOPLE LIVED
AS LONG AS TREES

▼▼▼▼▼▼▼

*"I hope the public will accept
the progress science can make."*

—Rosalyn S. Yatow
1977 Nobel Prize Winner in Medicine

▲▲▲▲▲▲▲

*D*octors like to say that 99 percent of all the discoveries in the history of medical science have been made in the 20th century, a claim that's probably true. Run down a list of diseases cured in the 20th century and you have an index to illnesses that routinely devastated the human race, diseases that killed millions of our ancestors before they ever reached old age. Yellow fever, scurvy, cholera, malaria, diphtheria, polio, meningitis, tuberculosis and smallpox, to name but a few. If there is one meaningful statistic about where 20th-century medicine has taken us, it's the one triggered by penicillin and all its descendant antibiotics. In 1940, infection caused 25 percent of all deaths. Today, it's less than three percent. There's another meaningful statistic that proves the same point. Man's life span was 48 years at the start of the 20th century. Today, it's 72 years.

The fast pace set in the first two-thirds of the 20th century for new cures and treatments will be hard to sustain but it will be done and even stepped up in fields like brain research, which are only now beginning to catch fire. So rapid will be the pace that children being born today can expect to live for 83 years, 10 years more than their parents, 20 years more than their grandparents and 30 years more than their great-grandparents.

There will be new drugs that lessen the need for radical heart surgery, artificial body parts that prolong the good health of vital organs and artificial organs that prolong life itself. People will not only live to be older, they'll enjoy more of their old age. There will be drugs that improve and even restore memory. They will come in nasal sprays and be so effective they'll set senility back 10 years. Nonaddictive painkillers will appear that are stronger than morphine, mood modifiers will come onto the market that not only elevate spirits but exhilarate them.

MEDICINE IN SPACE

Medicine will venture into outer space in the search for new cures and treatments in the years ahead. First to place an experiment aboard the space shuttle will be Johnson & Johnson, which wants to know what the weightlessness of space will do for the manufacture of serums and vaccines. Oil and water will mix in zero gravity. Liquids that can't be separated on earth will separate out in zero gravity. At the very least, completely pure and uncontaminated vaccines made in space will revolutionize the treatment of disease.

The fifth operational flight of the space shuttle in the fall of 1983 will carry a cannister built by McDonnell-Douglas for Johnson & Johnson that will be filled with human blood. By use of a process called electrophoresis, which separates liquids whose electrical charges are different, the cannister, when it is returned to earth, will contain a vial of pancreatic beta cells to treat diabetes and a vial of an anticoagulant to dissolve blood clots. Johnson & Johnson has reserved space on eight shuttle flights through 1985 to experiment with other serums. If the experiments work, they plan to send a five-ton satellite into space that will serve as the first robot pharmaceutical laboratory in weightlessness. Six months later, Johnson & Johnson will pick up the satellite and bring it home to earth, where they will market whatever serums and vaccines were made aboard the satellite. There will be more than new serums and vaccines tested in space by such companies as Johnson & Johnson, Eli Lilly, Merck and Pfizer. On an upcoming flight of the space shuttle, an astronaut will wear a sticky, dime-sized patch behind his ear that contains three days' worth of a prescription drug called scopolamine used to treat motion sickness. The drug seeps off the patch into the body in minute amounts that provide a continuous form of treatment. The sky isn't the limit for these skin patches. They'll be tested as a way to administer drugs to treat asthma, high blood pressure and angina.

NEW WAYS TO PREVENT BLINDNESS

Who knows what new medicines will become available when weightlessness is used to mix and separate liquids for the first time? After all, the thousand-year-long Bronze Age came from the discovery that copper and tin formed an alloy superior to either metal. Besides using robots in space medicine, aging astronauts seeking relief from their arthritis in the weightlessness of space could do the mixing and separating. They'll be an envied elite. By the year 2000, there will be three times as many arthritis sufferers in the U.S. as there are today. As one doctor puts it: "The jogging craze may very well lead to a generation of people with the strongest lungs and hearts in our history but with joints so worn and arthritic they won't be able to get out of bed."

There will be new ways to prevent blindness and deafness and will even be new cures for blindness, deafness and dumbness. Laser light will become a more important surgical tool than the scalpel ever was for the eye, ear, nose and throat, bloodlessly removing pressures on the eye that cause glaucoma and tumors from the ear, nose and throat that cause loss of hearing and speech. There will be pills that cure phobias. Fear of heights, crowds, strangers, elevators, closed-in places, even fear of flying will be phobias of the past.

Out of the world's pharmaceutical laboratories will come new mood-modifying drugs far more beneficial than the Tofranil and Lithium people take today. These new drugs will raise low spirits to new highs at the same time they cut down the habit-forming rate and side effects everybody identifies with mood-changing drugs. Gone will be the dryness of the mouth and nose, the fall and even loss of sex drive that walk hand in hand with today's mood modifiers. The "pleasure pill" George Orwell and Herman Kahn talked about is on its way. Development of these drugs is sure to go underground before the Food and Drug Administration approves them for use. They'll be sold as dope before they can be bought from a druggist.

GENE SPLICING

Not only will we feel better, we'll look better toward the end of the century. Men will take drugs to grow hair, women will take drugs to keep the color in their hair. There will be a nutlike snack that people can chew to keep teeth white, strong and free of cavities. There will be hormones to make people shorter, taller or thinner. Already being tested in Sweden to make dwarfs grow is a hormone called HGH, which stands for Human Growth Hormone. In years past, this hormone was extracted from the pituitary glands of human cadavers to treat dwarfism, but the world's mortuaries can only provide enough of the hormone to treat one dwarf out of six at more than $1,000 a treatment. The tests in Sweden involve the use of genetic engineering in which the genes of the Human Growth Hormone are spliced and rearranged to produce HGH in abundance at a fraction of what it costs to extract the hormone from cadavers. Not only will this new synthetic hormone help dwarfs to grow, it can make taller people out of short ones. Researchers say they are already on their way to manipulating the hormone in a way to make shorter people out of too-tall people who are embarrassed by their height. Next will be a way to use the hormone to control weight. The first true diet pill may be on its way.

NEW HORMONES FOR MEMORY

Studies at Tulane University show that a protein present in a hormone that helps tan the skin also helps people heighten their powers of concentration. Students scored higher on geometry tests after they were injected with the protein, which also gave mentally retarded students quicker comprehension of tasks they'd been learning. Some doctors now think that people who grow up with good memories are people whose bodies produce an excess of this protein. If they're right, you can expect prescriptions of this protein for people in need of better memories.

Another hormone named vasopressin that's made by the pituitary gland at the base of the skull may prove to be an even more striking memory aid. Doctors at the University of Liège in Belgium tried the hormone on men between the ages of 50 and 65 and found that three doses in three days were enough to improve almost all their scores on memory and learning tests. One man who'd been in a coma for 15 days after an automobile accident and remembered nothing about the accident for three months recalled all the accident's details after seven days of treatment with vasopressin.

How does vasopressin work? Even the doctors testing it don't know. First made synthetically in 1968 to regulate the body's water content, the hormone extract of the pituitary gland was suggested as an aid to memory by a Dutch doctor who noticed that rats suffered impaired memories when their pituitaries were removed. Rats who'd learned their way through a maze wouldn't get through after they lost their pituitaries. Where does it stand now? It's being tested to help adults regain their childhood memories and has already helped some people regain the use of foreign languages they'd forgotten.

Two things are holding up its wider use right now, especially its use as a tool against senility. Vasopressin raises the heartbeat and blood pressure of people taking it and it's a member of a class of chemicals called peptides, which can't be injected because they're broken down by enzymes in the bloodstream. They must be used as a nasal spray to be effective. Even so, the drug company that synthesized vasopressin predicts it will be safe enough and effective enough to be on the prescription market by 1985 and in worldwide use by 1990.

CHEMISTRY OF THE BRAIN

The hope that vasopressin holds for senility and amnesia victims illustrates the dramatic advances being made in the field of brain chemistry. Fewer than 10 years ago, doctors had identified six chemicals that took messages from one brain cell to another. They now know of 30 and suspect there may be as many as 200, each one promising to solve a mystery of how the brain works and how it breaks down. Understanding of how the brain works chemically is growing so fast that neuroscientists are on the verge of devising better treatments, based on new drugs and medicines, for depression, schizophrenia and drug addiction.

When a doctor named Solomon Snyder at Johns Hopkins University found in 1973 that opium and only opium attaches itself to certain cells in the brain, he opened the door to a potential cure for drug addiction. Out of his finding has already come a chemical called naloxone, which strips heroin and morphine right away from the brain cells they hold onto. Naloxone is now stocked in the nation's hospital emergency rooms, where it has saved untold heroin overdose victims. The drug is now being tested to see if it can screen out heroin addicts seeking treatment with methadone from addicts wanting a methadone fix.

NEW DRUGS FOR PAIN

More urgent than a treatment for drug addiction is the worldwide search now under way for a drug that kills pain with the same force as codeine and morphine but doesn't carry the price of addiction. Sol Snyder calls it the search for the ultimate drug. Already, the search has uncovered several chemicals that are produced naturally in the brain, some called enkephalins (Greek for "something in the head") and one called dynorphin (Greek for "power"), which kill pain 200 times better than codeine does. The theory is that these chemicals occur naturally in the brains of most mammals (humans included) to help them endure and ward off pain. And since they exist by nature in the brain, they are by nature nonaddictive.

Then why aren't they being used to kill pain? For one of the same reasons vasopressin isn't being used to improve peoples' memories. Like vasopressin, dynorphin and the enkephaline are peptides and are rapidly destroyed by enzymes in the bloodstream before they reach the brain. The enkephalins also have trouble breaking the body's blood-brain barrier, which keeps toxic chemicals from invading the brain. The enkephalins can't even be used in nasal sprays, as vasopressin can.

If that were all there was to it, there wouldn't be much point in spending the millions of dollars now being spent across the globe on enkephalin and dynorphin research. But doctors are convinced the brain chemicals are broken down in the blood by a particular enzyme, not just any enzyme. Finding that enzyme could uncover a chemical that blocks the enzyme's action; mixing that chemical with dynorphin or the enkephalins could be a means of getting the painkiller to the brain before it's destroyed by the enzyme. How close is medical science to doing this? One drug company is quietly testing an enkephalin derivative on humans in Europe. There could be a nonaddictive opiate, Sol Snyder's ultimate drug, in doctors' hands before 1990.

NEW CLUES TO DRUG
ADDICTION

There's another reason for pressing on with research on nature's painkillers. They could provide the clues to drug addiction. Doctors at Johns Hopkins are giving rats injections of morphine, then measuring the rate at which the natural painkillers are made and destroyed in the rats' brains in the time it takes for the rats to become addicted to the morphine. Doctors at Stanford University are doing the same thing with dynorphin, figuring there may be a shortage of dynorphin in addicts' brains which causes them to be addicted to the morphine.

Another chemical in the brain that promises major advances in the years just ahead is dopamine, which was found 10 years ago to occur in a part of the brain called the striatum which helps control body movement. Dopamine is produced by dark-stained nerve cells called *substantia nigra*, which project their fibers directly into the striatum. Doctors had known for more than 50 years that these cells were curiously absent in patients who had died from advanced Parkinson's disease but they were never able to isolate what it was in these cells that had a connection with Parkinson's disease.

Almost immediately after the discovery of dopamine, doctors began injecting Parkinson patients with it. Nothing happened. The dopamine never made it past the blood-brain barrier. Neurochemists then worked out the pathway dopamine takes through the brain and discovered that dopamine was being made from another substance called L-dopa, which did cross the blood-brain barrier. L-dopa's effect on Parkinsonism is one of the most dramatic advances in recent medical history. Just a few injections of L-dopa eliminate almost all the symptoms of this dread disease. The trembling, the shaking, the inability to move . . . all stop after treatment with L-dopa.

Ten years of research with dopamine have now convinced doctors it can treat more than Parkinsonism—for example, at least two symptoms of aging—senility and the growing inability to move with any speed. Injections of L-dopa into aging rats make the rats more alert. Old rats barely able to swim suddenly rip through the water after L-dopa injections.

THE CAUSE OF SCHIZOPHRENIA

Doctors also believe that dopamine may provide clues to the treatment of schizophrenia and severe depression, still the two leading causes of mental illness in the United States. Doctors know that Parkinson patients develop hallucinations and delusions, which are also symptoms of schizophrenia. Even Parkinson patients responding to treatment with L-dopa develop schizoid tendencies in five years, in part because L-dopa alters the brain's dopamine delivery system in some poorly understood way.

There is more evidence of a dopamine connection, though it's circumstantial. A few antischizophrenic drugs on the market work by blocking the nerve cells that act to receive dopamine in the brain. Nobody knows why they help. At the same time, doctors have found that moderate doses of L-dopa given schizophrenics worsen the patients' symptoms. The educated guess is that the ultimate cause of most forms of schizophrenia is some abnormality of the dopamine delivery system in the brain. Trouble is, nobody knows what that abnormality is. Again, the educated guess is that they will know before 1990.

When Sigmund Freud said 50 years ago that every event in the brain would someday be traced to chemical change, he predicted the wave of the future in brain research. Doctors now fully believe that aggression has a chemical base, that aggressive and violent behavior can be traced to a shortage of two chemicals, called serotonin and norepinephrine, found in the brain. Studies of Canadian enlisted men who had trouble adjusting to military life showed that those with the most trouble, those exhibiting the most aggressive tendencies, were those with the least amount of serotonin in their spinal fluid. Think of the treatment that might someday be used on hardened criminals. Injections of a serotonin derivative might be all they need to change their lives.

WHAT CAUSES FEAR

Fear itself may be triggered by a peptide recently found in the brain. In controversial tests at Baylor University and the University of Tennessee, rats were trained to move through mazes in the dark before being killed to extract this peptide from their brains. Each time the extract was injected into untrained rats, they experienced such intense fear of the dark they could not be trained to get through the maze. The same extract was injected into goldfish, who henceforth would not even venture into the shadows under rocks. Even our sense of time may be controlled by a chemical in the brain. Honeybees at Germany's Würzburg Zoological Institute were trained to feed from bowls of sugar water at precise times of the day. Once they had the timing down right, they were sacrificed and their brain tissue surgically inserted into both sides of the brains of untrained bees. Lo and behold! By the third day, 60 percent of the untrained bees were feeding at the same time the trained bees did.

Beyond the gains that will be made in brain chemistry are what promise to be even more striking advances in the treatment of injuries to the brain and spinal cord. For the last 100 years, the conventional medical wisdom has been that once the brain or spinal cord are injured, they stay injured forever or recover very little function. Every other part of the human body repairs itself or can be repaired. Torn skin grows back, broken bones heal themselves, even severed nerves in the wrist can be sewn back together using microsurgical techniques to regenerate the nerves and restore the use of a hand.

THE INJURED SPINAL CORD

The central nervous system, the fist-sized brain and the spinal column that runs from the brain stem to the base of the spine, cannot repair itself and cannot be repaired. There is no treatment to rejuvenate injured brain cells or regenerate an injured spinal cord. The 675,000 Americans who must use wheelchairs and the 1.5 million Americans who suffer complete or partial paralysis are testimony to this devastating fact.

Now, there is new hope for the paralyzed people of the world, whose ranks grow by the thousands every year from crippling automobile and diving injuries. First to raise this hope were doctors in England, where anatomists at Oxford University showed that damaged brain cells are not dead brain cells. Working for the last 15 years with rats, anatomists under Oxford's Dr. Geoffrey Raisman showed conclusively that injured brain cells don't die. They lose the connections that give them their function but they don't die.

In a brilliant series of clinical experiments, Raisman and his Oxford colleagues set out deliberately to damage brain cells by using a tiny surgical knife to sever the cell connections in four regions of the forebrains of rats. Then they used a powerful electron microscope to observe what happened to the damaged brain cells. To their utter surprise, the Oxford team witnessed what no other doctors before had seen or suspected. They saw the rats' brain cells lose their connections, then go out and establish new connections with other brain cells. The brain cells reestablished precisely the number of connections in precisely the same positions they'd lost from injury to their original connections. The rats were able to go through this process after being surgically injured a second and even a third time. Never did the rats take longer than six weeks to restore the brain cell connections they'd lost to the surgeon's knife.

REPAIR FOR THE SPINE

In a flash, 100 years of medical pessimism about the central nervous system's repairability had been rolled back. It was true that none of the new connections restored function to the brain but nobody in medicine was ever going to look for recovery of function if they thought the brain didn't recover its connections. When Raisman was ready to publish his results for the first time, he was in such a state of shock that he began to worry that he'd made a mistake. Raisman consulted an old Oxford don, who told him: "A man who never makes a mistake will never make a discovery." Raisman published and shocked the world of neurology. In the last 10 years, his experiments have been confirmed in dozens of neurological laboratories around the world and there is suddenly new hope for the victims of brain and spinal-cord damage.

Since proving that the central nervous system is capable of repair, Raisman has set out to prove that it's capable of restoring function. If anything, Raisman has set himself a more difficult task than he set himself the first time. For almost 10 years now, Raisman has been trying to transplant healthy nerve cells into damaged brain tissue to see if the undamaged cells can form a "bridge" that might restore function. After all, he reasoned, transplantation to repair injury is an accepted medical practice. Doctors have grafted skin on burns for years. Transfusing blood is nothing more than transplanting blood. For eight years, Raisman couldn't get the transplants to take. The transplants were not making contact with the host tissues. The transplanted cells were not taking root; they behaved more like potted plants than plants in the ground.

REGENERATE THE SPINE

In the last two years, Raisman has finally achieved survival of transplanted brain tissue and mingling with the host cells. He did it through a combination of persistence and ingenuity. It involved taking nerve tissue from embryonic rats and transplanting it into adult rats. Why embryonic rats? The embryonic brain, Raisman reasoned, is still flexible, adaptable and has room to grow. He was right. Raisman's transplanted brain cells are now surviving and growing consistently in the rats he's worked on. Raisman is now convinced he can get the transplanted cells to begin carrying messages to new cell connections in the brain that will restore function to the damaged part of the brain.

What would that mean? That would mean that Raisman would move his experiments from the rat's brain to the rat's spinal cord. If he demonstrates regeneration in the brain, Raisman is convinced he can demonstrate it just as quickly in the spinal cord. After that, he is just as convinced he can move on to the human spinal cord. The first beneficiary of Raisman's pioneering work may well be a boy of twelve who suffers an injury to his spinal cord in an automobile accident five years hence. If he can transplant nerves into injured spinal cords, Raisman says he can transplant tissue into damaged brains. He's thinking of construction workers who lost their sight or their speech when a load of bricks fell on their heads. He's thinking of people who suffered single penetrating injuries, like soldiers who get a piece of shrapnel in the brain or in the spinal column. Unhappily, he says, victims of multiple brain and spinal-cord injuries may never find help. Only single penetrating injuries to the brain and spinal cord will respond. If they're damaged in more than one place, the brain and spinal cord won't have enough undamaged nerve cell tissue left to support repair.

NEW VACCINES

At about the same time that Raisman or one of his colleagues performs the first successful transplant of central nervous tissue, virologists will be devising new vaccines to prevent a broad array of viral diseases that today cannot be prevented. In the last few years, a vaccine has been devised against infectious hepatitis and another is being tried out against the 14 strains of pneumonia that cause over 80 percent of all pneumococcal infections. Ahead lies a possible vaccine for tuberculosis and as many as three vaccines to immunize people from cancers whose cause is known to be a virus. Doctors talk now of vaccines to immunize people against their own tumors, the kinds of cancerlike breast cancer that appear to be caused by viruses and appear to run in families. To hear many virologists tell it, the cancer of the breast that attacks one out of every 14 women, triggers 100,000 new cases every year and still kills 25,000 women every year may be the first cancer to be brought under control by preventive inoculation with a workable vaccine.

What virologists cannot do with vaccines may be done by the geneticists working in what is now the most explosive field in medicine, genetic engineering. It started in 1952 when James Watson and Francis Crick identified deoxyribonucleic acid (DNA) as the molecular carrier of all heredity. Each one of the more than 100,000 genes we possess is made up of DNA, a double-helixed chain of nucleic acids in which the arrangement of the acids determines the function of the gene. Once geneticists discovered what DNA was made of, they quickly discovered the enzymes and proteins that break the double helix in very specific positions. In any of the two million species of life, their chromosomes can be broken in very distinct places, removed and replaced with other chromosomes. This means it might be possible to cut out a characteristic of one species and substitute it in another. Stretching it, give a cat's eyes to a dog. Make a bigger salamander. Breed a better horse.

A BIGGER BRAIN

Or even a better human being. Build a body immune to kidney disease, which victimized Albert Einstein. Create a Beethoven who wouldn't go deaf. There's a lot of anxious talk about how genetic engineers are tampering with life, but Harvard's Dr. Paul Doty is one of those who think it is inevitable: "We ought to be engaged in species innovation to create a new man, a better man. I'm thinking mostly of a man with a bigger brain. There's no reason not to strive for this."

GENE SPLICING

Striving to create a man with a bigger brain may be a long way off but striving to conquer disease through genetic engineering is here and now. It's called gene splicing and here's how it works. Take the section of DNA that orders the human body to produce insulin to chew up excess body sugar. Splice that section of DNA into a plasmid, then implant the plasmid into a bacterium where it reproduces each time the "bug" divides.

The idea is to implant the human gene that produces insulin into a microorganism that replicates rapidly. In 30 minutes, the bug divides and both microbes contain the gene that makes insulin. Another half-hour and the two bugs divide again. Soon, there are eight, then 16, then 32. In two days, one microorganism reproduces billions of copies of itself, except that now they're all producing insulin. This is no flight of fancy. Bacteria given the DNA codes to produce insulin have done just that at a fraction of the cost it takes to produce insulin the nongenetic way.

The drug factories of the future will be bacterial factories where the bacteria are implanted with spliced human genes. Besides insulin, the candidates for bacterial production include cortisone to treat arthritis, the anti-hemophilia fractions of the blood now taken from blood donors and the growth hormone used to treat dwarfism that is now taken expensively from cadavers. The list of diseases that can be alleviated by gene splicing is staggering. People suffering from inherited genetic disease may someday undergo gene therapy, in which an abnormal gene is removed or "turned off" and a normal gene spliced in to take its place. Genetic diseases are among the most burdensome afflictions facing contemporary society. An estimated 12 million Americans suffer from one of the 2,000 disorders of the genes and chromosomes. Huntington's disease, sickle-cell anemia and Tay-Sachs disease are among the worst of the genetic killers that may be eliminated by gene splicing in the next 20 years. Hemophilia is a genetic disease. So is Down's syndrome (mongolism), which is passed on to one out of 40 infants born to women over 40 years of age. The time may soon come when the number of persons disabled or killed by genetic disease begins to shrink dramatically.

The first big benefit of gene splicing will come from its use in producing an ample world supply of interferon, the natural protein the human body produces to fight off viral infections. Doctors have long known that patients with one viral illness almost never caught a second viral infection of that particular type, as if the first virus prevented infection by the second. In 1957, two doctors in London found that the body produced a protein in response to a virus attack that made subsequent cells immune to attacks of the same virus. They named the protein interferon, because of the way it interfered with virus infections and blocked the passage of the virus from an infected cell to a healthy cell. They had discovered the body's natural mechanism for immunizing itself against every virus from influenza to the common cold.

ASSEMBLY-LINE
INTERFERON

Then why isn't interferon being used to help the body fight these viral illnesses? For the simple reason that there has never been enough of it to test in clinical trials, let alone to prescribe it for everyday use. White blood cells, the main source of interferon in the body, produce the protein in infinitesimal amounts. What's more, interferon works only in the animals that make it. Only human interferon works in humans, a condition that will be academic in the years ahead because of the miracle of gene splicing. Already, the gene that tells the body to make interferon has been identified and implanted in rapidly multiplying bacteria. Assembly-line production of interferon is right around the corner. Its use against every form of viral attack from hepatitis to some forms of cancer is less than 10 years away.

Gene splicing is such a promising method of making new remedies and new cures that doctors can hardly decide where to start and what to work on first. They talk of new vaccines to ward off infections before they invade the body, new antibodies to fight infections that do invade the body and new antibiotics to kill infections that spread through the body. Vaccines will be made by gene splicing for such intractable viral and parasitic diseases as amoebic dysyntery, trachoma, hepatitis and malaria. One gene-splicing laboratory in the Midwest is on the verge of a vaccine that prevents foot-and-mouth disease in animals, an ailment that costs U.S. cattlemen alone more than $200 million a year. At the same time the foot-and-mouth disease vaccine becomes available, look for the first gene-spliced hormones to come out of the laboratory. Medical researchers predict great things for engineered hormones. Of the 48 human hormones identified as likely candidates for gene splicing, 38 are not used in medical practice because they have not been available in large enough quantities to be tested for their therapeutic use. Gene splicing will change that overnight.

Widespread use of interferon to fight viruses will spearhead a new chemical attack on disease that will lengthen the life spans of everybody growing up today. There will be new drugs to dissolve blood clots that clog arteries and cause heart attacks. There will be new drugs to halt the secretion of stomach acids that cause ulcers. There will be new drugs that dissolve gallstones and new drugs that prevent the buildup of cholesterol and glycerides that harden arteries and new drugs that flush the arteries clean like chemical roto-rooters. There is already a drug called a calcium blocker that lowers blood pressure, raises cardiac output and cuts down irregular heartbeat all at the same time. There is another drug called a beta blocker that slows the heart and diminishes its need for oxygen when it is struggling to pump blood.

BYPASS SURGERY

These new drugs will save lives by doing away with the need for life-threatening surgery that debilitates patients and their pocketbooks. If there are new drugs to free clogged arteries, there should be less need for coronary bypass surgery. While it's true that bypass surgery relieves the crippling pain of angina pectoris, there is no evidence that it prolongs life. Surgeons with scalpels to grind insist the bypass operation extends the lives of patients with heart disease. This is not true. Studies of 600 coronary patients at 13 Veterans Administration hospitals show that bypass surgery was no better at prolonging life than nonsurgical treatment of clogged arteries. Patients will grow weary of bypass surgery, which now costs $15,000 a patient and costs the United States more than $1 billion a year. They've already tired of bypass surgery in Europe, where surgeons now perform seven bypass operations for every 100 that American surgeons take on.

Gone and soon forgotten in the years ahead will be surgery to remove the gallbladder, the most frequently performed abdominal operation in the U.S. An experimental drug named chenodeoxycholic acid (CDCA) is now so effective in dissolving gallstones that there will soon be no need for gallbladder surgery, which is performed half a million times a year in the U.S. Next to go will be surgery to resect the stomachs of duodenal ulcer patients, 25 percent of whom go under the knife every year. Another new experimental drug called cimetidine is being used that blocks the secretion of acids in the stomach, the prime consequence of stress and gastric ulcer. Many doctors already believe that cimetidine will revolutionize the management of duodenal ulcers and eliminate the need for the 42,000 gastrectomies performed every year on ulcer patients.

Fewer women will undergo the two operations that cause them so much physical and mental anguish, the hysterectomy that removes the uterus and the radical mastectomy that takes off a breast. Even though half of American women have their uteruses removed by the time they're 65, according to Dr. Eugene G. McCarthy of Cornell University, who used data from the National Center for Health Statistics, the hysterectomy is an operation whose time has passed. Not only do many doctors believe it is needless surgery, a growing number of them are relying on hormone treatment to get women through menopause. Women themselves will have something to say about it. More and more women will say they want to be involved in their own medical decisions, which does not include coping with the psychological loss of the uterus if it can be avoided. The same thing will be true of women with breast cancer, where radical mastectomies now show no better survival rates than more conservative treatments such as modified mastectomy or lumpectomy, in which only the cancerous lump is removed. Wiser use of newer methods of radiation will help women with breast cancer to choose the more conservative treatment. Women have taken a bum rap from the male-dominated medical profession on any number of things. Studies already under way will prove that 35 percent of birth defects are due as much to an aging male sperm as an aging female egg and that the female athlete has as great a resistance to stress under pressure as has the male.

ARE TONSILLECTOMIES NEEDED?

Gradually disappearing in the years ahead will be two of the most frequently performed operations in America, the appendectomy and the tonsillectomy. Most doctors now believe that an inflamed appendix can be treated by giving the patient large doses of antibiotics. Surgeons at Johns Hopkins found that appendectomies could be reduced by one-third if they followed these practices. There is more debate about tonsillectomies but doctors now think tonsillectomies are needed only if the tonsils are so large they obstruct breathing or swallowing. Some doctors now think both operations are still performed routinely because they're misguided remnants of medical folklore, like using ice to treat frostbite.

While the frequency of many operations will be reduced, there will be new surgical techniques that leap to the fore in the 20 years ahead that also promise to extend life spans. Most of the new operations will involve the surgical implants of artificial organs. The artificial liver, spleen and kidney are not topics of idle conversation for medical students. They are real possibilities whose time is coming. The artificial heart and the artificial pancreas are possibilities whose time may already be here.

Treatment with insulin saves the lives of diabetics but it doesn't save them from the complications they run up against later in life. Kidney disease, blindness, nerve and blood vessel damage that come from diabetes may be caused by the fact that insulin treatment alone is not enough to control blood sugars. The answer might be an artificial pancreas that controls the blood sugar level at the same time that it produces and stores insulin. The University of Toronto is already using a device that draws blood, checks it for glucose and then releases the right amount of insulin through the veins and into the bloodstream. Trouble is, its instruments fill a bedside: the apparatus to draw blood, an instrument to measure glucose, a computer to figure the insulin dose and a pump to feed it. Boston's Joslin Clinic has developed an artificial pancreas that involves using living insulin-producing beta cells placed inside a small sac implanted under a patient's skin. The sac is covered by a membrane that allows sugar to pass in and insulin to pass out. The cells inside the membrane respond to the blood sugar level just like a normal pancreas.

ARTIFICIAL BLOOD

Besides artificial organs, medical researchers are developing an artificial blood. Suppose you're an accident victim with a rare blood type. Wouldn't you want the hospital where you're taken to have some on hand? Well, a Japanese company named Green Cross thinks it might have the answer in some of the world's blood banks in 1982. Green Cross has already tested its artificial blood (made from chemicals called perfluorocarbons) on animals and will perform some of the same tests in the United States and Germany later this year. Artificial blood will never be a substitute for real blood, which is a complex brew of red and white cells and numerous blood factors that perform a host of tasks for the body. But artificial blood looks more than capable of doing one crucial job: transporting life-sustaining oxygen from the lungs to the brain. There is little doubt that artificial blood can be used to keep a critically injured person alive while his body begins to restore his own blood supply. The artificial blood has other advantages. It can be kept as long as two years, can be given to people of any blood type, and carries none of the risks of infection that human blood carries.

The ultimate artificial organ is under development at the University of Utah. It is an artificial heart made of plastic and aluminum and powered by electricity. One of these days, Utah surgeon William DeVries will get a human patient whose heart is beyond help and precipitously close to failure. DeVries will cut away the heart's lower ventricles, leaving the upper atria intact. Then he will sew dacron fittings to the three main coronary arteries and snap the artificial heart in place. A plastic tube leads from both ventricles through the patient's abdomen to a console connected to an air compressor. While air is pumped toward each ventricle, it pushes a thin membrane upward that expels blood through the atria and out through the pulmonary artery and aorta. Will it work? Not long ago, a team of researchers at Temple University Hospital in Philadelphia put the Utah heart in a woman whose brain had already been declared dead. The Utah device maintained the woman's blood pressure and kidneys for two hours before doctors took it out for further study.

Tethering a patient to an air compressor might not seem like much of a breakthrough but Utah surgeons are talking about people who have no other choice. "These people are in terrible condition," DeVries told *Time* magazine. "They often have difficulty breathing, let alone anything else." While not perfect, the Utah heart is a beginning. Devices are already under development that will bypass the heart to allow it to rebuild its strength. There is talk of a device that will use a tiny nuclear battery to pump blood without having to use an outside power source.

LIFE SPAN OF 150 YEARS

The elimination of childhood disease will be the first step in the antiaging revolution. Most people who will become old 60 or 70 years from now will not have had childhood diseases. That's an important difference because aging is cumulative. Step two will be a change in habits with regard to diet, exercise and self-care. Per capita consumption of tobacco will drop precipitously, promising a decrease in chronic lung diseases that can only prolong life. Improved treatment of hypertension has already produced a dramatic decrease in cardiovascular disease, a major chronic problem of old age.

These breakthroughs, some of them imminent, others not far away, promise to add years to the average life span. How many? Children being born today will live for 83 years. Their children will live even longer, at least as long as 100 years and maybe a lot longer. Sometime around the turn of the century, medical researchers will have gained such command of the genetic codes that guide us through life that they will crack the code that determines how the human body ages. When that happens, research will devise a drug that slows down the aging process. The first anti-aging drug will raise life spans to 150 years; improvements on the first drug will lift life spans to 200 years. That's as long a life as trees have on earth. What if people lived as long as trees?

No matter how you look at it, living as long as trees would change how we mature, how we think, how we socialize, reproduce, plan ahead and govern in ways so profound that life on earth will never be the same. Never. People have always had a tough time responding to change. Imagine the first reactions of people when they're told they can live to be 200! The elderly will be angry and bitter, knowing they're too late to get the treatment that halts the aging process. The young will want the treatment immediately, demanding they lose not a year of their promised longevity. The middle-aged will be confused. If they get the treatment, will their life spans lengthen? Nobody will know the answer right away. More research is needed to find the answers to questions like that.

The issues surrounding the treatment will not be completely new. The precedent has long been the dialysis treatment for failed kidneys. Do we give dialysis to an 80-year-old Nobel Prize winner or to the 25-year-old mother of two? We'll face the same questions with the drug that extends life. Do we keep the Nobel Prize winner around because of his proven worth or do we spend the money on the younger person with another 100 years of life left? This will be a real social question that will be debated for years without our reaching any final answers. There will be other social questions that defy final answers. How do we decide how many people the earth can support? Do we begin by allocating children to families who want them? Will the number of children be decided on the way oil will eventually be rationed around the world? Will society be willing to deal with a large increase in the number of old people?

Nobody knows what this drug will be or when it will become available, only that it's on its way. Already, a cadre of precursor drugs are being tested on animals, so it's only a matter of time before the right drug pops out of the test tube. With a life-extending drug available, four generations of numerous families will be living at the same time. Great-grandparents will no longer be faceless people the youngest family members never knew. They'll be alive. Will the new strains of living longer divide the families in such ways that the elderly become outcasts? Or could it be that grandparents and great-grandparents become the well-springs of a new family life, keeping families intact at a time when the strains on family life will be greater than ever. Older family members may end up taking over more family responsibilities. It could be that the grandparents will raise the youngest children while the middle-aged parents go to work. The real strains will be on marriages. After all, how many people will want to stay married to the same person for more than 100 years?

Meanwhile, the government will announce that it won't dispense the life-prolonging drug for another five years to give everybody a chance to think about whether he or she wants the drug. Many people won't want it, thinking that a drug that extends life is nothing less than medical quackery. When the Futures Group, a professional forecasting organization, recently carried out a study on life-extending technologies, they found just that kind of reaction from many people who were to be involved in the study. Taking the drug is to be voluntary. The government will also announce a condition to giving the drug. Anybody who takes it must also take a sterility drug that will prevent him or her from conceiving any more children. Each person getting the drug is to be allowed one child, to be drawn from a sperm or ovum bank set up like a savings account in the names of everybody wanting to live to be 200. If you want more than a "replacement" child who will replace you when you die, you won't get the drug to prolong life. You won't be punished if you want children, you just won't be rewarded with the treatment against aging. Choices will be clear cut and final.

In the five years between the government's announcement that it has the drug and the time it starts dispensing the drug, the national psyche goes haywire. The birth rate soars. Women take fertility drugs so they can have multiple births, couples considered too old or too young to have children have them. Churches take stands against the drug because it's against nature. If God wanted man to live to be 200, He would have made it that way.

Suicide grows more common, especially among the old who won't be helped by the drug. Toward the end of the five-year waiting period, the divorce rate soars as people who know they're going to get the drug decide they don't want to spend the rest of their 200 years with the same spouse. Older people turn against their children, who will benefit from the drug while they won't. The young resent the old even more because they're against the drug. A dissident pro-death movement springs up, spearheaded by the old. A pro-life movement backed by the young rises up in opposition. Psychologists do a booming business as the old and young alike seek to explore their feelings about the drug and what it is doing to them.

The job market will be in chaos. Junior workers will feel they'll be stuck in the same spots for years because senior workers simply won't die. Employers will be outraged by the idea that incompetents will be around that much longer and go on a firing spree that results in a 25 percent layoff of the work force. Corporate planners will begin to emphasize products that last longer. Quality will come back, as will the environmental movement that died off during the Reagan administration. We predict that if people are going to live on Spaceship Earth for 200 years, then by God let's not let them muck it up. Government and industry together will scrap all retirement plans, substituting instead a new form of Social Security that allows older workers to contribute less as they work shorter hours. Young people will look forward to two centuries of life.

What will be the impact of longer life on pension funds? There will be longer periods of payout by pension funds to people living longer lives and less money coming in from smaller numbers of younger people still on the job. The only way the pension funds will be able to stay solvent will be to sell stocks, which could in itself be a stock market, buying stocks at depressed prices when everybody in the money market turns bearish on stocks. The Social Security system may borrow money to finance its growing deficit. One way to finance Social Security will be to raise the inheritance tax and turn over the money to the Social Security system. After all, if family size is going to be limited to one or two children, a raise in the inheritance tax won't hurt heirs as much if they don't have to share their inheritance with three or four siblings. We predict that retirement age will be raised. People who live to be 150 will work until they're 110. People who live to be 200 will work until they're 150.

Toward the end of the first decade of the drug, the first scandals will break out about its use. High drug-company officials will be exposed for having the drug prolonging life but not taking the sterility drug preventing them from having large families. A black market for the drug will unfold, where government officials will be bribed to help dealers sell the drug illegally to people wanting families.

The government will announce it is taking over the companies that produce the drug and moving production of the drug to the moon, where it can't be easily smuggled to the black market. The government announces that the penalty for illegal possession and use of the drug is suspension from the drug for five years for a first offense, ten years for the second and denial for life for a third offense. At the same time, the government announces that henceforth the drug that prolongs life will be blended in with a sterility drug so nobody can cheat on its use.

It will take 50 years for most people to adjust to the new life-style. The first shock will be that bold choice faced by everyone once the antiaging drug is produced. Do I want long life or children? After 10 years, all citizens will be required to commit themselves to the new way and be required to sign papers choosing long life or children. Many will continue to require psychiatric help in coming to terms with the new life. Divorce will continue to rise as people realize the implications of life with the same spouse for almost two centuries. Suicide will become common, in part because of sheer weariness or disillusionment with a 200-year-long life. Society will be kept in some kind of turmoil by unreconstructed people who choose death at 100 over life for 200 years.

Parents will choose to have their single child later in life, since the body will be so well preserved. Aging as we know it today will disappear because people won't look that much older. White hair, wrinkled skin and sagging muscles won't appear in life until late in middle age, say about 130. It will be all but impossible to tell a person's age under 120. You'll have to hook him up to a machine to tell how old he is. A new sexual freedom will be inspired by the new life. We predict people will say that if they're going to spend 200 years on earth, they will want to enjoy it with as many people of the opposite sex as they possibly can. People will enjoy active sex lives until they're well into their 170s, when the antiaging drug will begin to lose its potency.

74

There will be periodic cleansing treatments to flush bodies of all liquids from blood to bile and replace them anew to give people new vitality even in old age.

To pass time in the new life, people will turn from electronic games to recreational drugs, then take up sailing, walking and jogging as never before. Everybody will be an environmentalist and the environmental movement will become the organized religion of the next century. Even the clerics will embrace environmentalism, especially as they see religion's influence waning in a world that no longer fears death because life goes on for 200 years. Life will grow less private as the government turns from governing to regulating. Slowly but surely, we will be forced to get used to the idea that Big Brother knows everything about us. At the end of 25 years, the question of how much to trust the government may still be a burning issue but after 50 years it won't be an issue at all. Who else can you trust but the government? After all, who but the government is taking care of us for the next 200 years?

Soon, the world's population will begin to shrink as everybody everywhere goes on the drug. In time, the world will begin to achieve a social parity. People will begin to live alike, think alike and even look alike as they age happily toward 200 years. The Brave New World of 1984 will be here. The year will be 2050.

3
▲▲▲▲▲▲▲▲

ENERGY SOURCES
FOR TOMORROW

▼▼▼▼▼▼▼

*"We have seen
the past and it doesn't work."*

—Dwight David Eisenhower

▲▲▲▲▲▲▲

*E*conomists blamed an unchecked rise in consumption, sociologists blamed too many people burning too many lights and driving too many cars, businessmen blamed the ecologists for wanting to revirginize the land and ecologists blamed the businessmen for wanting growth at any price. The truth is, they're all to blame for the bind we are in that is now routinely referred to as the Energy Crisis. In a sense, it's more a fuels crisis than an energy crisis. The United States doesn't have enough fuel to satisfy our wants and the fuel we have isn't the right kind to fill our needs. We can't burn coal because it's too dirty to burn, we can't burn natural gas because it's too clean to waste, we can't burn oil because it costs too much and we can't burn uranium because it scares people to death. Pessimists think the energy crisis has no solution. Optimists think it can be solved only by facing up to an endless string of price increases and unhappy compromises over which combination of clean, dirty, expensive and frightening fuels to use.

What got us into such a fix? How did something called an energy crisis strike the world's richest country with such force? Where was our warning? Who in the White House, who in the Congress, academia, private industry and the media told us it was coming? It started coming in the late fifties, when nuclear energy was oversold to the country as a cheap fix for all future energy shocks. If it did nothing else, the overselling of nuclear power forced a

79

recession on the coal industry that lasted almost 20 years. From 1958 to 1968, not a single new underground coal mine of any size was opened in the United States. The number of operating coal mines fell from 6,000 in 1963 to 1,700 in 1973. When coal slumped, natural gas became the fuel of choice for industrial boilers and electric power companies. Feeding natural gas to boilers is like feeding caviar to a bum. The cleanest, most precious fuel we have is now one of the scarcest. Geologists figure that when Columbus landed in America, there were 2,000 trillion cubic feet of natural gas in the ground that at current use rates will be drained out of the ground by the end of this century.

BOTTOMLESS BUCKET

Meanwhile, an insatiable appetite for energy was growing in the United States. America became a superstate on a diet of cheap, plentiful domestic energy. Nobody had as much energy as we did, a bounty that lowered the price of electricity every year from 1946 to 1971. The power companies advertised that the more electricity you used the less it would cost. There was no bottom to the bucket. The average American filled his home with light, heated his rooms when they were cool and chilled them down when they were warm. We went on the same binge with gasoline, which for years never sold for more than 30 cents a gallon and fueled a car so heavy it got only 12 miles to a gallon. While population was doubling in the United States, energy use was growing more than five times. By 1970, six percent of the earth's population, all Americans, was using 33 percent of the earth's energy. As energy became a better and better buy, everybody used more and nobody looked ahead. We were out for a free lunch. Even as the storm clouds gathered, nobody saw the darkening of the sky. Nobody in the White House and nobody in the Congress. One prominent (and here nameless) U.S. Senator looked us in the eye one day more than 10 years ago and said: "Don't you understand that you can't deal with a crisis before it becomes a crisis?"

One thing that forced the situation to a crisis was the environmental movement, a nationwide crusade against polluted air and water so unforeseen that in 1967 one of the nation's leading futurists wrote a book about the future that scarcely mentions the environment. Mentioned or not, the movement hit the energy business like a *blitzkrieg*. It brought an instant halt to the Plowshare program to use underground nuclear explosions to release oil and natural gas trapped in tight rock formations, delayed construction for at least seven years of the Alaskan oil pipeline, forced a near moratorium on the building of dams and effectively killed the fast breeder nuclear program in the United States. Ecologists forced power companies to abandon scenic river and lake sites in no fewer than 30 states while forcing power companies in more than 30 U.S. cities to abandon coal for low-sulfur oil. By one count, ecologists caused more than 1,000 delays in the construction of nuclear power plants in almost every state of the union. The electric power industry did not do well in its matchups against the movement. For a period of more than 10 years after environmentalists blocked Consolidated Edison's attempt to put a pumped storage plant on Storm King Mountain in New York's Hudson River Valley, the electric power industry failed to win a single environmental court case anywhere in the United States.

BOTTOMLESS THIRST

A bigger trigger of the energy crisis is America's appetite for oil. Of all the things wrong with America, one of the worst of them is its bottomless thirst for oil. In the last 30 years, the United States burned 142 billion barrels of oil, more than twice what all Europe burned in the same time. During almost every year of the 20th century, our thirst for oil has grown. In the last 30 years, the United States consumed more than four times as much oil as it used in the previous 30 years. Today, the United States takes one third of the earth's oil production, burning more than 14.2 million barrels of oil every day. Americans fly in airplanes that suck up more than 46 million gallons of jet fuel and drive cars that swallow more than 360 million gallons of gasoline every day. That's every day! The United States produces 8.6 million barrels of oil a day from its own oil fields but must also import 5.6 million barrels a day to quench that bottomless thirst. Those imports are a strain on the world's oil fields, its tanker fleets, its banks and its patience. The United States reached its domestic production peak at the same time that Europe and Japan felt a surge in oil demand as their economies took off. That meant that the United States had to turn for oil to the Middle East at the same time that Europe and Japan had nowhere else to go for oil but the Middle East. The head-to-head competition for Middle East oil is at least part of the reason world oil prices have gone from $3.50 to $35 a barrel in the last 10 years, a tenfold jump.

Today's standard American car goes 18 miles on a gallon of gasoline, about as far as it went 60 years ago and nowhere near as far as Japanese and European cars go. The nation's 110 million cars run on engines that average 150 horsepower, almost twice the size of European auto engines using almost half the gasoline. Seventeen percent of the world's people own 88 percent of its cars. The rest of the world uses an animal, a bicycle or their feet to get around. India alone has 12 million oxcarts clogging the roads.

MORE THAN
SCHENECTADY

Most homes in America are so poorly insulated they're overheated in winter and overcooled in the summer. The typical American high-rise building is enclosed in glass walls that let heat out in the winter and let heat in during the summer. One of the worst examples of the high-rise American energy waster is New York City's World Trade Center, which draws 80,000 kilowatts of electricity every day for lighting, heating and cooling. That's more electricity than the entire upstate city of Schenectady uses for its 100,000 residents. A classic case of energy waste in America is the story of the Los Angeles office building manager who leaves the lights on in the building all night because it's cheaper than putting in switches to turn the lights out when everybody goes home at night.

The only way to discourage energy waste is to raise energy prices, something that's been done with a vengeance for the last 10 years. Oil, natural gas, coal, uranium, even wood and windmills cost as much as 10 times what they cost 10 years ago. In an age of double-digit inflation, no prices were pumped up the way energy prices were. New car prices, food prices, theater tickets, clothes, dinner for two at a restaurant, air and train travel, even housing prices—it makes no difference. None of them rose in price as fast as energy did. In fact, most inflation is rooted in energy inflation. The price of an airline ticket went up because the price of jet fuel went up. Our electric bills are sky high because the price of oil is sky high. Food prices are up because it costs more for heat to process food and for refrigeration to keep food from spoiling. Food prices are up because farmers pay more for fertilizer that comes from oil, for gasoline to drive their tractors and for propane and butane that come from oil that they need to dry their crops. If you'd like to, you can blame inflation on energy prices. If energy prices had not risen so dramatically, we would not have the galloping inflation we have today.

ENERGY WAS
UNDERPRICED

Why have energy prices risen so rapidly? We need to do another flashback to explain that. Twenty years ago, even 10 years ago, energy was underpriced because there was too much of it. Oil gluts were commonplace, gasoline wars even more so. No longer plentiful, energy is no longer cheap. Oil is the pacing fuel for pricing. If oil rises in price, natural gas, coal and uranium usually rise with it. Why is oil the pacing fuel? Because it's a liquid that's easy to handle and contains a rich mix of useful hydrocarbons ranging from asphalt to gasoline. Oil has risen in price because we have begun to run out of it. No matter what anybody thinks, there is not an endless supply of oil in the United States or even in the Middle East, where 76 percent of the world's oil reserves are estimated to lie. Why should there be? The oil America burns in one year took nature 14 million years to create and the oil we've burned in the last 60 years is the geological equivalent of what it took the earth 400 million years to create, which is only 200 million years short of the time that the earth's oldest decaying fossils began to form oil.

The first signs that we have begun to run out of oil were there for anybody to see. Ten years ago, American oil wells produced 10 million barrels of oil every day. Today, they pump a little more than eight million barrels a day and that includes the two million barrels of oil being produced in Alaska that we did not have 10 years ago. When oil was plentiful, its price was based on what it cost to produce, which ranges today from $15 a barrel in the North Sea to $12 a barrel on the North Slope of Alaska to less than $1 a barrel in Saudi Arabia, where it lies so close to the ground it almost seeps out by itself. No longer is the price of oil determined by its cost of production. Nowadays, the price of oil is fixed by what it costs to find new oil to replace the old oil we just burned. Again, the cost of finding new oil varies from place to place but it makes only a little difference these days. In 1980, we found two billion barrels of new oil in the United States and burned three and one half billion barrels of old domestic oil. Worldwide, oil explorers found 15 billion barrels of new oil while the world burned 18 billion barrels of its old oil. It should not take a mathematical genius to figure out why the price of oil is on the rise.

POLITICAL PRICE
INCREASE

Oil also has a political price. When Iran and Iraq went to war in 1980, the spot price for oil in the rest of the world went up in what was clearly a political price increase. Even though there was a modest oil glut at the time the fighting broke out, Iranian and Iraqi oil supplies were interrupted by the fighting. This was a signal to the rest of the world's oil producers that they could raise their prices, which many of them did. What was the size of the price increase levied by the Arab oil producers at the end of the Yom Kippur War with Israel in 1973? One could argue that the price of oil has never stopped rising since 1973 and in fact has risen 10 times since the Arabs embargoed their oil during the war with Israel.

Based solely on past events, we would have to forecast a price increase for oil anytime there is a precipitous political event in the Middle East. Suppose Saudi Arabian King Khalid's heart stopped one night. What might happen to Saudi oil, on which more than half the world depends, if there was a battle royal among the royal family to succeed Khalid? If Saudi oil was interrupted, would the rest of the world's oil producers stand idly by and not go about the business of raising their prices? What if the Islamic right-wingers who took over the mosque at Mecca in 1979 began blowing up crucial pumping stations in the richest Saudi oil fields? A couple of years ago, a fire broke out in the Abqaiq oil field in Saudi Arabia, decommissioning a single pumping station for three months. It cost $1 billion to repair and cut off the daily flow of five million barrels of Saudi oil for three months. The only reason a worldwide crisis was averted was that oil stocks were at new highs in many industrialized countries, which were suffering a mild recession at the time.

$10 A BARREL INCREASE

It does not have to be a crisis in Saudi Arabia that interrupts world oil flow and kicks off a new round of price increases. Suppose a warlike Iraq decides to invade neighboring Kuwait to get a stronger foothold in the toe of the Persian Gulf. Oil prices would hardly be the same the day after Kuwait fell. There's the possibility of still another Arab-Israeli war which could carry with it the same economic sanctions against the West that were imposed at the time of the 1973 war. This time, the sanctions could be more severe than an oil embargo that was violated in spirit if not in fact. If there was another embargo, a price increase of $10 a barrel at the end of the embargo is not an impossibility. More likely than an all-out Arab-Israeli conflict is the chance of a pan-Islamic war that pits the Sunni Moslems against the Shiite Moslems in a war that would enflame almost the entire Middle East. If such a war takes place, as onetime deputy energy secretary John O'Leary told us, "you have a scenario where Middle East oil is essentially ruled out" for as long as 20 years. Rule out Middle East oil for 20 years and you raise the worldwide price of oil to $100 a barrel and drop the industrialized world into its longest and deepest recession since the Great Depression of the 1930s.

Nobody can forecast how many of these events will take place or which ones will take place, but by putting our trust in history we think it is safe to predict that two disruptive events will happen in the Middle East in the next 15 years. (After all, there were two major disruptions in the last 10 years, the 1973 Yom Kippur War and the Iranian revolution that overthrew the shah. There were three if you count Iraq's war with Iran. There could easily be another revolution in Iran, a second war between Iran and Iraq and an Iraqi invasion of Kuwait. There could also be a civil war in Saudi Arabia and a coup d'état in Syria.) Harder to forecast is the size of the price increase that follows each disruption. Five dollars a barrel is not out of the question for each major disruption, which would translate to $10 a barrel if there were two such events. That would raise oil's price to $45 a barrel barring any further price increases for purely economic reasons. One thing is sure. A price increase for purely political reasons will stick. For some curiously unexplained reason, when oil rises in price these days because of political pressures, it never sinks back to its old price when the pressures ease up. Mexico and Venezuela both raised the price of their oil after the outbreak of the war between Iraq and Iran. Both countries apologized effusively for doing so but they stuck to their price increases. The only oil-producing country that does not adhere strictly to this rule is the biggest, Saudi Arabia.

WELLS DRY UP

If, by some miracle, there are no political disruptions in the Middle East, we are still forecasting higher oil prices for the next 15 years. Let's face it, the world's oil wells will continue to dry up and exploration costs will continue to escalate to put upward pressure on prices. The 8.634 million barrels of oil that American wells pumped as a daily average in June of 1981 marked the first time United States production was up in the lower 48 states in eight years but it also marked an upper production limit on domestic wells that the United States will never see again. Even the two million barrels we get every day from Alaska's North Slope will begin to drop later this year (1982) unless another new field the size of Prudhoe Bay is discovered in the next few years. The new fields being found in the North Sea are getting smaller in size with each new find, suggesting the North Sea has a limited oil future. Drilling costs on the North Slope and in the North Sea have climbed to over $1,000 a meter, meaning that new discoveries in these two frontier regions will be harder and harder to come by.

There is a lot of oil exploration going on, despite the rising costs of finding oil. Oil companies are looking for oil off the western coast of Australia, in Indonesia off the coasts of Java, Sumatra, Borneo, Sarawak and Brunei, off the coasts of China and Vietnam, in the gulf of Thailand, along the Siberian continental shelf, in the Gulf of Alaska and the Canadian Arctic, off both coasts of South America and along the entire Outer Continental Shelf in the Atlantic Ocean. There is even talk of exploratory drilling in the deepest depths of the ocean using the former Central Intelligence Agency submarine recovery ship, the *Glomar Explorer*. The outlook for all these adventures is hazy and questionable. The only countries that are sure to have sizable reserves of oil at the end of the 20th century are the Arab countries of the Middle East, especially Saudi Arabia and Kuwait. There are three kinds of recoverable oil in the world, the oil close to the surface that just flows out, the oil not too far beneath the surface that must be pumped out and the oil far below the surface that must be forced out by the underground injection of chemical detergents and hot steam. Most of the oil in the Middle East just flows out. Kuwait alone has better than a 40-year supply of close-to-the-surface oil. Saudi Arabia has almost half the world's recoverable oil.

$55 A BARREL

What will be the price of oil in the next 20 years? Some experts think it will be $50 a barrel by 1990, $75 a barrel by 1995 and $80 to $85 a barrel by the year 2000. We don't think it will go that high because we think that fusion power will be so close to demonstration by 1995 that it will put a brake on oil prices. We do think that oil will hit $55 a barrel by 1995. That is almost unavoidable. What will that mean to gasoline prices? The rule of thumb is that you add two and one half cents a gallon to the pump price of gasoline for every dollar you add to the price of a barrel of crude oil. So figure it out. If oil costs $35 a barrel right now, a $20 per barrel increase will add 50 cents to the price of a gallon of gasoline. Will there be enough oil at the end of the century? There will be enough oil to fuel ships, planes and the cars that are still propelled by internal combustion engines. An oil crunch when worldwide oil supplies start to dwindle rapidly will not come until 2010 or 2020. Those will be the years that Middle East oil starts to dry up. The social and psychological fallout of an end to oil and to gasoline will be severe.

FORGET WINDMILLS, SO LONG SOLAR

How will the world manage to make ends meet? How will we deal with higher and higher prices and less and less energy? We *won't* deal with it by spending hundreds of millions of dollars attempting to use the sun, the winds, the tides and the heat that's trapped under the earth to generate electricity. Solar energy, wind energy, tidal energy and geothermal energy are ideas whose time will never come. The same is true of other "exotic" energy sources like biomass, magnetohydrodynamics and most of the so-called synthetic fuels you can name. They're all losers.

The two biggest losers are the two "clean" exotics that were hailed not only as answers to the energy crisis but as the salvation of the environmental movement—the wind and the sun. How clean can you get? What more could we ask for? For a while, windmills looked like an answer—big space-age windmills with propeller blades made of exotic metals that were placed on tops of hills or even mountains to turn on the lights for entire towns. Trouble is, they cost too much, broke down too easily and made a noise that drove the townspeople a little balmy. In any case, most of these space-age windmills aren't turning right now and when they're not turning they don't turn on anybody's lights. Forget windmills, solar was going to be our savior. The government even established something called the Solar Electric Research Institute to explore ways in which we could harness the light and heat of the sun to generate electricity. Energy from the sun, a source so ideal it's as if it were sent from heaven. Trouble is, solar electricity requires exotic collectors and even more exotic solar cells to convert light to electricity that costs the equivalent of oil priced at $50 a barrel. Solar energy has been a sun-sized disappointment. Our forecast is that solar-powered buildings, those steel and glass monstrosities with their enormous glass panels facing the sun, will become the windmills of the 21st century.

GOODBYE GASOHOL

Another loser is gasohol, a fuel mix of gasoline and ethanol (ethyl alcohol) that some futurists have predicted will solve any gasoline shortage we might face. Nonsense. The futurists making this prediction would *like* to see gasohol catch on because it would lessen our dependence on gasoline. The facts are these. The

United States plunged into gasohol production after President Carter embargoed grain shipments to the Soviet Union as punishment for invading Afghanistan. Suddenly stuck with millions of bushels of corn, Carter scrambled frantically for a use for the corn. Brainstorm! Guarantee loans of up to $3 billion for distilleries to convert the surplus corn to 500 million gallons of ethanol, which could be pumped into cars with gasoline as gasohol. Make it a national goal to distill 11 billion gallons of ethanol from corn so we have it in reserve in case of a national gasoline emergency.

The further facts about gasohol are these. It takes at least 2.3 gallons of gasoline for a farmer to plant, fertilize, cultivate, harvest and transport enough corn to distill one gallon of ethanol. Put another way, the American farmer would have to import a barrel of crude oil to distill one-fifth of a barrel of ethanol to mix with gasoline to make two barrels of gasohol. Carried even further, the same American farmer would spend his last gallon of gasohol plowing his last cornfield to plant his last cornseed to make more gasohol if he had any left to drive his corn to the distillery. The futurists quote the Brazilian experience with gasohol as the model for the United States. In Brazil, they don't plow the cornfields with tractors, they don't use fertilizer made from oil and they don't spray the fields with insecticides and herbicides from oil either. They fertilize with manure from the horses and mules who haul the corn to the distillery. That would not work in America. The futurists still want gasohol for America's cars, pointing out that President Carter proposed a four-cent per gallon tax break on its use. If we ever met the national goal of 11 billion gallons of ethanol, it would mean a gasohol subsidy of $440 million on top of all the other reasons not to pursue it. Gasohol is a disaster looking for a bridge to jump from.

COAL IS BURNED OUT

Still another fuel that is not the answer to the energy crisis is coal. This may sound like heresy to some people but our forecast is that coal will not even begin to fill our energy needs of the next 20 years. Coal is out of step with the times. As Tennessee Valley Authority Chairman S. David Freeman put it once: "There are two things wrong with coal. We can't mine it and we can't burn it." Let's face it, coal is mined in ways that Americans no longer accept and it's burned in ways that Americans find a sore to their eyes, a danger to their property and a threat to their health. The nine million tons of sulfur oxides pumped into the air by burning coal as recently as 1970 were linked statistically with lung and heart ailments in almost every metropolitan region of the country. Do you know how victims of black lung disease walk upstairs? They walk up backwards because they lose their breath if they walk up frontwards.

The sulfur in city air was found to corrode metal 30 times faster than sulfur-free rural air. High-sulfur coal burned in outlying rural regions has been blamed for destroying everything from pine trees to potatoes. "One reason we're switching away from coal," an executive of Consumers Power Co. in Michigan explained 10 years ago, "is that we're tired of paying the celery farmers for the crops we kill." Nobody will ever know what sulfur pollution cost the United States before the laws on air pollution were tightened up but the Council on Environmental Quality in 1968 put the cost of air pollution at $20 billion. Three years later, the Environmental Protection Agency calculated air pollution costs at $16 billion a year, $6 billion for its ill effects on health, $4.9 billion for material and vegetation damage and $5.2 billion for property loss. If we go back and burn coal, we can expect to see the same kinds of damage reports in the years ahead.

Worldwide energy use doubled in the last 20 years,

with oil accounting for two-thirds of the increase. Since energy conservation is finally taking hold in heavy energy-using countries like the United States, most experts expect energy use to increase 50 percent in the next 20 years. We know that oil cannot account for another two-thirds or even another one-third of the increase in energy use. There just isn't enough oil to handle it. Will coal take up the slack? Forgetting that you can't mine it and you can't burn it, there's something else wrong with coal that prohibits its broad use in the next 20 years. You can't transport coal either. United States coal companies produced 800 million tons of coal last year (1981) and would like to triple their output to 2.4 billion tons a year. How? There aren't enough railroad cars, there aren't enough waterways, there aren't enough barges operating on the available waterways to haul the coal they produced last year. There aren't even enough coal yards to stock the coal they produced last year. The fastest-growing market for coal in America is the export market. Germany and Japan will take all the coal we can send them. Coal cars sit for as long as three months near coal ports waiting for ships to take the coal aboard. Empty ships wait for as long as one month outside coal ports waiting for the coal cars to reach the docks. People talk about coal being a source for synthetic gas and a synthetic liquid fuel to make it easier to use. The cost of either one of these synfuels today is the oil equivalent of $50 a barrel, about the same as solar electricity. Let's face it, coal is out of step with the times.

HEAVY OIL

If coal is so far out of step, what's going to get us through the next 20 years? Heavy oil is going to get us part of the way through. What's heavy oil? It's oil so thick it won't move out of the ground even when it's pumped. It's the kind of oil that, when it was found in earlier days, was written off as a dry hole. It is not what oilmen call recoverable oil. All that is changing. Oil companies have begun to consider heavy oil as recoverable. The fact is, there are 300 billion barrels of heavy oil still in the ground in Utah, Wyoming and California, two trillion barrels in Canada and three trillion barrels in the Orinoco oil belt in Venezuela. While we'll never get all this heavy oil out of the ground, we'll get enough of it out by forcing it to flow with injected steam that it will tide us over through part of our energy shock. It will cost money to do this but light oil at $35 a barrel makes the cost of extracting heavy oil reasonable.

NEW NATURAL GAS

Natural gas also will get us partway through the next 20 years. A quarter of a century ago, the United States had proven gas reserves in the ground that were equal to 21 years of production. Ten years ago, reserves fell to less than 12 years' production and five years ago were down to 10 years' production. We were not finding new gas to replace the old gas we were consuming and our consumption of gas was rising so rapidly that it looked as if we were consuming ourselves right out of natural gas. The patient is not out of the hospital yet but two new trends have pulled the patient out of intensive care. Gas consumption is not as high as it was ten years ago. At the same time, new gas has turned out to be easier to find than new oil, especially since 1978 when Congress passed the Natural Gas Policy Act putting price incentives into gas exploration. New gas wells produced 40 percent more new gas in 1979 and 50 percent more in 1980 than they did in 1978. Gas reserves are now equal to more than 10 years of production, the first time a downward trend was reversed in almost 20 years.

If it did nothing else, the Natural Gas Policy Act gave gas producers a price incentive to drill deep. Gas wells deeper than 15,000 feet that used to be too deep to drill at the prices producers used to get have turned out to be bonanzas. One out of three gas wells drilled more than three miles down in the Deep Tuscaloosa Trend in Louisiana has turned out to contain gas. Usually, 90 percent of the gas wells drilled in the United States turn out to be dry wells. The *Oil and Gas Journal* says the Tuscaloosa Trend may contain as much as five trillion cubic feet of gas, which is one-fourth of a year's production in the entire United States. Gas men claim that deep wells like Tuscaloosa contain as much as 26 percent of all the gas found before in the United States. If their claim is even half correct, natural gas will get us even more than part of the way through the next 20 years.

Oil will also get us partway through the next 20 years. Drilling for oil in deeper offshore water promises the most rapid return and stepped-up drilling in Alaska the second best. Both will cost money, but if we recognize that the only alternative is even more expensive foreign oil, we will accept the expense.

THE ATOM IS THE
ANSWER

What is really going to get us through the energy crisis is atomic energy, the oversold nuclear power of the fifties and sixties that will come back in the eighties to save us. Nuclear power will come back as more and more people come to believe that its benefits outweigh its risks. There is no longer any doubt that the construction and safeguarding of nuclear power plants requires a network of controls unlike any the world has ever seen but to most people the "Faustian bargain" will be worth it to maintain a high living standard and an economic growth rate that means jobs. Uranium fuel doesn't cost as much as the black gold that comes from the Middle East.

LET'S GET TOUGH

Not everybody can run a nuclear plant—that's been clear ever since Three Mile Island. We predict tighter operating requirements on nuclear power. Nuclear safety will become the overriding concern of the federal government, which may take away the operating licenses of any power company that doesn't live up to the highest safety standards. Let's face it, the Metropolitan Edison Co. of Pennsylvania was not competent enough to be running a nuclear power plant. It should never have gotten an operating license for Three Mile Island. There are other electric power companies that should not have nuclear operating licenses. Former Energy Secretary James R. Schlesinger once said privately that no more than half the electric companies in America were competent enough to run nuclear power plants. There will be a get-tough attitude in deciding which electric companies will be given nuclear operating licenses and which will not. Hard choices will be made. We think the Nuclear Regulatory Commission will have enough remote monitors at every nuclear plant in the United States to turn off the reactors and cool them down from a distance if the people inside a plant are not working it right. The NRC will also have a S.W.A.T. team ready to go directly to a plant in trouble to straighten out whatever trouble it has.

Another hard choice that must be made is what to do with our radioactive waste. This is a question that's been successfully avoided by the last five American presidents, starting with Eisenhower. Technically, it is not a difficult question. It has been successfully answered in Germany, the Soviet Union, Australia, Sweden, and the United States. First, you harden the waste and change it into a glassy material or you enclose it the way Australian geologist Ted Ringwood did in a synthetic rock that can withstand a lot of heat for a long time. Next, you bury it as far down as you can in a cavern near no underground rivers in a part of the earth that hasn't felt an earthquake for centuries. There are millions of locations in the United States that fill this bill.

BURY THE STUFF

The tough part of the radioactive waste question is political. Arizona Congressman Morris K. Udall once started out a speech to the nation's 50 governors by asking them to raise their hands if they'd accept a burial ground for radioactive waste in their states. Not a hand went up. Not a single governor was willing to take on a nuclear garbage dump, even though there are three states that already qualify as atomic burial grounds. One is Washington, where the United States has buried the waste generated by the military nuclear power plants at Hanford for more than 30 years. Another is Nevada, where the United States has exploded hundreds of atomic weapons underground for almost 30 years. The third is Alaska, where the Aleutian island of Amchitka was used to test a five-megaton weapon below ground as recently as 1970. Why not bury our nuclear waste at Hanford, on Amchitka and in the Nevada Test Site. We must think they're safe. There's already as much buried radiation at all three sites as there is in all the country's operating nuclear power plants. What are we waiting for? Pick one of the three as the nation's nuclear repository or, better yet, bury the stuff in all three. All it takes is a presidential decision. We forecast that it will be made by President Reagan.

Finally, the United States must make it harder for a country generating nuclear power to use it to get into the nuclear weapons club. The United States must find a way to contaminate the uranium it sells to the world so that the plutonium it produces cannot be used to make atomic weapons. It is not impossible or even difficult. Making it harder to make plutonium bombs will revive the now-dormant fast breeder reactor that burns uranium to produce plutonium for electricity and is a necessary bridge between nuclear fission and nuclear fusion. The United States will build a commercial fast breeder reactor by 1986. Breeders are needed because 80 percent of the uranium fuel breeders use can be reused. By using breeders, we are saving our uranium. The technology is here. Experimental breeders have been working very nicely for the last 30 years. We need breeders if we're to extend nuclear power far into the 21st century. Without breeders, we will run out of uranium soon after we run out of oil. That is not a pretty possibility to contemplate. When President Reagan makes a decision on where to bury nuclear waste, we are forecasting that he will also decide to speed up commercialization of the breeder.

FUSION, NOT FISSION

The breeder will do more to get us through the energy crisis than anything else—except fusion. In fact, the crisis will be a cause of concern until somewhere between 1995 and 2000, when fusion power will be demonstrated so convincingly that the price of oil will fall for the first time in 25 years. Fusion is not fission. In fission, we explode atoms. In fusion, we combine them. Since we're combining atoms, there is no radioactivity being released and no radioactive waste left behind. Not everybody believes that commercial fusion can be demonstrated before the turn of the century but we are forecasting that enough breakthroughs will be made in the next 20 years that fusion energy will go commercial in the first few years of the 21st century. The fuel for fusion is deuterium, which exists in nature in sea water. When burned in a fusion reactor, the deuterium in one gallon of sea water is equal to the energy in 300 gallons of gasoline. A few pounds of deuterium will run a large city for weeks and the world will never run out of deuterium because the world will never run dry of sea water. What's more, fusion power doesn't involve use of uranium or plutonium, which can be made into bombs. There is no fallout from fusion over nuclear weapons. There is a waste issue but it's a simple waste issue. A fusion power plant would be strongly radioactive after 40 or 50 years of being bombarded by neutrons escaping from the reaction that fuses deuterium atoms together with such force it lights up at a temperature of 100 million degrees. There's a simple solution to the radioactive fusion plant. Cover it over with dirt and concrete at the end of its 50 years of useful life. Make a mausoleum out of it, a move that will cost the world far less in money and anxiety than not building fusion plants wherever we can. Anytime a nation, a state or even a community has voted to close down a nuclear power plant, other voters have turned out to keep it open. The same thing will be true of fusion.

The Congress has consistently voted for fusion every year for the past 10 years, overwhelmingly passing the Magnetic Fusion Engineering Act of 1980 that set the stage for a $1 billion fusion pilot plant to be working by 1990. A $314 million plant called a Tokomak (the Russian word for doughnut—the machine is shaped like a doughnut) is under construction at Princeton University and in 1985 is expected to reach a temperature of 100 million degrees Celsius, surpassing the 82 million degrees reached by a smaller Princeton Tokomak a few years ago. What's magic about 100 million degrees? That's the break-even point where the energy generated by the device is more than the energy needed to create a fusion. At about the time the big Tokomak is ready in 1990, the U.S. may decide that the doughnuts are too big and too cumbersome to make commercial power plants. No matter. Alternatives to the Tokomak abound. Magnetic mirrors are being developed that are smaller, cheaper and easier to maintain. Laser fusion is another strong alternative for the future. Fusion's strong point is its simplicity, no matter what method we use to produce it. In a fusion reactor, a plasma no bigger than a basketball can generate the electricity for 3,000 homes.

THE ELECTRIC CAR

The arrival of fusion will mean abundant, inexpensive electricity and will turn the entire world to an electric economy. Oil will no longer be needed. The electric car will appear, not the tiny experimental electric car we sometimes see today that never moves faster than 40 miles an hour and whose batteries have to be recharged every 50 miles but a normal-sized electric car whose batteries or fuel cells require recharging every 250 miles. That's acceptable. After all, we fill up our gas tanks every 250 miles so why should we object to recharging our batteries every 250 miles at the same gas stations we now use to get gasoline. The arrival of electric cars could even mean electrified highways where the cars attach themselves to an electrified rail by the side of the highway the way subway trains operate. That way, cars could run on highways for an indefinite time without having to recharge their batteries. Hooked up to an electrified rail, a motorist wouldn't even have to stay behind the wheel of an electric car on the highway. All the cars on the highway would be moving at the same speed, keeping the same distance between them. We think France will be the first country to try out this scheme. Not only does France have the longest experience with an electrified railroad network, it is also turning rapidly to an all-nuclear, all-electric economy. While we are forecasting an electric economy that produces electric cars, we are not forecasting an end to the internal combustion engine. There will always be cars that run on gasoline, though they will cost twice what electric cars cost. By the year 2010, oil will no longer be the world's main source of energy. The price of oil and its availability will determine when electric cars make a widescale appearance. If the price of oil levels off or comes down before it begins to run out, the electric car will be postponed. As soon as oil begins to disappear and the price runs up again, the electric car will be here to stay.

PLASTIC CARS

Oil will continue to drive ships and planes that cannot be plugged into electrical lines. Huge inland ferries and giant lighter-than-air vehicles will do what trucks do today, hauling the world's produce from place to place. We even see the time when coal is carried from the United States to Europe by lighter-than-air vehicles making the trip in 30 hours. Car bodies will be made of fiberglass and plastic and weigh half what they do today. Even the cars that burn gasoline will get twice the mileage they do today. There will not be gasoline rationing in the United States anytime in the next 20 years unless there is a major Middle East interruption of oil before the fast breeder and fusion power plants start to drive down oil prices. Driving will diminish, mostly because new techniques of communication will eliminate the reasons for as many as 25 percent of all trips. There will be a luxury tax on new gasoline-driven cars, which will no longer be designed with planned obsolescence in mind. The average car will be driven 10 years before it gets sold or junked.

These are our predictions for energy in the next 20 years. We think they're sensible and plausible. We don't think the world has to make any drastic new changes in its life-style to accommodate itself to the energy crisis. Remember, it is a crisis brought on by the world's dwindling supplies of oil. The time has come to move away from oil. We do not think the solution to the energy crisis will come from the extreme measures being taken by Interior Secretary James Watt, whose answer to the oil shortage is to open up one billion acres of offshore federal lands to exploration by the oil companies. Even the oil companies don't like that. They couldn't possibly explore 200 million acres of offshore land every year for five years, which is what Watt proposes they do. There are simply not enough people, money, and oil-well-drilling machinery available anywhere in the world to do all that.

4
▲▲▲▲▲▲▲

THE CRYSTAL GLOBE– WHICH NATIONS WILL SURVIVE?

▼▼▼▼▼▼▼

*"If we could first know where
we are and whither we are tending we
could
then better judge what to do and how to
do it."*

—Abraham Lincoln

▲▲▲▲▲▲▲

*I*n the 37 years since the end of the worst war in history, more countries have changed than were changed by all the previous wars in history. Nations have fallen, risen, disappeared and reappeared with a frequency that makes it impossible to record all the change. There's been the fall of fascism and the rise of communism, there's been the end of empire and the start of socialism. There have been civil wars, revolutions, coups d'etat and military juntas in every corner of the earth through every decade of the last three. The colonial counties of Europe no longer own a single colony. The greatest empire in history, the empire on which the sun never set, now consists of England, Scotland, Wales and Northern Ireland, where the sun sets no more than an hour apart every evening. If you ponder the stability of nations over the last 20 years, ponder the countries of Africa. They've changed their names more than 100 times in those 20 years.

If the last 20 years were unstable times for the family of nations, what will the next 20 years be like? If the last 20 years could not be predicted, how can we hope to forecast the next 20? The answers aren't simple, except to say that many of the events that shaped the makeup of nations over the last 20 years were themselves predictable, just as predictable as the events that will change national makeups in the years ahead.

GERMAN AND JAPANESE REBULDING

The reasons why Germany and Japan prospered so mightily after suffering catastrophic defeat in World War II are not difficult to explore. They were allowed to reindustrialize by their conquerors, decisions made deliberately in the cabinet rooms of the United States, Great Britain and the Soviet Union. What they were not allowed to do was research on atomic weapons, rockets and aircraft, decisions that saved the Germans and Japanese enormous amounts of money, which they used to rebuild their steel mills and shipyards. Today, the factories of Germany and Japan are still new and still use up-to-date machinery. The factories of the United States are no longer new and their machinery has long been outdated.

Why did France leave NATO? Because France decided to defend its colonies in Indochina when the British pulled out of Malaysia, Hong Kong and India, thinking the United States would bail them out if they got into trouble. Instead, the United States waited until after the French defeat at Dien Bien Phu to move into Southeast Asia. France never forgave the U.S. for that delayed move, pulled out of NATO and ordered U.S. troops off French soil in retaliation.

A COUNTRY'S VITAL SIGNS

The trends that help to shape national events are always influenced by a country's vital signs, which are just as important and just as easy to check as the blood pressure, temperature and pulse of a person. No matter where we live on earth, our normal body temperature is still 98.6 degrees Fahrenheit. So it is with nations, which have normal and abnormal vital signs. The vital signs to look for in a country are the signs that indicate political, economic and social stability. These signs include a country's birth rate, how it takes care of injustice, its treatment of dissidents, its relations with the press, the frequency with which it changes commercial regulations and goes out on strike, where it sends its elite to be educated, what it pays in salaries to its military officers.

The most frequently quoted vital sign is a nation's per capita disposable income. Every survey of national stability uses per capita income as its guide. But how important is per capita income? What does it tell you about a nation's stability if you know the average amount of money the average person is earning? Of far more importance is the income gap between the top and bottom tenths of a country's population. It's bad to have the very rich and the very poor in the same country. It's like the man with his feet in the oven and his head in the refrigerator. His average temperature may be 98.6 degrees but he's not going to last very long if he stays that way.

The top tenth in the United States earns roughly 11 times what the bottom tenth makes, not the best in the world but far from the worst. The most stable country in the world based on income gap is Sweden, where the uppermost tenth make two and one half times what the lowest tenth earn. Using income difference as a guideline, the most unstable countries of the world are Saudi Arabia, Indonesia and Argentina, where the upper tenth earn more than 40 times what the lower tenth makes. We're not forecasting imminent revolution for any of these three countries, but we do point out that Iran fell in part because the earnings of the upper tenth rose to where they were 38 times what the lowest tenth earned.

IRAN'S INSTABILITY

Just as important a vital sign for any country is its unemployment rate. Not just unemployment through the entire working population but the unemployment of the males between the ages of 18 and 28 who make lots of trouble when they're penniless and restless. These are the men who left the rural regions, maybe got an education and then came to live in the city to get a job. Except there are no jobs. They don't have a place to live, they don't have money for food and they don't have wives. They're educated enough to know that things should be better. When the shah fell in Iran, there were hundreds of thousands of men like this who settled in Iran's largest cities. They were the backbone of the revolution that broke the shah.

Other vital signs changed in Iran that helped break the shah, the kinds of changes that always imply the onset of instability. The shah doubled the salaries of his military officers in the two years before he fell. What does that tell you? That the shah was no longer buying military strength, he was buying loyalty. You can't buy loyalty. Not to a cause and not to a country and not to a shah. Still another indicator of growing instability in Iran was how the shah began to treat dissidents. The shah's response to dissent was to beef up the size and strength of the SAVAK, the brutal Iranian secret police force whose answer to dissent was imprisonment, torture and murder.

Expectations are an important vital sign. If everybody is poor, no one minds being poor. If everybody gets a fair share of even a little wealth, it's all right. The shah never fed his people's expectations. In 1973, he stopped payments to the mullahs and ayatollahs who ran the Moslem religion in Iran. His wife began taking a percentage of all the contract money pouring into Iran after the shah began using his oil revenues to industrialize the country. This meant the corrupt low-level officials could no longer count on their small share of the proceeds at the same time the mullahs were being cut off the dole. So what happened? The mullahs showed up among the merchants in the bazaars demanding one percent of the proceeds. In one fell swoop, the shah had lost the clergy, the merchants and the bureaucrats who were the backbone of Iran's middle class. The shah took away the country's religion, then its middle class. When you lose the middle class, you lose the country.

DETERMINING POLITICAL STABILITY

Which countries will be the most stable at the turn of the century? Which will be unstable in the year 2,000? What countries will undergo such dramatic change in the two decades ahead we won't be able to recognize them?

In forecasting the future of the family of nations, we shall use some of the same vital signs and indicators we've already told you about as guides to reckoning national stabilities. Think of them as facts in a computer, all arranged in a way that points the reader of the machine's printouts in the right direction. We'll use other signs, too. In determining political stability, we'll want to know how well each country transfers power from one regime to the next, we'll want to know a country's level of administrative competence and we'll want to know how its people accept central authority. Take Argentina, for instance. They don't accept central authority at all. Each state, each province has more control of its people than the government in Buenos Aires ever does.

To figure economic stability, we want to know if they export more than they import, if they have more than one natural resource, if they produce any of their own energy supply and what their rate of inflation is. Take Israel, one of the toughest and potentially one of the world's most unstable nations. Why? They import five times more than they export, they have a little bit of one natural resource (potash), the only energy source they produce is the solar energy they get from the sun. Israel has no oil, no natural gas. It gets its coal from South Africa and its uranium from the United States. Its inflation rate last year was 131 percent, the year before 129 percent.

IDEOLOGIES AND RESOURCES

There is also national unity to consider. Are the people who make up a nation in cultural conflict? Put another way, how many different factions make up the country? Iran had Christians, Jews, two differing sects of Moslems, Kurds, Azerberjanis, Baluchis and the Marxist Tudehs, all in opposition to each other when the shah fell. Is there a unifying ideology present in the country? Argentina gets the lowest marks for unifying ideology. Most Argentines are German, Irish, Italian and Spanish and dislike each other intensely.

Finally, there are world trends to consider to define the directions nations are taking. Take population. A country whose people increase at two percent a year is less stable than one whose population grows at one percent a year for the simple reason that it's producing too many new mouths to feed. A country where most of the people live in the cities is unstable because it implies overcrowding, unemployment and not enough farmers growing food for the people in the cities. How much food is available? Is a country's population getting all the calories it needs? Is its protein intake sufficient? What about energy supply? Generally, a country producing more energy than it consumes is more stable than a country using more than it has.

Go on to raw materials. A country with one natural resource is certainly less stable than a country that has two, three, even four different raw resources to draw on, refine for its own use or export to earn foreign exchange. A prime example of an event illustrating this trend is a little thing like corn. Research has produced a sweetener from corn that is cheaper and sweeter than the sugar that comes from cane. When this happened, five countries whose sole crop was sugar fell from the Third World into the Fourth World. An exception was Jamaica, which lost its sugar market to corn sweetener but which still had bauxite to sell to the world's makers of aluminum. Jamaica stayed in the Third World.

THE STABLE COUNTRIES

A crucial trend in rating national stability is a country's exploitation of science and technology. An example of a stable nation is one whose labor force can absorb the most advanced technology available. An unstable country is one whose labor force is technologically illiterate and still does most of its work by hand. Consider a country's degree of industrialization. A nation producing more than $50 billion in finished factory goods is stable. A country whose factories produce less than $10 billion in goods is not stable regardless of size. While only one indicator of stability, the $10 billion figure is a kind of "critical mass" that indicates instability if a country falls below that figure. National aspirations have something to do with stability. One should not be too optimistic about the future of Iran and some other countries with large numbers of Shiite Moslems because their self-image is so high they will kill and die for their beliefs. Even a country's geographic position influences its stability. A nation commanding an important sea or land route to one of the world's superpowers is going to be more stable then one with no such access, for the simple reason that the superpower is likely to provide protection to the country with access.

In a nutshell, here's what we see for the Spaceship Earth ten to twenty years hence. The strongest, most stable country in the world will continue to be the United States. Second, third and fourth will be Australia, Canada, and the

United Kingdom. Fifth will be a reunited Germany. Then France and the Soviet Union, whose fortunes will slip because they've been late in recognizing the technological revolution that is transforming world economies. China will be more of a world power for the same reason Japanese influence will wane. China has its own coal, oil and minerals. Japan has none.

Great Britain will make a comeback because of North Sea oil and gas and a tougher political stance. The Arab countries will no longer hold the world hostage to their oil but neither will they slip back into oblivion. There will be a single Indochina, run by Vietnam. On the other hand, the Fourth World countries with no oil, no minerals and too many people, the countries like India, Pakistan, Bangladesh, Sri Lanka, Niger, Chad, Eritrea, Mauritania and Bolivia will be lucky if they still exist as separate or independent states.

GERMANY

The single most important political change of the next 20 years will be the reunification of Germany. Expect it. The process has already begun. West German Chancellor Schmidt made his first state visit to East Germany after the Polish strikes began. It won't be long before Schmidt makes that visit. The next step will be a policy that allows people of both countries to cross borders freely and visit their relatives, then a tearing down of the Berlin wall followed by a loosening of the trade barriers between the two and a relaxation of emigration rules. The final step will come when Soviet troops begin to exit East Germany. Expect that in 1990 and reunification by 1995. By that time, the Russians will welcome reunification. Why? To get West Germany out of NATO, open up a buffer zone free of nuclear weapons between East and West and force the united Germanys into the world's unaligned bloc of countries.

The forces that will help to bring about Germany's reunification are already loose. West Germans can now visit their East German relatives and the two countries have begun to exchange goods. Lutheranism is making a strong comeback in East Germany, where Christmas trees and Tannenbaum wreaths can be had for the first time in years. The guilt West Germans felt about the Holocaust and which helped keep the two Germanys apart is disappearing. The East German government no longer adopts the hard line of the last 20 years. The Soviet Union does not come down as hard on East Germany as it once did.

German reunification will take place when the Soviet Union allows it, a process that has already begun. Soviet oil is being sold to West Germany and a pipeline to carry Soviet natural gas into West Germany is being built for the first time. What's significant about that? Germany could end up just as dependent on Russian gas and oil as France is on oil from the Middle East. A strong analogy would be the nuclear research reactor France built for Iraq that was air-attacked by Israel early in 1981. France gets one-third of its oil from Iraq. Why wouldn't it build a research reactor for Iraq? The natural gas pipeline into West Germany is the first step of a Soviet scheme to keep the Germans on the fence. The Soviets also have begun to realize they need West Germany. They need consumer goods, especially consumer goods with a high-technology base. What better goods than German goods? Why not barter Soviet gas for these goods? There's another inevitable process taking place. The members of the ruling Politburo that remembers the German destruction of the Soviet Union in World War II average 72 years in age. They will soon retire and die off, giving way to younger men whose memories aren't imprisoned in Stalingrad.

RUSSIA

The Soviet Union itself is in for somewhat tougher times. It continues to support an arms race at the expense of consumerism, a mud-mired attitude that sucks the lifeblood from the Soviet economy year after year. It has all but ignored the civilian technology revolution sweeping the rest of the world and finds itself falling further and further behind the rest of the world. Except for arms, the Soviets don't have a solid technological base. They gave the contract for the Siberian oil pipeline to Caterpillar Tractor because they don't know how to build it themselves. Their space program is crude and at least five years behind the American program. The Soviets had the world lead in fusion research 20 years ago and are falling behind in the race today. Russians still suffer food and housing shortages with routine regularity. Moscow motorists still keep their windshield wipers in the glove compartments of their cars for fear they'll be stolen. They're growing weary of it all. There's another thing soon to take place. In 1985 the Russian race will be a minority in their own country for the first time and the Soviet Union will face the severe instability that usually comes with minority rule.

CHINA IS LEAPFROGGING

In contrast, look at China. As undeveloped 30 years ago as any country on earth, China has leapfrogged that dismal episode and stands to enter the 21st century stronger than it has ever been. Unlike Japan, China has its own oil and minerals. It's not even paying the money to extract its oil from the ground. China has told the American oil exploration companies to drill for the oil with the understanding they'll be paid in the oil they find. China is also moving into the electronics age lock, stock and barrel by buying entire U.S. plants and importing U.S. managers to run them until Chinese managers can take over. A country with only two million telephones for almost one billion people, China will install fiberoptic telephone lines to start a major expansion of its phone network. It plans to have at least two communications satellites acting as switchboards in the sky by 1990 and has already begun using the largest tractors in the world to cultivate farms and make China self-sufficient in food. Even social change is making its impact on the new China. To cut down its population, China now allows a tax deduction for the first child, none for the second and takes back the first deduction when a third child is born. A third child also brings removal from the Communist party, a harsh penalty indeed.

What we've tried to do is outline the vital signs essential to national health. We've also attempted to paint a broad picture of what those vital signs mean for the major countries of the world in the years ahead. Now, let's go into more detail of what we think lies ahead for the countries whose position, size, population, degree of development and influence make them important pieces of the global puzzle. We'll leave out some countries because they're too remote, too small or too much like other countries that exercise more impact on world events. Finland, Norway and Denmark are classic examples of the latter. They mirror Sweden, they follow Sweden. Therefore, we'll talk about Sweden with the implication that we're discussing the future for all of Scandinavia. New Zealand is another country we'll leave out, simply because in forecasting the future of Australia we think we're tying that future with New Zealand's as well.

THE MIDDLE EAST

Let's start with the Middle East, the hot spot of the entire earth, the source of almost half of its oil, at least half its tensions and most of its misunderstandings. There's an old story that goes something like this: There was a scorpion standing on the west bank of the Jordan River when a fish swam by. The scorpion called the fish over and said: "Look, I'd really like to get over to the other side but I can't swim. Will you give me a ride over on your back?" Well, the fish gave the scorpion a very fishy eye and said: "Are you kidding? As soon as you get on my back, you'll sting me and I'll die." Whereupon, the scorpion replied: "Why would I do that? If I did that and you died, I'd drown. I'd be crazy to do something like that." The fish thought about that for a moment and said: "Okay, climb on my back." The scorpion did as he was told and the fish took off for the east bank. Halfway across the river, the scorpion couldn't contain himself any longer and gave the fish a deadly sting. Dying, the fish looked up at the scorpion and said: "Why in God's name did you do that?" Shrugging, the doomed scorpion answered: "I don't know. This is the Middle East and it's in my nature."

There is no place on earth like the Middle East, where the Zionist state of Israel sits surrounded by the oil-rich Moslem countries who call Israel their sworn enemy. There have been three major outbreaks of war between the Arab countries and their sworn enemy and a steady state of tension between them all that was perhaps typified by the Israeli attack in June 1981 on a nuclear research reactor that had just been built by France for Iraq about 12 miles from its capital city of Baghdad. Nowhere else on earth had any country attacked a foe's nuclear reactor. It suggests that the Middle East is the height of instability, which it is.

THE HOUSE OF SAUD

There isn't a country in the Middle East that doesn't show at least some instability, even Saudi Arabia. The upper tenth of its population earns at least 40 times what the lowest tenth makes, not a sign of stability. The oil sheiks and the royal family members of the House of Saud all live in palatial homes, spend their money conspicuously, export their gold to Western banks and drive either a Rolls-Royce or a Mercedes Benz, which they often junk when it breaks down because it's easier to buy a new one. The one million Yemeni and Pakistani "guest workers" pose something of a political threat, though nowhere near the threat constituted by the 250,000 Palestinian guest workers in the country.

The Saudis are bothered enough by this threat that they're now attempting to control the number of "overstayers" by limiting their time in the country. Saudi Arabia will always have a severe shortage of native manpower. Therefore, there will always be guest workers in Saudi Arabia, raising the possibility of civil war or revolution in the years ahead. The Saudi army is pathetic. It is comprised mostly of 20,000 Pakistani mercenaries, who could be beaten in five days by any kind of invading force unless the United States checked in on their side. Look for the U.S. to do that if there is any threat of force against Saudi Arabia in the next 20 years. If there is no U.S. presence in Saudi Arabia, its hopes for permanence will plummet precipitously. Saudi oil and the moderate Saudi voice at Middle East peace tables are too important to U.S. interests.

Nevertheless, the world's largest oil producer will go on making remarkable strides improving the everyday lot of the Saudi people. Hospitals, highways and schools will be more than adequate for the next 20 years and while housing is expensive, home ownership is helped by 25-year government mortgages. Where else in the world can you get a mortgage without paying any interest? Despite a small clique of dissidents who took over the mosque in 1979, there is still no organized opposition to the House of Saud. There are still no labor unions or political parties or dissatisfied student groups. The military has still never interfered in affairs of state. Does Saudi Arabia sound too good to be true? The real danger to royal rule will come when radical factions of the royal family develop a following among dissidents who see traditional Islamic values being compromised by Western life-styles. Saudi Arabia may sound like a desert Utopia but it isn't. There's trouble ahead.

IRAN

If trouble comes to Saudi Arabia, it could come from Iran, where almost anything is possible in the next 20 years. Among the possibilities for Iran are a coup that brings back the young shah; the dismissal of the elected parliament (the majlis) and president by a more feeble Khomeini; and a total dismemberment of the country by the Kurds, the Azerberjanis and a radical left Islamic coalition that includes the Tudeh (Communists), the Fedayin and the growing Islamic socialist organization, the Mujaheddin. Iran's political scene will be chaotic for at least the next 10 years. If dismemberment doesn't come, the country will go on being dominated by the radical right-wing Islamic Republican party, which will attempt to export its revolution when Khomeini dies and a younger firebrand takes his place. Economically, Iran will hurt. Expect dwindling oil revenues, high unemployment and an inflation rate that doesn't fall below 50 percent. As bleak as the 1980s appear for Iran, the 1990s appear even bleaker. By then, there may not be enough oil wealth left in Iran to give the country a second chance at the industrialization begun by the shah and stopped by the Ayatollah. With 30 million mouths to feed, industrialization is the only hope for this seemingly hopeless country.

LIBYA

If Iran doesn't fill the role as troublemaker for the Middle East, Libya may well step in and take over that role. In many ways, Libya has already assumed that mantle. Qaddafi's adventurism seems only to grow with time. His witch hunts for dissidents, his murder of exiled dissidents, his incursions into neighboring Chad cost him his embassies in the U.S., Nigeria, Niger and Mauritania. Qaddafi finds himself friendless in Gambia, Senegal, Sudan and Mali and has no friend in Egypt, which would love an excuse to annex Libya and acquire its oil wealth. France has long since given up trying to keep Qaddafi under control, now seeing him as an enemy making trouble in the French-speaking countries of North and West Africa. There is still plenty of low-sulfur oil to pay for Qaddafi's schemes, but there are signs that Libyan reserves are not as great as they were once thought to be. One sign: Libya has begun to search for oil in contested border areas where there could be conflict.

Despite some obvious signs of instability, Qaddafi's Libya shows a remarkable national unity. Adventurous he may be, a terrorist, a fervently radical Moslem, but Qaddafi is a charismatic leader whose five million people seem to worship him. He's also one of the youngest leaders in the Middle East and will probably be around for a while. As far as anybody knows, there has never been an attempt or even a plot to assassinate him. Nevertheless, Qaddafi is his own worst enemy. Right now, he has allies in Syria, Iran and Moslem Lebanon and that's it. If his adventurism grows or if he gets in a serious quarrel with Egypt, there is no guarantee Syria would come to his aid in a conflict. Should that happen and one almost expects it to, Qaddafi and Libya could collapse. Look for Egypt to do Libya in. With Sadat dead and Egypt still on friendly terms with Israel, there would be nothing to hold Egypt back from annexing Libya and its oil.

ISRAEL

There can be no mention of the instabilities of the Middle East without a serious discussion of the instabilities that menace the state of Israel. The only thing that keeps Israel intact is its first-class war machine and its chutzpah to use it in preemptive strikes against its enemies. Take a good look at Israel. It has none of its own energy, almost no natural resources, an economy that's chronically ill, no water, and the highest inflation rate in the world. Its major exports are flowers and citrus fruit which it sells to western Europe. If Spain and Portugal win entry to the Common Market as is expected, then Israel will lose the export market for its flowers and citrus because Spain and Portugal will move theirs into the Common Market at preferential prices.

Politically and religiously, Israel is a divided country. Nothing illustrates those differences more strikingly than an incident at the outset of the Yom Kippur War in 1973. The first Israeli casualties in that war were soldiers on motorcycles who were killed on their way to the front by chains that had been strung across the road by Orthodox Jews who objected to their going to war on the Sabbath. Israel's vital signs are not healthy. More and more, there are violent clashes between Jews and Arabs in the occupied territories. There is also a huge disparity in birth rates between Israel's Jews and Israel's Arabs. Jewish women are now producing an average of 1.1 children, Arab women are up to an average of 6.8 children. Not only does this increase already aggravated tensions, it will make Israeli Jews a minority in their own country by the year 2000. There's growing friction among the Jews themselves. Reports of discrimination against the Sephardic Jews by the ruling Ashkenazic Jews are more and more frequent. But among the Jews, the Sephardim are by far the fastest-growing group, suggesting the Ashkenazim will not be able to maintain their political and economic domination much longer.

On top of all this, Israel's friends in the West are losing patience with Israel's uncompromising policies over the occupied territories, the settling of the West Bank and the Palestinian issue. Israel is at a major fork in the road of its existence. It can forfeit the West Bank and allow the settlement of Palestinians in a separate state and can make a major attempt to get along with its Arab neighbors. Its solid technological base could then be used to forge new trade ties with its neighbors. If all this happened and it developed a major export market for its modern weaponry, it could enter the last decade of the 20th century as strong as it's ever been. If it continues its uncompromising policies, it will forfeit the sympathies of an oil-hungry West and be at the ultimate mercy of an increasingly angry Arab world eager to destroy Zionism. One nuclear bomb placed between the major Israeli cities of Tel Aviv and Jerusalem, and Israel will cease to exist as a nation. On the other hand, Israel, because of its high levels of technology, management, and education, has made the desert literally bloom. When the canal between the Mediterranean and the Dead Sea is completed, the Israelis say, dams on the canal could be used to generate 600 megawatts of hydroelectric power in addition to the tremendous irrigation potential. When either desalinization and/or fusion come to fruition in the late 1990s, Israel is again expected to become one of the most stable countries.

COUNTRIES OF THE FOURTH WORLD

As unstable as the Middle East will be, it will not be as shaky as we expect most of Africa will be for the next 20 years. No continent on earth has more unstable countries of the Fourth World whose only resource is their people. Unfortunately, too many people. Mauritania, Chad, Niger, Eritrea, the Central African Republic, Senegal, Mali, Gambia and the Upper Volta are all African countries that chart out very low on the stability scale because they have no raw materials and no energy in the ground. There are only three with the potential for true global stability. They are Nigeria, South Africa and Zimbabwe, formerly the white-run British colony of Rhodesia. Even these three face major periods of instability. The runaway population growth of Nigeria will strain its food supplies and its oil money, the racial policy of apartheid will strain South Africa's political stability and the numerous tribal factions fighting each other will tax Zimbabwe's political staying power.

NIGERIA

The success of the Nigerian effort to stay a strong member of the Third World seems to be dependent on too many miracles. An importer of food to feed its still-growing population (currently 60 million people), Nigeria has embarked on a green revolution to become self-sufficient in food but has not earmarked enough money to do so. At the same time, the northern deserts are encroaching on existing farmland. Nigeria still doesn't have enough native skilled manpower to capitalize on its oil and may end up importing too many guest workers to do so. Its oil-pricing policy is erratic, leading to oil surpluses and sudden layoffs of oil-field workers that do not promote internal stability. Its young civilian government is making a halting transition to civilian rule, in part because there are so many rifts in what are too many major political parties. How many? At least two parties in each of Nigeria's 19 states can rightly be called major political parties. Even now, the civilian government is faced with demands that it create more new states, that it keep the size of the bureaucracy from spiraling out of control, that it accomplish "even" development among the many states, that it hire an "even" number of bureaucrats from each state. The list of demands goes on. The government may not be able to cope with any of them.

The schism between the north and south is wide and getting wider. The drive for universal primary education (UPE) is an immensely popular idea but it will do little to right the imbalances between north and south. Already better educated, the southerners are rushing to take advantage of the new education policy while the northerners are not. There is a shortage of teachers everywhere but a far worse shortage in the north. Too many people have moved from the countryside to Lagos, whose population will reach four million by 1986 and whose unemployment and crime rates are rising as rapidly as the population. Nigeria is afflicted with a disease one might call "rising expectations." Today, it is oil rich. Unless it can find massive new oil reserves that so far have not been tapped, Nigeria will not be oil rich in 10 years. If the day comes when Nigeria is not oil rich, it will become a land in chaos that will revert back to the bloody civil wars that marked the country 10 years ago.

ZIMBABWE

Zimbabwe is a country facing major near-term stability questions but it could be a more stable land than Nigeria by the turn of the century. In the year since Robert Mugabe took control of the government from the whites, few of the worst and few of the best expectations about the new government have been realized. The tiny white minority, still the core of the country's technocracy, did not leave the country when Mugabe took over. Mugabe seems prepared to honor guarantees that there would be a certain number of white seats in the parliament, to compensate white farmers for land turned over to blacks and white civil servants passed over for promotion by blacks. At the same time, thousands of guerillas roam the hinterland fighting each other instead of their old white rulers. The foreign investment needed to exploit the country's vast resource wealth is lagging, in part because of a wait-and-see attitude by investors watching Mugabe's progress. Mugabe has mentioned nationalizing the mines, which has more than a few investors skittish at the thought.

Mugabe has promised free primary education and health care, even though there is already a shortage of teachers, doctors and nurses. Like Nigeria, Zimbabwe suffers from the rising expectations disease. Unhappily, it will spend the next few years in near chaos waiting for order to come. But come it should. Great Britain, Canada and the U.S. are all pulling for Zimbabwe to make it and are prepared to supply the help it needs to get there. The country's black majority is well aware how rich their land is in natural resources and seems uncommonly willing to put the nation's interests before their own to exploit that wealth.

SOUTH AFRICA

In a continent of contrasts, no country shows such vivid contrast as South Africa. Western investment appears to have returned to South Africa, making its booming economy one of the strongest in the world. Its emerging policy of neoapartheid at last suggests subtle changes in its racial policy. Exports of gold, minerals and food are at all-time highs. Though the country is attacked daily by the black African press, South Africa has never enjoyed as much trade with black Africa as it does today. The terrorist attacks of 1980 that destroyed several of the country's Sasol (liquid coal) plants were not repeated in 1981. Possessing the world's fifth largest coal reserve, South Africa also owns the world's most advanced processing plant to convert coal to a usable liquid fuel. Because it's so rich in minerals, it supplies employment to hundreds of thousands of black workers from Botswana, Lesotho, Zimbabwe, Angola, Swaziland and Mozambique. It also supplies telephone service and electricity to those countries, which may be one reason the terrorist raids have slackened off. South Africa is clearly enjoying a breathing space right now, which we expect will last through the eighties.

At the same time, there are some troublesome signals of instability throughout South Africa. The white police still show no shame in killing blacks to break up riots. Blacks are still shackled in poverty and restricted to rural regions. The country is obviously in the process of building nuclear bombs, if it hasn't already done so. There are no signs anywhere that the National party, which has been in power for 30 years, is in any danger of losing that power. Despite a growing range of opinion within its ranks on apartheid, support for whatever racial policy the National party chooses to follow is at an all-time high. Unemployment among blacks stays high, which it must do as long as access to the skills needed in South Africa's technological economy are denied to them. There aren't even enough skilled whites in the work force. If South Africa must use its army at any time in the near future, this scarcity of skilled manpower will worsen and the booming economy will boom no longer.

While South Africa may be in for a breathing space, it won't be a long one unless major changes are made in racial policies. If the policies don't change, the terrorist attacks on the gold mines and Sasol plants will resume. The terrorists will have a juicy new target: South Africa's uranium enrichment plant. If it is destroyed or even damaged by terrorists, it would be an enormous psychological defeat for the ruling regime. It must be emphasized that whatever world influence South Africa has it derives from its economic power. Any change in that and all bets are off on

South African stability. If South Africa's whites cling to their fanatic dedication to maintaining a separatist society, the minority white government will be toppled sometime in the decade between 1990 and the year 2000. Count on it.

INDIA

Few regions of the world will be more unstable in the next 20 years than the subcontinent of Asia. In examining their vital signs, it's almost impossible to forecast any kind of stability for India, Pakistan, Bangladesh and Sri Lanka. How these countries manage to survive as separate states is a mystery. None of them has any energy supply, none of them has any raw materials to speak of, none of them possesses any industrial might. The only thing they have in common is an overabundance of people, whom they barely manage to feed. The only things that keep India going are its size and position on the globe. Because it's still the largest democracy on earth and because of its position commanding the Indian Ocean, India is very adept at playing the East and West blocs off against each other and acquiring aid from both. The same thing is true of Pakistan on a smaller scale.

Besides a near-stifling poverty, India suffers from too many internal tensions. Its urban population despises its rural population. The Hindus hate the Moslems. The caste system prevents the formation of any middle class that might bootstrap the country out of its poverty. There are so many languages spoken in India that the country has no sense of national identity. Even its reputation for democracy is suffering. The most momentous legislation of Indira Gandhi's new term was the passage of a new preventive detention act to restore order and repress opposition. Gandhi's biggest mistake was in pouring money needed for irrigation projects into developing an atomic bomb. The explosion of the first Indian atomic bomb infuriated East and West, India's only sources of long-term survival funds. The only other things the Hindu Indian bomb did was to encourage Moslem Pakistan to start its own development of an atomic bomb, a move by the poorer Pakistanis that may prove to be a bigger mistake than the Indian bomb. The only thing India has going for it is the amount of aid it can squeeze out of the Soviet Union and the United States. The only thing Pakistan has is the money it gets from the Moslem world to continue development of a Moslem nuclear bomb. This nuclear development contest with India will almost surely escalate, possibly leading to a nuclear exchange between the two. If that happens or not, the outlook for India and Pakistan is grim. By the year 2000, both countries may be splintered into a number of smaller states, more than one of which might be nuclear armed.

AUSTRALIA

When one thinks of the grim future facing India, it's hard not to contrast it with the bright future ahead for another former colony of the British Commonwealth. Everything India doesn't have, Australia has in abundance. Coal, oil, natural gas, uranium, bauxite, copper, iron, chromium—name the raw material or the energy source and Australia seems to have it. The only thing India has is too many people. One of Australia's great strengths is its underpopulation of 14 million people, most of whom live in the big cities along the coasts and make it an extremely stable country. Almost all of Australia's vital signs point upward. It has one of the most stable political systems, has a strong sense of national unity, no great division of race, creed and religion and everybody speaks the same language. Australia has even had the good sense to open the country to Indochinese immigration and recognize the rights of its own aborigines.

If anything, Australia will get stronger as times march

on. Its resource boom is just getting under way. Self-sufficient in all forms of energy, it will be exporting coal, uranium and half a dozen different minerals for years to come. It has enough iron and natural gas for heat to mill steel that will be competitive in price with any in the world. Even food will be a major Australian export, making Australia the breadbasket of the entire Pacific region. Almost immune to attack, Australia's lone weakness may be one of the world's smallest armies for a country of its stature. In the two decades ahead, Australia will be the most prosperous of the world's nations, emerging as an influential regional leader whose standard of living will be one of the two highest in the world.

JAPAN

The rise of Australia in the years ahead is a key to the declining status of Japan. No matter how much the Japanese might disbelieve it, the Japanese economic miracle is coming to an end. The miracle really is the length of time Japan was able to stay on top. The country in the world most dependent on imported energy, Japan has no minerals or raw materials at all to fall back on. The mightiest exporting country in the world must import every raw material it uses to produce those exports. As bad as it is now, things will only get worse. Today, Japan imports 96 percent of its energy. In 1990, it will be 98 percent.

Japan faces new challenges as well. Its aging population will retire 20 to 25 percent of the work force in the next 10 years at 80 percent of their basic pay. Japan will be hard pressed to afford it. No longer can its work force expect wages to rise to match its increase in productivity. Why? Because the productivity of these amazing people is finally leveling off. Toyota has already announced a freeze on the salaries of workers over 40 years of age, effective in 1985.

Datsun is expected to ask a similar freeze. Japan will be forced to turn to robotic automation to keep up productivity, a move that will raise Japan's unemployment rate from its current two and one half percent to as much as 12 percent by 1995. Production is also expected to fall. Up 10 percent a year only 10 years ago, Japan's production gains fell to five percent last year and will be down to less than two percent by 1990. Clearly, the miracle is nearing its end.

Still, Japan will remain a major stabilizing force in Asia and throughout the industrialized world. Many of its vital signs will continue to point upward. It has one of the highest literacy rates in the world and values education as do few countries of the world. Japanese have one of the world's longest life expectancies, in part because their crime rate is one of the world's lowest. Nonetheless, there are defects in the Japanese life-style. The country is still frightfully over-crowded and polluted, which could someday cause a decline in life span. Its aging populace will surely place greater stress on health care and social security, which could lead to higher taxes. Higher unemployment could raise the crime rate. In the face of all this, it must be remembered that the population will not age, its productivity will not fall and its technology not fail overnight. Japan is a resilient country that snapped back completely from the only military defeat in its history. Japan will long be one of the earth's most competitive countries.

CHINA IS LOADED

As Japan's influence wanes in the years just ahead, China's influence will wax as strong as it's been in modern times. Just as Japan has none of its own energy sources, raw materials, or agricultural capabilities, China is deep in oil, gas, coal and just about every mineral it needs to grow industrially. It also has great agricultural potential. China is 30 years behind the rest of the industrialized world, in part because Mao decided China had to shut itself off from the rest of the world to cleanse itself of the corrupt policies of the past. As Japan will not decline overnight, so China will not rise up overnight. But remember one thing about China. Its vital signs include a stoic acceptance of delayed goals that few countries of the world can ever hope to match. China is in no hurry to outstrip its neighbors but outstrip its neighbors it will. The Chinese are keen mathematicians and physicists with great respect for education. They are bound to catch up with the rest of the world. What China needs is less people and more bureaucratic competence. Programs to achieve both have already begun. A major change that has already taken place has been the separation of the government from the Communist party. Party leaders will no longer hold government positions and vice versa, a change that is sure to improve the efficiency of both. Look for China to become more Socialist than Communist in the years ahead. Even now, the Chinese are turning back to their ancient belief that a person puts one-third of his money into land, one-third into running his household and one-third into his savings to take advantage of opportunity when it strikes. Together with their strong acceptance of delayed goals, this philosophy will make the Chinese of the future more like the Puritans of yesteryear. It's the old Protestant ethic, if you will, and a hard ethic to beat.

SOVIETS AND SATELLITES

What lies ahead for the Soviet Union and its satellite bloc in Eastern Europe? The Soviets will stay a world superpower, make no mistake about it. Despite a chronic shortage of grain that may never end because of the Arctic winds, the Soviet Union is more or less a self-sufficient nation. It has enough oil and gas, enough coal and uranium to export energy westward. The

Soviet Union is not short of raw materials. Politically, its vital signs are those of a fit but aging athlete. Its leaders are getting old and will soon be succeeded by next-generation leaders. The only questions are, how competent will the next generation be and which direction will they take? Revamping the economy to place more emphasis on consumerism would appear to be a must. The great weakness of the Soviet Union is its ignorance of the consumer instincts of its citizens. What travelers to the Soviet Union have not been asked to sell their blue jeans, panty hose and dollars? One suggestion of how to attack the Soviet Union has been to have B-52s drop Sears-Roebuck catalogues printed in Russian.

The ability of the Soviets to exercise international power in the two decades ahead will depend not only on themselves but on the willingness of the West and the Chinese to let them do so. A unified Germany will help Russian influence, but a chronically dissatisfied Poland will weaken Russian influence. There is a great deal of uncertainty ahead about Soviet relations with the Warsaw Pact countries, not just Poland. Yugoslavia and Rumania have already broken loose from the mother ship; Hungary is thinking the same kinds of thoughts. If others follow in their wake, Soviet world influence will decline.

EUROPEAN STABILITY

Western Europe will undergo some subtle shifts in stability but no real major changes. West Germany will stay near the top of the charts for the same reasons it's at the top right now. No matter what vital signs you plot for West Germany, they come out high. It has a strong economy, the most stable politics in Europe and a healthy, disciplined and educated people. It has no cultural conflicts of any kind. The only ethnic disturbance Germany suffers are its estimated two million guest workers, most of them Turks, Yugoslavs and Italians. So stable is Germany that many of its second-generation guest workers have become German citizens. Why not? Its inflation rate of six percent is the lowest in Europe and the mark is one of the strongest currencies in Europe. The only real trouble Germany has is the same trouble facing almost all the rest of the industrialized world. It must import a lot of its energy, though not nearly as much as its neighbor France.

FRANCE

France is a country that must expect a modest decline in the years ahead. Its industrial productivity will fall somewhat, mostly because France suffers from an excess of smaller family-run concerns. Politically, it is stable for the next six years even with a socialist government in charge for the first time. Its dependence on Persian Gulf oil doesn't help it but its emphasis on nuclear electricity doesn't hurt it either. Along with Germany, France will become a major exporter of breeder nuclear power plants and earn vital foreign exchange. France has one major economic hurdle ahead of it. In 1988, the infamous gold bonds of Giscard d'Estaing come due and the French treasury will take a beating. Giscard put the bonds on the market and offered real gold for their redemption at a time when gold sold for less than $500 an ounce. It was not a wise marketing move on Giscard's part.

GREAT BRITAIN

While we expect France to falter, we expect Great Britain to rise. It's true the United Kingdom is now in difficult economic straits but Thatcher's policies show signs that they will work if given enough time. We think she'll get that time, if only because of the growing rift within the opposition Labour party. The British still have a high standard of living, in part because of North Sea oil and gas and the preeminence of the country as one of the world's financial capitals. It has few ethnic problems, except for the chronic headache in Northern Ireland and a growing problem with black immigrants from Asia and Africa. The separatist movements in Wales and Scotland seem to have abated and will stay that way through the next 20 years.

ITALY

The countries with the biggest troubles ahead in Western Europe are clearly Italy and Spain. Second only to Japan in dependence on energy imports, Italy also suffers from chronic political instability, a high inflation rate, a growing disparity between the rich and poor and a wave of terrorism that has brought Italian justice to its knees. Italian industry is hamstrung by Italian politics, whose 41 governments in the last 35 years have allowed Italian workers an extra month's paycheck, Christmas bonuses, excessive vacation benefits and guarantees against layoffs even in the worst of times. Italy is still not a unified country in the minds of its people, whose voters include the largest Communist party and the largest monarchy party in the West.

SPAIN

Spain's troubles are a lot like Italy's. Basque and Catalan terrorists may yet force a separation of the two states. Spain is almost as energy poor as Italy. It has its own coal but it is of poor quality. If Spain does not win entry into the Common Market and if Europe's economy falters badly enough to bring crowds of

Spanish guest workers home from the more industrialized countries, Spain is in for big trouble.

CANADA

One of the two most prosperous countries in the world in the 20 years ahead, outside of the United States, will be Canada. Like Australia, Canada has an excess of energy supply and a seemingly endless quantity of raw materials in the ground and will continue to be a major agricultural exporter. Canada's only problems are political. The liberals have all their strength in the cities, the conservatives have all their strength in the provinces. The same divisions exist in the minds of the people. Canada's wealth lies mostly in its western provinces, which may someday in the next 20 years form their own country. If they do, it will be the richest in the world. The separatists in Quebec will be quiet for a few years but if a separatist movement springs up in the west Quebec can expect to become vocal on the issue again. Canadians do have an identity crisis. They can't make up their minds who they are and who they want to be. If Canada splits up into different states, expect the two maritime provinces in the east to join the United States.

LATIN AMERICA

Latin America has long been the repository for misplaced and forgotten countries. Mexico is the strongest of the lot because of its oil and gas but that strength is weakened by an overpopulation relieved only by illegal entries of migrant workers from Mexico into the U.S. Colombia still sells its coffee beans at good prices but its stability is threatened by its ties to drugs, which now match the country's coffee exports in size.

Inflation and political instability are the two curses on Brazil and Argentina. On top of chronic student and worker strikes, Brazil saw the formation of six major new political parties last year, hardly a barometer of political stability. Meanwhile, inflation topped 100 percent in 1980 and 1981. Its city slums continue to swell as displaced farm workers flock to the cities where they find no jobs, no housing and no access to education and health care. The same problems exist in Argentina, except on not such a grand scale. The poorest outlook for all of Latin America is in Bolivia. Literacy will never top 60 percent and its pool of doctors and nurses will decline in the years ahead from the already inadequate numbers they have today. Spanish is still the official Bolivian language even though the Indians are in the majority. The outlook for Bolivia is so bleak that we expect it may no longer exist as a separate state in 1995.

If countries like Bolivia are to survive, the industrialized nations of the world must get together and decide to support them with foreign aid. Every industrialized nation must give three percent of its gross national product to a foreign aid pool if the Fourth World is to stay intact. Sweden already gives nine-tenths of one percent of its GNP to foreign aid, the other Nordic countries turn over about half of one percent to the same cause. The U.S. gives only one-tenth of one percent to foreign aid, the Soviet Union gives even less. There must be a change in the way rich countries support poor countries for the poor to avoid slipping off the side of the earth. The stability of *all* nations depends on it.

THE NEXT 20 YEARS

In summary, here's a list of the most stable countries today and our projections for the next 5 to 10 years and the next 10 to 20 years.

In order of *decreasing* stability, the most stable countries *today:* United States, Federal Republic of Germany, Australia, Canada, Japan, France and the United Kingdom.

The most stable countries the *next 5 to 10 years:* The United States, Australia, Canada, the U.K., the U.S.S.R. and Germany. The most stable countries *10 to 20 years hence:* the U.S. stays first, Australia second, Canada third and the U.K. fourth; Germany moves to fifth and France to sixth. The Soviet Union slips to seventh and Japan to eighth.

Some of the most dramatic changes in outlook affect those nations now in the midrange of stability. Rapid *deterioration* is anticipated for: Poland, which drops from ninth to twenty-fourth in stability ranking; Italy, which drops from eighth to twentieth (from eighth to twenty-fourth in the long term); Spain, which drops from fifteenth to twenty-fifth; and Israel, which drops from fourteenth to twenty-third, then rises to eighteenth.

Major *gains* in stability will be established by: Zimbabwe, rising from twenty-fifth to eighteenth (short term) and then to eleventh place (long term); South Africa, rising from twenty-second to eleventh; Nigeria, rising from twenty-first to twelfth, and then to tenth; and Libya, rising from seventeenth to eighth, but then falling again to nineteenth.

5

▲▲▲▲▲▲▲

WILL THERE BE WAR OR PEACE?

▼▼▼▼▼▼▼

*"If we open a quarrel
between the past and the present,
we shall find that we have lost the
future."*

—Winston Churchill

▲▲▲▲▲▲▲

The year is 1990 and world population exceeds 5.3 billion souls, all striving to get through the next 10 years and into the 21st century. Electric cars dart through the streets of New York, the first city in the world to wire one million computers into the workplace. The silicon chip drives elevators and subways, turns thermostats, runs operating rooms and changes traffic lights. The jobs people have, the games they play, the purchases they make, the funds they transfer, even the food they cook start with the silicon chip.

Oil is no longer king and the Arab oil producers of the Middle East no longer wield the power and influence they once did. Electricity is king, coming as it does from nuclear furnaces everywhere in the world. But if much has changed since 1980, so much else has stayed the same. Power rests in the same enormous hands it's rested in for 45 years. The superpowers are still the superpowers. The United States and the Soviet Union still rule each end of the roost. No other country challenges their military leadership of the East and West blocs of the world.

There have been no major wars, but the Soviet Union and the United States are again at odds after a brief spell of detente that ends with the Soviet invasion and occupation of Iran. The North Atlantic Treaty Organization (NATO) is dissolved and replaced by the North Atlantic and Pacific Treaty Organization (NAPTO), a group that includes Japan but not West Germany. The West Germans abandoned

NATO in 1988 to begin reunification talks with East Germany. German reunification seems inevitable. North and South Korea were reunited the year before after 42 years of being apart.

Reunification. One Germany again—the price the Soviet Union paid for driving West Germany out of NATO. On achieving their goal, the Soviets turn their attention eastward, tightening their ties with Vietnam and still scorning the Chinese tiger to the north. Vietnam now occupies part of Indonesia and has turned over the Indonesian naval base at Surabaya to the Soviet fleet. At long last, the Russians have a warm-water base in the Pacific. Where are the Chinese? The Chinese play a curiously passive role through all this, choosing to stay out of conflict while they strengthen themselves at home. Meanwhile, the rest of the world is primed for trouble. The threat of conflict is everywhere.

Black African radicals in Zambia, Mozambique, Zimbabwe and Botswana mass troops along their borders for war games in preparation for an all-out assault on South Africa. Across the South Atlantic, Brazil and Argentina are locked in a race to develop a nuclear weapon after refusing to sign the treaty of Tlaltilco banning nuclear weapons in Latin America. Pakistan explodes a 10-kiloton atomic weapon underground, prompting India to set off a 50-kiloton bomb in the atmosphere over the Great Indian Desert. First Libya, then Egypt, then Israel and then South Africa openly test nuclear weapons and send ripples of fear across the Dark Continent and the Middle East. Just as suddenly, the eyes of the world are on Saudi Arabia, where a threat of revolution threatens the oil lifelines of Japan and Western Europe.

Oddly, the United States is less concerned with civil war in Saudi Arabia than with civil strife in Mexico, which now supplies the U.S. with 70 percent of its foreign oil. The culprit in Mexico is an aging Fidel Castro, who supplies money, arms and terrorist training to a band of Mexican revolutionaries eager to strip out their share of Mexico's oil wealth. A single spark seems all it would take to set fire to any of these conflicts. There comes a spark in the fall of 1990. Yugoslavia applies for partnership in NAPTO, the defense umbrella that has succeeded NATO. It is a move felt round the world.

RUSSIA INVADES TURKEY

Background: On Tito's death in 1980, Yugoslavia begins to drift back into the Communist camp as a kind of nonaligned junior partner to the Warsaw Pact. The Soviets busily encourage an indecisive Yugoslavia to take a full partnership, in part because the Russians covet Yugoslavia's warm-water ports along the Adriatic and the indestructible submarine pens built into the cliffs north of Dubrovnik. By 1988, the Yugoslavs move so close to the COMECON countries that the West silently writes off Yugoslavia from the unaligned.

Two things happen to change that. The Soviet Union occupies Iran, and Yugoslavia installs a new leader, a man as strong in mind and independence of will as Tito had been. He brings the Yugoslavs together, telling them they can't trust the Russians because of their move into Iran. Taking the entire world by surprise, the new Yugoslav leader renounces his country's commitments to the Warsaw Pact and pledges a new allegiance to the North Atlantic and Pacific Treaty Organization. The Soviets are caught as much by surprise as anybody else, then in a cold fury decide they can no longer live with the frustrations that come without a warm-water port in the Mediterranean. On Eid-el Adha, the Feast of the Sacrifice, the Moslem Christmas, the Soviet Union invades Turkey. Striking from the east with six tank divisions to tie down Turkey's Third Field Army at Erzurum, the Soviets pour two full field armies through Rumania and Bulgaria to trample Istanbul and to reach Ankara in less than a month. A NAPTO country is under Soviet attack, bringing certain retaliation from Turkey's NAPTO allies. For the first time since 1939, the world stands on the brink of total unthinkable war. Could that really happen in 1990?

WAR GAMING

Yes, it could really happen. War can always happen. The scenario you've just read is no idle plot schemed into being by fiction writers. The scenario you've just read has been discussed at length by senior military officers and planners at the various U.S. War Colleges, where real responses to potential hostilities anywhere on the globe are carefully plotted out by America's military leaders.

Every military school in the west—Sandhurst, West Point, St. Cyr—is war-gaming a major Warsaw Pact invasion, either across Europe or through Scandinavia. In addition, every military college in Asia and the United States is playing the North Korea invasion of South Korea war game. The Russian invasion of Turkey that you have just read about is just one hostile act that's been war-gamed at these service schools. At least six others have received the same treatment. While still just scenarios for potential conflicts, each of the seven is treated as a real possible outbreak of hostilities involving the U.S.

Clearly, a Soviet invasion of Turkey would be a stronger threat to world peace than anything that's happened since the Cuban missile crisis of October 1962. Turkey is a NAPTO nation, a member of a mutual defense force that demands retaliation. But consider the following possibilities for conflict, all of them real in the next 10 to 15 years. The Soviets invade Yugoslavia and/or Greece for the same reasons they move into Turkey: access to the Mediterranean Sea. Or the Soviets invade Australia, using their newly acquired Indonesian naval base at Surabaya as the springboard into Down Under. Don't sneer when you read that.

By moving into Australia and blowing up its railroads and oil refineries, the Soviets would be denying the Western countries access to Australian iron, copper and uranium for the critical last decade of the century. If Australia can't move its iron and uranium from its inland mines to its seaports, there's not much sense in mining these resources.

The Soviets don't pose the only threat to world peace in the next decade. There is the real possibility of an all-out black African offensive against South Africa, which is sure to defend itself with nuclear weapons. How would the U.S. react? Would it side with the black nations of Africa against the atomic weapons of apartheid? Or would it move to South Africa's side to protect the vital mineral deposits so badly needed by the U.S.? Fidel Castro might like nothing more in his later years than the neighboring island of Jamaica, which was turning tantalizingly close to Castro's kind of communism before the 1980 Jamaican election turned things back the other way. Suppose Castro decides to make trouble in Mexico. What better way than to sabotage the oil field in Campeche Bay, Mexico's biggest money-earner and the oil lifeline of the United States?

How would the U.S. respond to either one of Castro's moves? Eight years of Republican conservatism in the U.S. is sure to force U.S. relations with Cuba into deterioration, which means the U.S. is likely not to sit back and watch while Castro creates mischief in the hemisphere. Could the U.S. tolerate a Cuban invasion of Jamaica? Not likely. Lyndon Johnson sent 14,000 American troops into the Dominican Republic in April of 1965 to put down a civil revolution under the guise of protecting American lives and property. How would the U.S. tolerate a Cuban-supported terrorist attack on the oil fields of Campeche Bay? Not even as well as it might tolerate an invasion of Jamaica. By 1990, the Campeche Bay fields will be supplying the U.S. with as much as 70 percent of its oil imports. Take a guess at how the U.S. would react to a terrorist attempt to cut that lifeline.

SOVIETS INVADE
AUSTRALIA

Let's start with the conflict many people might think is the least likely to happen in the next 10 years, a Soviet invasion of Australia. Australia? Not even the Japanese set foot on Australian soil during the height of their success after the start of World War II. Why would the Soviets invade Australia? It's a country as big as the United States with a population smaller than California's. What's to invade? Why would the Soviet Union even think of invading Australia?

Think ahead 10 years. Jamaican bauxite is no longer freely available to the U.S. because of Jamaican unrest and Cuban interference. Africa's uranium mines don't export as much as they used to because African politics is against the free export of uranium. In 1990, the U.S. gets most of its bauxite and most of its uranium from Australia. There has also been a resurgence of the British Commonwealth. India and Pakistan have rejoined the Commonwealth and Australia supplies those two countries with most of their food. What better mischief could the Soviet Union provide than to cut the U.S. off from Australian bauxite and uranium and India and Pakistan from wheat and meat?

Australia is not a member of any mutual defense treaty organization like NAPTO. It sits at the bottom of the South Pacific, enormous, impossible to defend, alone except for tiny New Zealand. Its endless beaches make Australia easily accessible to invading forces. What allies it has are thousands of miles away. At the same time, its military might is laughable. Australia has a standing army of 32,000 men and 90 tanks. Its air force is made up of 150 tactical airplanes. Its navy has one aircraft carrier.

Staging six divisions out of Vietnam, Iran and the Indonesian seaport at Surabaya, the Soviets attack Australia from the sea on Christmas Day. They mine the ports at Melbourne and Sydney, blockading the small Australian navy. They drop two airborne divisions outside Melbourne and Sydney to prevent troop movement. The six seaborne divisions enter the country through the Northern Territory, where they quickly occupy the uranium mines and the coal and iron fields. Soviet aircraft spray Agent Red all over Australia's wheat fields, ruining the harvest. They blow up the rail junctions and oil refineries, which has the effect of crippling the country. Any land as vast as Australia must have railroads to move goods. Things come to a standstill.

The Soviets remove their troops from Australia in three weeks but the damage is done. By the time the Russians go home, they have sabotaged the uranium mines, wrecked the railroads and blown up the oil refineries. The uranium, the bauxite, the copper, the iron are all useless without railroads and fuel to move them. It takes years to get the country moving again, the U.S. is without a backup uranium supply and a resurgent British Commonwealth suffers a major setback because two prodigal members (India and Pakistan) are denied their food supplies.

Clearly, the U.S. took too long to react to the Soviet invasion of Australia. While deciding what to do, the White House debated using the neutron bomb against the invading Russian armies. By the time the U.S. decides to warn the Russians about the neutron bomb, the Soviet troops are gone. Canada, Great Britain and New Zealand, the military backbone of the Commonwealth, are just as surprised and just as slow to react to the invasion as the U.S. and the Soviet Union gets away with one of the greatest thefts of history.

By 1990, the threat of a limited nuclear war is a steadily growing one. Atomic genies have popped from their bottles the world over. More than a dozen countries have tested atomic weapons, at least another half dozen are nearing that phase of development where they are planning a test. Nuclear sabers are being rattled everywhere. One can hear rattling sounds in Libya, Egypt, Iraq and Israel. Back in the

Commonwealth, India and Pakistan both possess nuclear weapons. Taiwan has a bomb. So do the reunited Koreas. South Africa has a small arsenal of tactical nuclear weapons, including the fearsome neutron bomb. The question is not how to stop the spread of nuclear weapons but how to stop one of these countries from using a nuclear weapon against a neighbor.

ARGENTINA BOMBS BRAZIL

The first nuclear salvo to be fired in anger since Nagasaki is fired by Argentina. Furious that its giant neighbor Brazil has gone ahead with the construction of three huge dams along the contested Rio de la Plata, land which Brazil had acquired from Argentina under a previous agreement, Argentina drops a 20-kiloton bomb on a rural region of Brazil. The choice of target is a careful one, a region so sparsely populated the bomb kills few people and burns and contaminates nothing but undeveloped land. But the explosion does two things: It expresses Argentina's festering discontent with Brazil and announces that Argentina has created an atomic bomb before Brazil. Unless Brazil halts construction of the dams, a second bomb will fall on Rio de Janeiro. Live with the consequences, Argentina says in a terse diplomatic note— we face the future unafraid.

Argentina follows up its nuclear salvo with conventional strikes on Itaipu and Sete Quedas in the Rio de la Plata basin but Brazil quickly moves troops to the border to protect its hydropower projects. Already, the war has its comic aspects. Brazil's army and air force are each more than twice the size of Argentina's but it is Brazil who plays out the role of David while Argentina is acting for all the world like Goliath. As if it suddenly notices the disparity, Brazil takes the offensive and moves its men across the Rio de la Plata into Argentina. Brazilian leaders dare Argentina to call a nuclear strike on Rio de Janeiro.

While all Latin America holds its breath, the U.S. decides to move on its own. Wisened a little by the Soviet invasion of Australia, the U.S. tells the Organization of American States it plans to move into the zone of conflict as peacekeeper. U.S. objectives are simple: Prevent a nuclear exchange and terminate hostilities. A rapid deployment force comes in fast using a major new U.S. weapons system. Lighter-than-air vehicles carrying more than 1,000 men apiece land along the river basin and disperse troops across the river into Argentina, which is clearly the aggressor and clearly the more nervous of the two combatants. Nonlethal gases are pumped in along both borders to neutralize combat troops on both sides. An airborne division is dropped to surround the site suspected to be the Argentine nuclear depot. The OAS backs the U.S. move in full.

To the surprise of most of the world, the bold U.S. move against the Argentines works. Hostilities cease, the OAS hauls the two combatants before the United Nations and a serious debate begins. How did such a bizarre little war begin? Argentina concedes it felt a growing bitterness toward its bigger neighbor, especially over Brazil's exclusion of Argentina from joint ventures. Not once did Brazil indicate it wanted to share the hydroelectric projects along the Rio de la Plata. Venezuela and Mexico, the region's two oil powers, did little if anything to help. Seemingly, they shared Brazil's contempt for Argentina and sided with Brazil and the one-sided hydroelectric project. A beginning was made. The two largest countries of South America are brought a little closer together by what was almost a catastrophic misunderstanding.

BLACK AFRICA *VS.* SOUTH AFRICA

Back across the South Atlantic, another nuclear confrontation is taking shape. Black African radicals are massing troops along 3,000 miles of border that South Africa shares with Zambia, Mozambique, Zimbabwe and Botswana. Western intelligence indicates these are not war games or guerrilla moves. An all-out offensive is in the offing, one that will stop only when Pretoria falls to the blacks. South African response is knee-jerk. Pretoria warns the black Africans it will defend itself with nuclear weapons, hinting at the same time that its defense force includes neutron weapons. Few in the West doubt that South Africa possesses a neutron bomb. The Central Intelligence Agency warns the blacks of the fearful consequences a neutron bomb attack could bring. The blacks decide to call Pretoria's bluff and move in force across four borders toward certain holocaust.

Black Africa's move on South Africa comes at a bad time. There is no country left in Africa to act as mediator in the dispute. Nigeria had once been able to conciliate the two sides, but no longer. Out of control politically, over-populated and no longer as rich in oil as it had been, Nigeria is not a power in African politics. A panicked Great Britain knows that it cannot act alone. Hat in hand, Britain calls on the U.S. to come in with it in a last-ditch attempt to stop the holocaust. The U.S. finds itself in a quandary. Emotionally, the U.S. is on the side of the black Africans. How can it support South Africa militarily? Says the chairman of the U.S. Joint Chiefs of Staff: "You want me to order my troops to defend South Africa? Half my men are black. They might turn their guns on me."

But the U.S. also knows that if it doesn't defend South Africa, the South Africans will use their neutron weapons against the blacks. What follows the use of neutron force? Nobody can predict what might follow. The Chinese might intervene, the Soviets would surely intervene. Nuclear attack on South Africa from Libya and Iraq is a certainty, and if that happens Israel would join South Africa in all-out war against the aggressors.

Difficult as it is, the U.S. knows it must bite the bullet. Quickly forming 10 divisions made up entirely of white troops, the U.S. uses the rapid deployment force to get the men into South Africa before the holocaust begins. The U.S. air-drops irradiated materials along a broad front 30 miles ahead of the invading black forces to seal off the South African heartland, then uses some of the same nonlethal gases it used in Argentina two years before to neutralize the advancing black hordes. At the same time, the U.S. and Great Britain turn around and tell the white government of South Africa in no uncertain terms that the time has come for an end to apartheid. If South Africa is unwilling to bend on this issue, the U.S. and Great Britain will abandon her.

While the whole world watches, a drama of capitulation unfolds. Two black African leaders secretly enter South Africa, where they hold day-and-night talks with their white counterparts. No holds are barred in the discussions, which are mediated by the roving British and American ambassadors. After what seems like months, the talks stop and a joint communiqué is issued. Black Africa's troops are called back from South Africa and an end to apartheid is declared. A peacekeeping force of American troops stays behind in South Africa to ensure that the end is orderly. Hopes for African, even world, peace rise as one of the deadliest threats to that peace begins to dissipate.

CIVIL WAR IN SAUDI ARABIA

Two years after the end of the troubles in South Africa, a new trouble spot flares up. It is Saudi Arabia, still the largest oil producer in the world and home to 1.5 million Yemeni and Palestinian guest workers. In a land of four million people, that's a lot of guest workers. The economic gap between the guest workers and the native Saudi population is enormous, having widened every year since 1980. Oil revenues are dwindling as the rest of the world has learned to live with less oil and as the drive to demonstrate fusion nears an end. There is unemployment in Saudi Arabia, a growing source of friction between the Saudis and their guest workers. Dissidents are at work and the Soviets have begun to supply them secretly with arms. One day the roof falls in. A gang of Palestinian guerrillas ambush the king and crown prince of the House of Saud and machine-gun them on their way to the airport at Riyadh. Insurgents attack Riyadh and Jidda. The House of Saud calls on the United States for help. A civil war seems almost a certainty. The oil lifeline of Japan and most of Western Europe is about to be severed.

The 20,000 Pakistanis who protect the royal Saudi family assemble in Riyadh and the 50,000-man Saudi army drives out into the desert to meet the guerrillas, whose numbers are surprisingly strong. The U.S. response is immediate. Striking from the Negev Desert and a staging base outside Cairo, a rapid deployment force of four divisions moves into Saudi Arabia from the air and the sea. Their first move is into the oil fields to protect them from sabotage. The next move is to position troops and tanks alongside the pipelines to make sure the flow of oil doesn't stop. Fighter planes roar out into the desert to provide air cover for the Saudi army, which is struggling to hold its own with the insurgents. Two more divisions are called in to back up the Saudis in the desert. A battle royal is joined that lasts for a week. Tank and air superiority win the day for the Saudi-American force, which gets by in the desert by tapping secret artesian well water northwest of the huge Saudi oil fields. The Soviet response is to threaten to move on the Strait of Hormuz but they back down when Japan and Western Europe send their own peacekeeping forces into Saudi Arabia. Full-scale war is averted but the U.S., the

Japanese and the Europeans are in Saudi Arabia to stay for several years.

CUBA INVADES JAMAICA

As compelling as the need would be for the United States to intervene in a civil war in Saudi Arabia, imagine how compelling it might be to intervene in a war that begins 600 miles from our shores. What kind of war is that? A Cuban invasion of the island of Jamaica, that's what kind of war that is. Nowhere near as farfetched as it sounds, a Cuban invasion of Jamaica could come before 1990. How would it come? A repressive government comes to power in Jamaica, there is civilian unrest that leads to rebellion and the Jamaican government invites Cuba to dispatch troops into Jamaica to help put down the rebellion. Naturally, Cuba responds to the invitation and six regiments of Cuban soldiers land on Jamaican shores and crush the rebellion in a bloody manner.

The first thing the Cubans do is to nationalize Jamaica's bauxite deposits, cutting off bauxite exports to the United States. The threat to U.S. interests is no longer a perceived one, it is very, very real. Not only are 30 percent of U.S. supplies of aluminum done away with overnight, the Cuban incursion into Jamaica is more than just Cubans helping out their island neighbors in an emergency. U.S. security is threatened, hemispheric security is threatened. The U.S. decides it can no longer tolerate Cuban expansion. Something must be done at once. But what? After all, Jamaica's legitimate government invited the Cubans in to deal with the rebellion. How can the U.S. counter with a military attack?

Despite these obvious drawbacks, the U.S. decides it must seek a solution to the Cuban problem and mounts a massive sea and air blockade of Cuba and Jamaica. The import of essential foodstuffs is all that's allowed to come into both islands. Ships carrying bauxite from Jamaica and sugar from Cuba are turned back by high-speed patrol boats and submarines. The U.S. justifies the blockade by invoking the Monroe Doctrine, declaring that it will not loosen up on the blockade until every Cuban soldier has left Jamaica. At the same time, the U.S. recognizes a Jamaican government in exile and puts pressure on the Organization of American States to do the same thing. Finally, Mexico and Venezuela denounce the Cuban invasion of Jamaica because they fear the Cubans will be encouraged to move on them if they succeed in Jamaica. The pressure works, the Cubans get out of Jamaica at the same time there is a bloodless coup in Kingston that deposes the pro-Cuban government. The blockade is lifted and things slowly and nervously return to normal.

CASTRO'S TERRORISTS IN MEXICO

The same script could be written sometime in the early 1990s for the Campeche Bay oil fields in the Yucatan Peninsula of Mexico. By this time one of the richest producing oil fields in the hemisphere, Campeche Bay supplies the U.S. with 70 percent of its imported oil. That fact alone encourages the rise of a Mexican terrorist organization that gets its training, its money and its weapons from a Fidel Castro now nearing his sixty-fifth birthday. Political events in Mexico do little to discourage Castro from fomenting trouble. Mexico's ruling PRI party becomes more and more dependent on the Mexican military to keep its hold on power. Rumors of rigged elections are rampant and while Mexican oil exports bring in record amounts of foreign exchange the rural and urban poor have nothing to show for it. Radical movements gain in popular support while the government loses its popular support. The time is ripe for trouble. In the words of Fidel Castro: "One man's terrorist is another man's Freedom Fighter."

The trouble comes out of the Caribbean, where Mexican terrorists and their Cuban mentors, disguised as fishermen, leave Cuba and early one morning quietly enter Campeche Bay. One by one, the oil workers are marched off the platforms and onto the Cuban boats. Then, the terrorists place time bombs on the platforms and mines on the platform legs. In a matter of hours, Mexico's richest oil fields are rendered useless as platform after platform is blown up in an operation the Cubans have code-named Thunderbolt. Eight billion dollars in oil-producing equipment is destroyed in one fell swoop.

How does the U.S. react to the Cuban-planned destruction? Nobody in the Mexican government invited the Cubans in to terrorize the oil fields so there is not the same U.S. reluctance to take direct action on the terrorists. On the other hand, the Mexican government does not have the popular support of the Mexican people so important to successful intervention. The U.S. decides it must act anyway for the same reasons it mounted a sea blockade of Cuba after the Jamaican invasion. Moving fast, a rapid deployment force supports a Mexican retaliatory attack on the terrorist bases in Cuba, smashing them the way Israeli commandos went after Palestinian camps in Lebanon. Another blockade is mounted on Cuba. Mexican commandos move onto Cuban soil in an operation code-named Lightning and begin to set fire to the sugar fields. There is a danger that a fire will be lit all over the hemisphere that will be impossible to put out.

A NUCLEAR FREE ZONE

What you've just read are scenarios for possible conflicts that lie ahead in the next 20 years. That doesn't mean they have to happen or that there won't be any other conflicts in the world. The most explosive potential confrontation still exists in Europe, where the Soviet Union faces Western Europe. However, a reunification of West and East Germany would defuse such a conflict. No longer would the Soviet Union have a corridor through Poland and East Germany right into the West. No longer would the Soviet Union have to be worried about nuclear weapons being moved into West Germany. Terms of the reunification would make the reunified Germanys a nuclear free zone. The Soviets would never accept a unified Germany without that guarantee. The question is, Will the new Germany look like Sweden or Finland? Sweden, nonaligned but more acceptable to the West, or Finland, nonaligned but more acceptable to the Soviets. The two Germanys will be nonaligned members of a new Third World suddenly made more prestigious by the German move to Third World status. Suddenly, Germany is at the head of a nonaligned Third World that has more to say about the directions of world peace than it ever did before. Germany as peacekeeper. Think of it. As curious as it might sound to the ear, a peacekeeping Germany will be a source of great strength and hope to world peace.

What else lies ahead for world peace? Some of it will be good, some not so good. The trend is toward more nuclear disarmament but the new weapons of the next 20 years will make peaceloving souls long for the day when MIRVs were the worst weapons in world arsenals. Neutron bombs that kill with enhanced radiation will be commonplace stockpile items. Both the U.S. and Soviet Union will have tested successful laser weapons and pulsed-beam weapons, to be used either in space or as antimissile or antiaircraft defense. The two superpowers will have also tested nonlethal chemical and biological weapons that can stun and even paralyze thousands of troops at a time. The Soviets will continue to rely on a deterrent based on massive nuclear warheads for use against a handful of America's largest cities while the U.S. will keep as its mainstay the smaller warheads for use against the many Soviet cities they will be targeted on. The

U.S. will have a STEALTH bomber, the Soviets will not. The U.S. will have a busy space shuttle taking reconnaissance satellites back and forth, the Soviets will have no space shuttle at all. Laser weapons will be positioned in space by both countries as the first effective antiballistic missile weapon ever developed.

THE U.S. A LITTLE STRONGER

There will be other new weapons systems developed by the U.S. to go with a rapid deployment force. Huge lighter-than-air vehicles that can cross oceans at 100 to 150 miles per hour with as many as 3,000 troops at one time. Silent helicopters that can strike without warning. Ballistic missiles kept on lake and ocean bottoms, where they can be moved to avoid detection and where they're just about invulnerable to hostile missile attack. Young men will not be drafted into the U.S. Army in the foreseeable future. President Reagan will have begun a program that pays skilled volunteers three times what unskilled volunteers are paid. It will be enough to attract a higher caliber of solider and keep the volunteer army a strong one. The U.S. will be a little stronger and the Soviets a little weaker, making for an even balance. The main reason the Soviets will be weakened (though not by much) is their population shift. By 1985, the Russian people will be a minority in the Soviet Union for the first time. The 120 other races that make up the Soviet Union will be the majority. It will be enough of a shift to cause the Soviets to pay more attention to themselves domestically and to look inward, a change in attitude that will leave its mark on the Soviet Union for a long, long time.

One other thing will happen that will help the U.S. in the years ahead. Before the two planes carrying the 53 released American hostages from Iran had arrived in the U.S., the new American president had already announced to the world a new policy on hostages. Ronald Reagan stated in no uncertain terms that henceforth the U.S. will treat all kidnapped diplomats as it treats prisoners of war. Henceforth, only volunteer diplomats will be sent to countries like Iran. Most attachés in U.S. embassies in troubled, changing or Third World countries will be career military or diplomatic people who will be well aware of the risks they run in Third World lands. The kidnapping of diplomats will cease the day the news is ignored and ransom payments unmade. In some ways, it will be a heartless policy to pursue but it will be the only one that makes sense.

ISLAMIC REPUBLIC TOPPLED

Look for another surprise to take place in the next few years. It all depends on how long the 82-year-old Ayatollah Khomeini lives. At his death, either by natural causes or political assassination, the Islamic Republic will be toppled by a coup d'etat that returns more reasonable government to Iran. Moslem mullahs will still be represented in the new Iran but they won't dominate the Iranian parliament the way they did in 1980 and 1981. There won't be any shah to lead like a strongman. It will be a more moderate government, like the government Mossadegh led before the shah came to power. When that happens, the Iranian diatribe against the United States will stop and a really curious thing will happen. The U.S. will reopen its embassy in Tehran, the same battle-scarred building where 53 hostages were kept for the better part of their 14 months in captivity. At the same time, the White House will announce a kind of Marshall Plan to get Iran back on its feet. Why do all of this for a country that Americans learned to hate in 1980? Because we need Iran on our side. It is too close to the Soviet Union, in too strategic a spot controlling one side of the Strait of Hormuz to lose. We need its oil to keep energy costs down; we need its location to monitor the Soviet Union and keep it in its place.

THE GREAT EUROPEAN WAR

There is one war we'd like to leave out. Nobody wants this war, nobody. Trouble is, the conditions of this war already exist. The policy decisions that make this war possible have already been made. The contingency plans that nations have to make to pursue this war have already been arrived at. The die is cast. The war we're talking about is the Great European War that begins when the Russians strike across the inter-German border against the NATO divisions holding the long thin line of Western defense. How did it start? This dramatic and unexpected invasion is the aftershock of the dramatic uprising of the captive nations of Eastern Europe. It is the war that started with the Iron Curtain and the Berlin Wall, the Berlin Airlift and the revolts in the streets of Budapest, East Berlin and Prague. It is the war that begins with Solidarity in Warsaw.

For years, Communist economics had run the cities of Poland while free enterprise flourished in the countryside. For years, the Catholic churches in Poland were full and the party halls empty. That was the deal the Poles struck long ago with Moscow. We'll chafe under communism if you let us be ourselves. Then, along came Karol Wojtyla, Pope John Paul II, the first Polish pope. While nothing the new pope said was different from what the last pope said, he said it all in Polish. Solidarity demanded more and more, they wanted to be "Yugoslavized." They wanted worker-management committees to have equal or almost as much control over production as the Communist party. Tension builds between Moscow and Warsaw until one day late in 1982 Polish priests are forbidden to read papal messages from the pulpit. A week later, party goons prevent the people from entering the churches. Propagandists visit the schools, deriding and satirizing the church. One day, a party man arrives in the seaport city of Gdansk for his antireligion class, bringing a string of new leaflets showing the pope wallowing in dollars and pulling at the blouses of admiring women. Nothing like it had ever been seen before. Later that day, crowds of furious parents break into the party building and burn it to the ground.

The local police are called to establish order and refuse to do so. Security police are airlifted in from Warsaw and are mobbed by the entire town. The Polish army is called in but refuses to fire a shot. By the evening of the second day of the Gdansk uprising, the miners of Silesia are involved and all of Poland is in an uproar. The Polish government no longer has an army or a police force to call its own and can't even respond to an urgent call for help from the Soviet Embassy in Warsaw. The embassy is surrounded by 25,000 people holding up posters of the pope, surging through the gates toward the embassy walls. In less than an hour word comes from Moscow. Two Russian tank divisions in Poland will seize the airports at Warsaw and Krakow; airborne troops are on their way from the Soviet Union to crush the Gdansk rebellion. Four East German divisions and another two Soviet divisions are moving into Poland from East Germany to restore order.

When the news from Moscow reaches the streets of Warsaw, the people swarm to the barracks of the three Polish divisions around the city. Quickly, the soldiers, most of whom have family members in Solidarity, join the revolt. In hours, army units surround the bases of the two Soviet tank divisions while others move to the German and Russian borders to defend Poland from attack. Every airfield in the country is occupied by troops or workers' militia. Trucks park on the runways so Soviet planes cannot land. Poland is in the hands of an insurrection. While the Soviets were ready for the Polish revolt, they had no inkling of what would come next. After all, hadn't they crushed uprisings in Hungary and Czechoslovakia without fear of intervention from the West?

The Czechs are first to rebel. Building huge roadblocks at all exit points, Czech army troops and tens of thousands of armed Czech workers surround the bases of the five Soviet divisions in Czechoslovakia. The next day, the same thing happens in Hungary and four more Russian divisions are bottled up. That same day, East German troops are driven out of Poland by the furious firepower of two Polish tank divisions. The Kremlin can't believe it, starts to recall reservists all over the Soviet Union to bring its 168 divisions to full battle strength. At the same time, home divisions based in European Russia drive west into Hungary, Poland and Czechoslovakia. Their goals are Budapest, Warsaw and Prague. Resistance is continuing eight days after the Gdansk uprising; half of Eastern Europe is in flames.

Now in a panic, the Kremlin decides it must crush the revolt by crushing the West. Forty Russian divisions storm across 600 miles of the East German border into West Germany, where they are met head-on by 360,000 men from Germany, Denmark, Holland, Belgium, Great Britain and the United States. The Soviets have rehearsed this blitzkrieg a thousand times. First, the Russians launch small feinting attacks all along the line, then sweep in from the flanks with massive numbers of tanks and men. Predictably, the Belgians cave in and the Dutch retreat while the Germans stand fast. The British and Americans fight well but theirs is an infantry defense practiced to meet a direct attack and no more. The Russians know all of this. Bypassing the British and Americans, thousands of Russian tanks outflank the NATO troops in a strategy as stunning as Patton's march to the Rhine. In the skies above, NATO is winning the air war but the heavy fog of winter prevents them from providing any real kind of air support to their brothers on the ground. Within 48 hours, Russian troops are deep inside West Germany.

In fact, the Soviet troops have gone too far. Already,

they are running out of food for their men and fuel for their machines. Most of them don't know what they're doing and why. Troops dispersed to forage for food and fuel are met by guerrilla and sniper fire. One Russian division finds itself 10 miles from France and without any orders to stop keeps moving toward the French border. Suddenly, the French president authorizes the use of 36 tactical neutron bombs against the advancing Russian troops. In the only diplomatic move of the last 10 days, the French president warns the Kremlin he will unleash the missiles if the Soviet troops move onto French soil. Don't forget, France is not a member of NATO. In a flash, the Russians realize where things stand. Even though Russian troops are deep inside NATO soil, NATO has restrained itself from using its nuclear weapons. The Soviet president suddenly realizes that Moscow still stands untouched and unscathed in the first step of a war that could escalate into nuclear holocaust.

Still unaware of what is happening in Europe, the American president knows only that it would be weeks before U.S. troops could enter the war in numbers. He picks up the red phone in the Oval Office and gets the Soviet president just at a time when the Politburo senses what is about to happen. Let's talk, the American president says. Go ahead and talk, the Soviet president replies, I'm listening. While the two men talk, the word goes out to the battlefronts. Cease your fire, cease your fire. In 24 hours, the terms are agreed to. The Soviet troops are fed by an airlift organized by the Americans and allowed to withdraw back to East Germany. A new constitution for Poland is drafted, Soviet troops withdraw from Hungary and Czechoslovakia, Berlin is declared a free city and reunification talks between East and West Germany are to begin in 1983. Moscow and Washington praise each other for their restraint and statesmanship. Happily, the Great European War is over before it had a chance to begin. We shall have war and peace but no U.S.–Soviet nuclear exchange; in fact, the U.S. and Soviet Union will end up as police partners protecting the world against nuclear terrorism.

6
▲▲▲▲▲▲▲

RELIGIONS
OF THE FUTURE

▼▼▼▼▼▼▼

*"As no man can be very
miserable that is master of a
garden here, so will no man ever be
happy who is not sure of a garden here-
after."*

—British Writer John Evelyn

▲▲▲▲▲▲▲

*E*ven though there are gods without religion, such as theism, and there are religions without God, such as Buddhism, we still feel of all the ideas that have shaped the cultures of humankind, none has had more impact or been more permanent than man's unshaken belief that there is a God. There have always been people who profess to be atheists and agnostics but there have always been more people who believed in God. There were times when men worshipped the sun and the moon and things he didn't understand like fire, but through most of their four-million-year history humans have worshipped the unseen deity they call God.

We predict that people will go on needing God, that religion is here to stay. They will need God for solace and comfort and an unhesitating assurance that there is something more to their existence than life and death on Earth. People need their God to ritualize their passage through life. Birth, adolescence, adulthood, marriage, parenthood, death, they're all ritualized in baptisms, confirmations, matrimony, funerals, all of which take place inside a church, mosque or temple. People need these rituals to mark their time on Earth. There are questions that everybody asks, yearning for answers. Who am I? Where did I come from? Where am I going? People's belief in God and the religions they create to sustain that belief help them to understand that yearning. Put simply, God will never die. Man won't let Him die.

Forecasting the future of religion is another matter. The indicators we can use, the trends we can track to help us with our forecast, are not found in a computer's memory bank. Nonetheless, religion can be watched, followed and predicted. Usually, religion follows the same paths the rest of a culture takes. If a country's culture hasn't changed for years, its dominant religion probably hasn't changed either and probably won't change. Take Ireland, for instance, where the culture and Catholicism go hand in hand. Resistance to change is enormous in Ireland, one of the few countries of the world still to ban the open sale of birth control pills. How strong are the ties between church and state? If they're loose and there is real separation of church and state, change has probably come to whatever religion is dominant in that state. If there is no real distance between church and state, change has probably not come at all. Iran is a classic example. Iran's brand of Islam may be more resistant to change than any other country where Islam predominates. If conservatism is the dominating politics today, conservative religion will flourish today. So it is and so it will be for the next 10 years. It is the day of the Moral Majority. Which are the fastest-growing churches in America today? The Southern Baptists and the Mormons, both rock-ribbed in their conservatism. Which churches are losing members? The Presbyterians, the Lutherans and the Methodists, more or less a large segment of the liberal wing of American Christianity. Reform Jews are dwindling in number, Orthodox Jews are on the rise. The least liberal, the least tolerant religion in the world is now the fastest-growing religion in the world. There are now 450 million Moslems on earth, five million in the United States alone. That means there are twice as many Moslems as there are Presbyterians in America.

THE DECLINE IN
CULTURAL CONFIDENCE

It's no accident that cults like Scientology, Hare Krishna, the Unification Church, the Worldwide Church of God and Way International are thriving today. Harvard University psychiatrist John G. Clark, Jr., says the most fundamental factor behind the growth of cultism is the decline in what he calls cultural confidence. By cultural confidence, Clark means the way in which society has positive attitudes toward its fundamental values, beliefs, institutions and achievements. Until recently, most Americans had confidence in their culture. They believed in family ties, traditional religion, sexual restraint, the work ethic, free enterprise and the natural superiority of the American way. No longer. Clark says that almost all of these old values have been challenged, first in literature, then in behavior and now even in school curricula. Says Clark: "This process of value change has seriously affected young people. They do not get clear guidance when they look to the adult world for fundamental values. Young people are particularly receptive to the appeal of new nonestablishment groups which offer a ready-made sense of community and an idealistic world view providing clear rules of daily conduct and a purpose in life."

Cults do just that. Cults don't appeal to free-thinking liberalism, which is out of favor right now. Who joins cults? One study found that 30 percent of cult membership came from children of Jewish parents, probably the most liberal parents children can have. The main appeal of the cults is that they remove doubt, confusion and contradiction by invoking strict authoritarian rules. There is often an authoritarian figure at the head of a cult, like the Reverend Moon or the Reverend Jim Jones. We've seen this throughout history, we saw it with Hitler where the Germans had an inadequate father image after the First World War. They were ashamed of their fathers so they elevated Hitler into their image of what the ideal father should be and then became totally subservient to him.

In our attempt to forecast the future of religion, we've turned for help to people like Harvard's John Clark, one of the nation's leading authorities on cultism in America. We've consulted with rabbis, priests and ministers, we've talked with theologians and social historians whose bailiwicks and whose main interests are religious trends. People like Rabbi Arnold Fink of Temple Beth El, Alexandria, Virginia; Dr. David Scott of the Episcopal Church's Virginia Theological Seminary; Professor Philip K. Hitti of Princeton University; Dr. Charles Curran of the Catholic University of America; sociologist Richard Schoeenher (pronounced Shaner) of the University of Wisconsin; and California Congressman Tony Cuelho, who dropped out of a Jesuit seminary when he found out he was an epileptic. Congressman Cuelho thinks one of the main religious issues of the next 20 years will be the separation of church and state, in which he strongly believes. Says Cuelho: "The United States was founded on this issue and while I'm personally opposed to abortion I vote against all the limitations on abortion because of my role as a legislator. The trouble is, there are so many groups in America today who are trying to force us to make moral judgments instead of legislative judgments. They come to you and say, look, we really want a separation of church and state but we also want you to vote the way we morally believe you should vote. Well, that isn't separation of church and state when you do that. I think the Moral Majority really is an outgrowth of the concern that religion isn't based on fear anymore and that it's kind of a last desperation attempt to force us back to that fear."

While we attempt to deal mostly with the future of mainstream religions in America, we've also talked with experts on the Mormon church and on Islam for their views of what will happen to these two fast-growing worldwide religions. The Mormon experience is no longer a Salt Lake

City experience or even just an American experience. Twenty years ago, there were two million Latter Day Saints in the world, almost 90 percent of them Americans. Today, there are almost four million Americans and roughly one million who are not Americans who call themselves Mormons. The Mormons have built temples in Great Britain, Japan, New Zealand, Brazil and Switzerland and are now building temples in Australia, Tahiti, American Samoa, the Philippines, Chile, Mexico, West Germany and Sweden. Mormonism will be a major religious force throughout the world for years to come.

MORMONS PROVIDE
CLEAR RULES

Why Mormonism? Why a church that forbids drinking and smoking, that until recently had closed its doors to black members, that still bans women from its priesthood and extracts 10 percent of its members' income in tithing every year? The answers are complex and reflect the insecurity and secularity of the times. Like the cults, the Mormons provide clear rules of conduct and purpose in life. There are few doubts, confusions and contradictions in Mormonism, which is after all a church founded on a conservative belief. Brigham Young University's Tom Alexander (then a missionary, now a historian for the Mormon Church) remembers that the Mormons won many of their first foreign converts in the 1950s when refugees flocking into West Germany from Eastern Europe became converts to Mormonism to rid themselves of a shattering sense of dislocation. Alexander says there is something similar going on today in Japan, Korea and Taiwan, where Mormonism is growing very fast and where traditions are changing so fast that many people feel uprooted and dislocated. It's not the same kind of dislocation felt by East European refugees after World War II but the feelings it triggers are the same. Says Alexander: "I think certain Mormon teachings and beliefs provide a sense of stability and identity and I think many people in countries like Japan and Korea have felt a challenge to their traditional roles that they don't feel in Mormonism."

In a sense, the Mormons (and to some extent the Southern Baptists) have replaced the Roman Catholics as the most aggressive religious missionaries throughout the world. Every two years, the Mormon church sends 35,000 young men and women into the world as missionaries. The sole purpose of these young Mormons, who volunteer two years of their lives to the missions, is to convert people to Mormonism. Their success is best measured in numbers. There are more than 250,000 new Mormon baptisms in the U.S. alone every year. If the trend keeps up, the Mormon church will double its membership before the year 2000.

ONE BILLION MOSLEMS

The fastest-growing religion in the world today is Islam, whose conservative appeals to ancient values are fueled in the oil-rich Islamic countries of the Middle East. There are now 450 million men and women of every race representing every one of the six continents who call themselves Moslems and who follow the Prophet. Islam is the dominant faith in a broad swath of the earth that runs from Morocco in the west to Pakistan and across India to Malaysia and Indonesia in the east. Islam doubles itself in Africa every 25 years. The number of Moslems making the *hadj*, the holy pilgrimage to Mecca, increases by 100,000 every year. There are no signs this surging growth will slacken. The way the Moslem faith is spreading, the way the Moslem populations are growing, Islam may embrace almost one billion people by the year 2000.

Why in this age of spiritual doubt should Islam be so

vibrantly alive? Where in this time of religious confusion is Islam getting its astonishing vitality? In part, Islam has caught fire for some of the same reasons that cults and Mormonism are heating up. Islam is a fundamentalist religion, a church that teaches basic tenets, has only two affirmations (there is no God but Allah, Mohammed is his prophet) where Christianity has as many as fourteen. In return, Islam offers the answers without doubt or contradiction. Its ethical doctrines are austere and simple, something similar to what the Quakers believe. Its universal appeal has also let it cut across barriers of race, tribe and caste, which is another reason for its rapid growth in places like black Africa and black America.

Ironically, Islam is the religion most akin to Christianity and Judaism, the two religions Islam seems to have gone to war with. The late Professor Philip Hitti, one-time head of the Semitic Literature Program at Princeton University, told us that the alienation between Islam and the Judeo-Christian worlds is more one of politics and economics than it is of ideology. In a sense, Hitti said, Judaism is the essence of the Old Testament, Christianity of the New and Islam of a Third Testament, enshrined in the Koran. If the New Testament reads like the life of Christ, Hitti went on, the Third Testament is the life story of Mohammed, the Prophet. People tend to think of Islam as an Arabian culture, a notion Hitti said is not correct. "Except for the Arabic language through which it was disseminated, the Arabians contributed almost nothing," Hitti said. "Islam is a compound of ancient Semitic, classic Greek and medieval Indo-Persian."

One reason Westerners find it so hard to understand and accept Islam is that it has always threatened and challenged the West. Christianity doesn't challenge the West because Christianity is a part of the West. Judaism is too small and too tribal to pose any challenge to the West. Hinduism and Buddhism don't challenge the West because they're too ethereal. Only Islam is a threat, as it has been economically for the last 20 years, politically for the last 180 years and militarily for the last 1,500 years. Islam is confronting us again, in Iran calling us Satan for supporting the shah and challenging us in the rest of the Moslem world for supporting Israel. Think back to the hostages. No swami, no Dalai Lama, no guru and no rabbi ever threatened us the way the madjis and the Ayatollah did.

Another reason Islam is so inscrutable to Western eyes is that it runs on what we feel are outdated practices and principles. The whippings, the stonings, the mutilations and the executions meted out for violations of Islamic law are anathema to the Western mind. Why are bribes a way of life in the Moslem world? Why must women wear veils? Why can't women take jobs? Why must Moslem women walk behind Moslem men? Why can't they change? Why can't the Moslems be like us? There's a third reason why the West finds it so hard to accept Islam. There is no separation of church and state in the Moslem world. The state is the church. For Islam, God is Caesar and Caesar is God. There can be no distinction between church and state in the Moslem world, where criticism of Islam is seen as an injury against the state and society. Criticism of society is a criticism of the Moslem faith. It's more than criticism, it's treason. For this reason alone, there can be no easy accommodation between the West and a large segment of the Moslem world. The Moslem challenge to the West will continue as long as Islam's oil riches fuel its growth, which will last for at least another 15 years.

STIFF CHALLENGES

Closer to home, the traditional American religions face far stiffer challenges than anything they might meet from Islam. Not a single organized religion is exempt from these challenges. Catholicism, Protestantism and Judaism face them. What will the role of women be in these churches? Will the churches accept homosexual members? Will they raise homosexuals to the ministry? Will Catholic priests be allowed to marry? Will the churches' attitudes change toward divorce, birth control and abortion? Should clergymen become congressmen? Will there be a showdown between the fundamentalist right and the liberal left wings of the Protestant church? What will happen to ecumenicism? Will some churches merge? Will more churches split further apart? These are some of the issues facing the organized religions of America in the next 20 years. These are not issues that can be ducked, or that anybody expects will go away.

BIRTH CONTROL

More than any of the rest, the Catholic church faces the stiffest challenges on these issues in the years ahead. Catholic theologians agree that their church is not immune to a single one of these invasive issues. Divorce, birth control, abortion are all major issues in the Catholic church. The Catholic church has condemned birth control for so long that it's no longer an issue. A vast majority of America's 50 million Catholics practice birth control without hesitation. These Catholics would rather their church change its position on birth control but have decided they can no longer wait for that change and so have taken their religion into their own hands. Catholic University theologian Charles Curran puts it this way: "Most people have already made up their minds about birth control. To me, the significance of birth control is how the church's hierarchy deals and lives with it. Because the church doesn't change its stand on birth control, what's going to happen with divorce, which is becoming a much bigger issue than birth control to many Catholics?"

DIVORCE

To a lesser extent, Catholics are taking the matter of divorce into their own hands as well. More and more divorced and remarried Catholics are ignoring the church orders that excommunicated them and are attending mass, receiving communion and feeling free to be a part of their church. Still the church's answer to the rising tide of divorce among its members is to modernize and streamline the court procedures for annulment. Some theologians feel that is not the answer, that it's no more than a Band-Aid treatment of a wound that's getting deeper, and the reason the wound is deepening is simple. More and more Catholics are divorcing. More and more people are being touched and moved by these divorces. It is not just the people getting divorced, it is their parents and grandparents, their children, their relatives and their friends. Divorce will soon touch a majority of American Catholics.

Will the Catholic church change its stand on divorce? Ask first if the church will change itself on birth control. Will there be a change on the birth control issue? Yes, but not for another 10 years. The change will be agonizing and will meet intense resistance all along the way from the right-wing laity who see any change in church doctrine as a deadly threat to church tradition. The right wing will have the support of much of the church hierarchy, who see the birth control issue as an awful challenge to their authority. But so many Catholics will have repudiated the official church position on birth control that change is bound to come. All it will take is time.

But if it's going to take so long to bring about a new Catholic position on birth control, how long will it take to get a new stance on divorce. The answer: a lot longer. About all one can expect from an institution as large as the Roman Catholic church is an agreement to make one social change at a time. The answer is there will be no immediate or even foreseeable change in the official Catholic policy on divorce. The 21st century may see a new divorce posture but until then, more and more Catholics will leave their church or practice their religion and celebrate their sacraments on their own, regardless of sanctions.

ABORTION

Abortion is a different matter altogether. Abortion is a deeper and a more complicated issue than birth control or divorce—and will continue to be. Far more Catholics are against abortion than are against free sex, divorce or birth control. Liberal Catholics who believe that people are entitled to their own views on anything involving their sexuality blow the whistle on abortion.

Most polls of Catholics show that the majority still refuse to endorse abortion on demand, though most of that same majority are ambivalent about laws that ban federal aid for abortions and even favor abortion if the birth of a child involves rape or incest or if it threatens the mother's life. These are majority views that are unlikely to change with time. The church itself is even less likely to change on the abortion issue, especially since it knows it has the support of so many of its members. It is a safe matter to forecast on these pages that there will be little or no change in the Catholic church's position on abortion. The only question is, will the church be able to stay out of politics or will it make a bold attempt to change the nation's abortion laws. So far, the church has kept the issue in the pulpit.

CELIBACY

Within its ranks, the Catholic church is up against still another issue that will refuse to go away any time in the next 20 years. It is the issue of whether priests will be allowed to marry and it involves more than the issues of celibacy and married priests. It involves the rising rate of dropout priests and the dwindling numbers of men who seek to be priests. It also involves the delicate and undiscussed issue of homosexual priests. The church's official attitude toward homosexual priests is that they don't exist because the church still demands celibacy of its priests. The church makes no distinction between heterosexual and homosexual priests; it demands only that they all be celibate. That's the public position of the church.

The church will try to do something about its shrinking number of priests. As many as 10,000 priests have resigned their ministries in the United States alone in the last 10 years. Abroad, the dropout rate is even higher. There are entire parishes in heavily Catholic regions of France and Germany whose churches have no pastors. At Germany's University of Tübingen, there are 600 men taking advanced degrees in theology. No more than 10 plan to go on to the priesthood. There was a time not too long ago when more than 90 percent of Tübingen's Catholic theology students moved on to become priests. There is little doubt as to why priests are dropping out and why so few new priests are coming in. Clearly, the main issue is why they have to remain celibate and why they cannot get married. The University of Wisconsin's Dr. Richard Schoeenher found that of all the American Catholic priests who resigned their ministries in the five years ending in 1970, fully 70 percent had married. Even that high statistic is misleading. Schoeenher did his study in 1970 and found that 87 percent of the priests who had resigned four years before had married. Only 41 percent of the priests who dropped out in 1970 had married that same year. No matter what year they resigned, 43 percent of the dropout priests married dropout nuns. Almost all of them still considered themselves Catholics.

The next question is, What is the church going to do

about it? Will the church let priests marry to stem the rising tide of dropout priests and recruit more new priests? It may happen but not during the next 10 or 15 years. The decline in the numbers of priests is going to have to accelerate even further before the church hierarchy will do something about it. The trouble is, priests make up a small minority of the Catholic church and as a minority they can't bring enough pressure to bear to force change. Most of the Catholic laity doesn't care if priests get married or not. In fact, a large number of conservative Catholics like things the way they are. Priests have never married before. Why should they marry now? Pope John Paul II shows no signs of moving on this issue either. In fact, there are signs he doesn't understand what all the fuss is about. Liberal European theologians have said that Pope John Paul has written off Western Europe, saying that the reason European Catholics have so few vocations is that they don't have faith in their religion anymore. Married priests are a long way off. Maybe in the next decade. Certainly not in this decade.

WOMEN'S ROLES

Thorny as the issue of married priests is, it is nowhere near as thorny an issue as the future role of women in the church. Episcopal theologian David Scott says: "The place of women in the Roman Catholic church is going to be one of the presiding issues for them for the next 50 years." Catholic theologian Charles Curran says it more strongly: "At one time, even 10 years ago, I would have said the big problem was celibacy. That's not the big problem because there aren't that many people interested in it. But you've got at least half your people interested in the woman's issue and therefore the bureaucracy can't sit back and say, look, we've stonewalled this for 2,000 years and we can stonewall it again. You might do that on celibacy, you might even do it on married priests but I see no way the woman's issue can be avoided, no way."

Women no longer cherish the roles they're given in the Catholic church, which is to say nuns, nurses, teachers, social workers and housekeepers. Until recently, there have never even been altar girls in the Catholic church, only altar boys. "Choirboy" has been the expression of choice, never choirgirl. No bishop, no priest, no deacon, in the Catholic church has been a woman for almost 2,000 years. More perhaps than any other feminist issue, Catholic women want that to change. They want to be choirgirls and altar girls, they want to be deacons and they want to be priests. Though they stayed silent until recently, a large number of the 150,000 American women who are nuns want change. How do we know that? Because the National Sisters Vocation Conference in Chicago says that as many as 3,000 women drop out of their convents every year, at least in part today because they feel like second-class citizens in their own vocation. While the frustrations of being unable to crack the all-male club are in some way a unifying force for these women to stick together, they are also a reason many women leave and an even bigger reason many women no longer want to join a convent.

Does that mean the Catholic church will change its 2,000-year-old policy on women? Don't count on it happening in the 20th century. The Curia (the Catholic church's ruling body in Rome) believes the women's issue is an American issue. "Rome keeps saying, we don't have this problem in Africa, we don't have this problem in South America," says Charles Curran of Catholic University. "This issue is typical of your rich, first world, consuming society." Part of the reason Rome identifies the women's issue as American is that the feminist movement makes its stronghold in the United States. Outside the United States, there is less agitation for change on women's issues. Also, the nuns who have begun to speak out on women's roles in the church are mostly American nuns, a trend that Rome might be misreading. American nuns constitute the bulk of the world's educated nuns, so it should come as no surprise they would be first to speak out on the women's issue. Even most European nuns are nursing nuns, with little more than a nursing education. In contrast, most of the nuns in the United States are teaching nuns, many of them with advanced degrees. There are signs that the winds of change are blowing eastward and westward from New York and Los Angeles on the woman's issue. Says Catholic University's Curran: "I think Rome is wrong on this issue and I think they're going to find out soon that the issue is worldwide."

JANE-IN-THE-PULPIT

The Catholic church isn't the only church in America struggling with the woman's issue. Women have only begun to step up into the pulpits of Methodist, Lutheran and Presbyterian churches. There are only a couple dozen women rabbis among Reform Jews and none in the Conservative and Orthodox branches of Judaism. There are no women priests in the Mormon church and few women preachers in the Southern Baptist church. Despite its liberal reputation, the Episcopal church in America has only 200 women priests. The black Baptist church has almost no women preachers. The Greek Orthodox church and the Russian Orthodox church in America have no women priests. Catholic University's Charles Curran tells of the time 10 years ago when he overheard an Episcopal priest discussing the woman's issue with a Catholic priest. Curran said the Anglican turned to the Catholic and said: "I've got to tell you very openly that if the Anglican church ever ordains women I'm going to have to become a Catholic monk." Curran said he turned to the Anglican and said: "If I were you, I wouldn't become a monk, I'd become Greek Orthodox. They're never going to change."

WOMEN RABBIS

The outlook for women is not good in any of the Orthodox churches, some of which haven't changed since the sixth century. The outlook for women isn't good in the Mormon church or in the black Baptist church, both of which may be the last to accept women in the pulpit and may in fact never do so. Episcopal theologian David Scott puts it this way: "There will be lots of resistance along the way to the ordaining of women and I think the problem will be with us for a long time because it raises fundamental questions about sexual identity."

The only Protestant churches dealing successfully with the issue of women in the pulpit are the Methodist, Lutheran and Presbyterian churches, where Scott says the concept of women's ordination "has been accepted." Reform Jews are also among the first to accept women rabbis. While there are fewer than twenty practicing women rabbis in America today, almost one-third of the 200 rabbinical students at the three branches of Hebrew Union College in Cincinnati, New York and Los Angeles are women. "What this means is we'll be changing our models of authority because authority is generally conceived in male terms," says Rabbi Arnold Fink of Temple Beth El in Alexandria, Virginia. "There will be greater and greater acceptance of women in pastoral roles but we'll be shaking the role images and that is going to take time. After all, Moses had to keep his people in the wilderness for 40 years before they went to the promised land. You can't rush things like this."

Somewhat akin to the women's issue is the place of homosexuals in the church, on either side of the pulpit. Here, the outlook is less hazy than it is for women. Chances are that open homosexuals will not be acceptable in most

congregations and certainly won't be acceptable as pastors.
Homosexuals will have to continue to form their own
churches or stay in the closet if they want to attend a
"straight" church. Episcopal theologian David Scott
doesn't think there ever will be homosexuals filling pastoral roles in conventional churches. Says Scott: "I have
serious doubts about how willingly the average American
churchgoer would accept a practicing homosexual in the
pulpit and in the rectory. I mean not only now, I mean in
the future. Here I go back to the basic structure of society,
that the family and the heterosexual-biological comple-
mentarity is so built in that it's hard for me to see our
culture dropping all of its resistance to the advocacy of
homosexuality as an alternative life-style that's just as good
as heterosexuality. If life is a continuity from generation to
generation, there is no continuity in homosexuality."
Rabbi Arnold Fink thinks most churches and synagogues
will find it very hard to accept avowed homosexuals in their
congregations. "The law says who ministers, priests and
rabbis can marry and who they can't. When the day comes
that two gays bring me a legal marriage license, I'll deal
with it. Until then, I don't have a problem."

An upsurge of people are changing their religions, moving from an orthodox branch of their religion to a more
liberal wing or from a more liberal branch to a more
orthodox wing. "More people now look for a church that
will accommodate their own attitudes and life-styles,"
Episcopal theologian David Scott points out. "If they don't
find it, they'll find the thing closest to it and relate to it the
way they want to." More and more, we are witnessing a
move towards what Catholic University theologian Charles
Curran calls a "greater pluralism" where religious authority becomes less centralized and where different religions
take more different directions from each other than they
have in the last 20 years. The latter we see already in the
growing number of rifts between the modern and traditional wings of the same churches. Orthodox and Reform Jews

are increasingly at odds over their interpretations of Jewish law or what is called *hallacha*, which often deals with the definition of what a Jew is. By Orthodox law going back 1,900 years, a Jew is a person born of a Jewish woman. Reform Jews believe that a Jew may be a person born of a Jewish woman *or* of a Jewish father and raised as a Jew. Right now, there is a determined effort inside the reform movement to redefine Jewish identity to include converts, people who had neither a Jewish father nor mother but who married Jews and wanted to become Jews themselves. "If that happens, the 'Jewish paternity issue' could be the wedge that splits Reform Jews away from Orthodox Jews for a long time to come," Rabbi Fink says. "It would redefine Jewish identity in a way that is unacceptable to Orthodoxy." Incidentally, it should be noted that 31.7 percent of the Jewish population and 40 percent of the Catholic population marry outside their faith.

SISTER CHURCHES

In a strong sense, we are beginning to see at least a temporary end to the ecumenical movement that began in the Roman Catholic church almost 20 years ago with the papacy of John XXIII. One thing is clear: There will never be a superchurch of Roman Catholics, Eastern Rite Catholics, Greek and Russian Orthodox. There are too many doctrinal difficulties to contend with and too much leftover church bureaucracy to deal with. On paper, a merger between Greek and Russian orthodoxy and Roman Catholicism looks possible. In practice, it will never happen because the two Orthodox churches are tied so tightly to the past. They cannot change because they do not want to change. What we may see as a substitute for ecumenism in the future is a concept of "sister church" of the kind that brings the Anglican and Roman Catholic churches closer together but never so close that the next step is merger. The Catholics and Lutherans are coming much closer together. The Lutherans have begun to use the term "bishop" and to accept the role of bishops in the church and have said they would have no difficulty accepting the idea of some kind of Petrine office whereby St. Peter's in Rome is the adopted Holy See. What they cannot accept are all the historical developments of the Holy See, such as papal infallibility. That will never go over with the Lutheran church any more than a redefinition of a Jew would go over with the Orthodox Jews. Times are changing but not that fast.

RELIGIONS WITHOUT GOD

In some cultures, times never change. We're thinking of the Oriental cultures that have produced Confucianism, Taoism, Buddhism and Hinduism, which are truly religions without God and which have infiltrated Western thought in subtle ways over the last century. We think they will continue to infiltrate the West. Notice we did not say undermine the West or even threaten the West. None of these Oriental religions threatens the West the way Islam does. They've been taken up by Westerners seeking a different way through life. As time goes on, as we near the turn of the century, we think more Westerners will try the Eastern approach to life's numerous turns. There must be something to the Eastern way. Over half the world's population call themselves Confucianists, Taoists, Buddhists and Hindus.

The oldest of these four ancient religions is Confucianism, which probably began right after the master's death 479 years before Christ. Confucius believed in old rituals because rituals have values of their own and the rituals he believed in emphasized man's duty to man. In brief, Confucius preached nothing more than an elaborate, more humanistic version of the Golden Rule. Children owe obedience and respect to their parents. The parents owe love, sustenance and respect to their children. The right behavior, that's what it is—what might in some Western circles be called sincerity. Husbands owe the right behavior to their wives, brothers owe it to their sisters, friends to their friends, superiors to subordinates. The same rules hold for everybody. There is no place for power, no place for money and no place for sexual power games.

One example of the Confucian approach to today's ethics might come under the heading of sexual harassment. To the Confucian, sexual harassment is clearly unethical because it places power above the rules. This makes it exploitation—even worse, it makes it insincerity. The Confucian would make no distinction between an executive forcing his secretary to submit to his advances and the 17th-century diarist Samuel Pepys forcing his wife's maids to submit to his. It would make no difference to the Confucian that the secretary can quit rather than submit. To the Confucian, the executive and Mr. Pepys are clearly guilty of the grossest insincerities and are to be dealt with equally. Is there anything wrong with the Confucian approach? Absolutely nothing. But because it is an ethic for individuals, Mao outlawed Confucianism. For the Confucian, law can handle only the rights and objections of collectives. Ethics are always a matter between individuals. A religion with such values will always survive and will always have a future. Even now, China's new leaders have relaxed the bans on Confucianism. After all, it's no threat to the state. Why not encourage a religion with such basic and unthreatening tenets?

In a different way, the same is true of Taoism and Buddhism. The Buddhist religion began in India, then moved to China and Japan, where it was embraced in different ways. Buddhism was forced out of India in favor of Hinduism, which believed in a caste system. Buddhism took hold in China and Japan because Buddhists preach that anyone can follow "the path," provided he or she exercises self-discipline. The word *Tao* in Taoism literally means the Path, which means very simply the basic way of life. No religion is more simple than Taoism, which preaches that all attempts to behave by strict rules are artificial. The philosophy of Taoists is to conform to nature's way. Buddhists are more conformist but they're not ritualistic about it. It's true they erect temples to Buddha and it's true they have monks but they don't worship, they meditate. So alike are Confucianism, Taoism and Buddhism that in a single day a man could pay his respects to the heroes of the past, attend a Buddhist pageant showing a jeweled lord saving more humble souls from hell and practice the gymnastics and breathing exercises taught by the Taoists to prepare us for the transfiguration.

There is nothing but a bright future for Buddhism and Taoism in the Orient, in part because both religions so deeply reflect how Orientals believe in themselves. Outside the Orient, there will be a growing awareness of all Oriental religions as East and West mix more and more, as Japan and China trade more with the West and as China undergoes more liberal change.

We cannot predict as bright a future for Hinduism. In fact, we can only say that Hinduism will never escape the bondage of its caste rules that bind it up in India and keep that country so backward. The only thing that keeps Hinduism going even in India is its belief in reincarnation, that the soul leaves the body at death to put on a new body and then another one as time goes on. A good life leads to rebirth in a better life, an evil life dictates return to a worse life. Not bad as precepts but not enough to catch on as one of the world's great religions. We think the great religions of the future will preach more humanism and more individualism. With six billion people living in the world in the year 2000, it may be the only way we can look ahead.

7

▲▲▲▲▲▲▲

THERE'S PROFIT IN PROPHECY

▼▼▼▼▼▼▼

"How pleasant it is to have money!"

—*Arthur Hugh Clough,*
British poet

▲▲▲▲▲▲▲

While the Bible warned that it was the root of all evil, nothing takes a stronger hold on us than money. Like it or not, we want money and we need money. We need money for more than the food and drink in our stomachs, clothes on our backs and roofs over our heads. Psychologically, money provides a healthy outlet to almost every mental trauma we suffer through life. Money buys the car that gets us out of the house when we're bored, the airplane ticket that gets us away from our jobs when we're exhausted and gets us to the distant beach or mountain that renews us for the time ahead. British novelist William Somerset Maugham said it all when he described our need for money. "Money is like a sixth sense," Maugham said, "without which you cannot make complete use of the other five."

The origins of money go back a long way. For all we know, banking may be an older profession than the profession usually described as the world's oldest. Before there was money, of course, there was barter, which is still used in primitive cultures where food is traded for weapons or a field cleared in exchange for building a house. Barter was a big improvement over a state of affairs where everybody had to be a jack-of-all-trades. In a sense, barter represented a major turning point in the growth of civilization. "A great debt of gratitude is owed to the first two ape-men," observed Nobel Prize economist Paul A. Samuelson, "who suddenly perceived that each could be made better off by giving up some of one good in exchange for some of another."

Nevertheless, barter had to go. Barter gave way to money when metal coins came along as a substitute at about the same time that barter got too unwieldy. Though they increased in value by reproducing, cattle were not divisible into small change. So along came metal coins, to become the money of many a realm for a long time. Coins had to go for the same reasons barter had to go. Paper came along as a substitute at the same time that coins began losing their luster. Iron was too heavy. Besides, it rusted. Silver tarnished quickly in air. Gold kept its sheen but was too soft for the constant handling that money requires. Gold was also so scarce it had to be made into coins that were too small for ordinary use. So along came paper, which began as receipts for metal coins but was soon substituting for coins with the invention of the printing press. The age of commodity money had given way to the age of paper money.

Paper money grew into widespread use because of its countless conveniences. It's easily carried and just as easily tucked away. Printing more zeroes is all it takes on a bill to increase its value. Careful engraving makes it easy to recognize and difficult to counterfeit. The fact that private individuals cannot create it at will keeps it scarce. Karl Marx once said that paper money was valued "only insofar as it represents gold" but that may never have been true. "The public neither knows nor cares whether its currency is in notes or in copper or nickel coin," wrote Paul Samuelson. "So long as each form of money can be converted into any other the best is as good as the worst."

Right behind paper money came bank money. More than 90 percent of all transactions today go through by check and by credit card, which after all is only a more convenient way of writing a check. Living on checkbooks allows people to "live on the float," which means that if we get paid on Monday we can write a check the previous

Thursday knowing that by the time it clears the bank it will be Monday and our money will be deposited. Living on the float promises to choke our banking system. Our check load is now so enormous that more than 40 billion checks are being written every year in the United States. The number goes up at a predictable seven percent every year. At its normal rate of increase, that adds up to 50 billion checks by 1984, 60 billion checks by 1987, and 70 billion checks before 1990. They don't make bank tellers' armies big enough to handle that number of checks.

Following the simple rule of substitution which we have used to illustrate some of our forecasts, it is easy to predict that we will soon enter a checkless and cashless society. Someday soon, only diehards will use cash, paying a penalty for the privilege because cash will require special handling. Almost all transactions will be done with plastic. Funds will be transferred by voiceprint and almost nobody will have to shop in person. Two-way television in the home will let you dial a store, check prices on your screen and order by credit card or checking account number. The merchant will push a button that lights up green if you have enough funds in your account and red if you don't. People will still be able to live on the float. The machine will light up yellow if you've deposited the funds to cover your purchase even if the deposit is in the process of clearing your bank.

ELECTRONIC FUNDS TRANSFER

The substitution we're now able to make for paper money is, of course, electronics. Though the checkless and cashless society has not arrived yet, we are already in the midst of a precursor banking revolution called electronic funds transfer. Again, cost and convenience are the rules for substitution. If it can do the job cheaper and more conveniently, the substitute method will win out over the established method every time. Banking has never been cheaper or more convenient than it is under electronic funds transfer, which is changing the banking business in ways that nobody fully understands.

The largest banks and corporations have transferred funds electronically since the first days of the teletype machine but its use was confined to the technologically elite banks and their largest corporate customers. What is new about electronic funds transfer is that it is the first effort by commercial banks to use the fastest and newest computers to bring their financial services right into the hands of all their customers. Banks now use EFT terminals they call automated teller machines which are located on their outside walls, the ground floor of an apartment complex or right in the middle of a shopping center. These automated tellers work 24 hours a day and let customers deposit money, withdraw it, transfer savings funds to checking accounts, repay bank loans, pay utility bills, make credit purchases, check the balance of an old account, open a new account and apply for a loan. The speed of the robot teller is matched by its convenience. The terminals are reached through a plastic card that carries relevant information about the bank's customer on a magnetic strip. When the card enters the terminal together with a secret code given by the bank to the customer (the PIN number—the Personal Identification Number, given by the bank to each customer), the transaction begins.

BRANCH BANKS OF THE FUTURE

Electronic funds transfer is sweeping the country like wildfire. The banks of every major city are walled with automated tellers. So many banks are installing them at such a rapid pace that it is impossible to estimate their number, which ranges from 18,500 to 19,000 at the end of 1980 according to Linda Zimmer, who keeps track of these things for the EFT industry. What the banks spend on the machinery to make EFT work they more than save on the brick and mortar it would take to open up a new branch. The time is coming when banks will abandon their branches. Automated tellers are the branch banks of the future. Electronic banking is so fast on the move that Citibank began last summer to test a home-based computer console that 100 of its New York City customers can use by plugging it into their cable television sets. Citibank's test customers pay their utility bills, their rent or mortgage payments and transfer funds by using the computer keyboard. Citibank has already tested a similar service in 200 homes in New York's suburban Westchester County and figures that more than half its 2.5 million customers will be using the service by 1990.

Citibank is thinking of going national with this service (called Videotex) next year, a move that is sure to be followed by Chemical Bank and Chase Manhattan Bank, to name two of the nation's largest commercial banks. The banks figure that customers will flock to electronic banking because they will save money, not only on gasoline they won't burn to drive to their banks but on anticipated price increases banks are sure to pass on to their customers as they begin to charge more for clearing checks. Because banks pay higher interest rates on checking accounts, they will soon charge as much as 70 cents to handle a check. Electronic banking will bring the charge down to 20 cents a check. Banks won't be the only institutions using electronics to do business. J. C. Penney and Sears Roebuck are testing electronic shopping catalogues. One retail chain is experimenting with a home service whose security code is the customer's voiceprint. The voiceprint is the banking and retailing security system of the future. It was tested in Vietnam to keep the Vietcong out of American air bases and it worked.

While an EFT society is a far cry from a checkless and cashless one, it's a giant step in that direction. One thing holding people back from a checkless society is that a canceled check or the hard copy record of a credit card purchase is a proven record of redress against merchants if we have a complaint. Bankers and retailers have held back for a different reason. Electronic transactions mean there is only one set of records, not one for yourself, a second for your partner and a third for the Internal Revenue Service. These are obstacles that will shrink with time. A checkless, cashless society is inevitable. No longer will people be robbed or beaten for their money. Here is our timetable for the banking system of the future. Until 1985, you'll get a discount for paying with cash. Between 1985 and 1990, you get no discount for cash if you choose to pay cash instead of using an electronic funds transfer. After 1990, you'll be charged extra for paying with cash.

SINGLE-DIGIT INFLATION

No matter how much we're charged and how we pay, the money we're being charged and paying out will be worth less in the future because of inflation. Helped by a stronger dollar and smaller increases in food, oil and producer prices, inflation ran at about 9 percent through most of 1981. Pay increases ran less than 10 percent and the 1982 labor settlements in steel, autos and rubber promise to be modest enough to keep the "core" inflation rate down to a single-digit raise. What's more, Americans showed signs they were breaking their bad habit of buying everything on borrowed money. Americans borrowed a little more than 15 percent of what they earned in 1980, down from a 1979 high of 18 percent. We predict the borrowing rate will fall to less than 13 percent in 1982, which will ease the pressure on inflation and the money supply in the months ahead. We also predict that the inflation rate will stay close to 8 percent till the end of the century.

In general, we think President Reagan's policy of lower federal spending and reduced estate, business and personal income taxes will put more downward pressure on inflation. It's important to keep the pressure on inflation to ease the pressure on interest rates. The big fear about high interest rates is that they will stay so high they will trigger a deep recession late in 1982. After all, high American interest rates caused the American dollar to increase in value in 1981, forcing other governments to raise their interest rates to protect their currencies. Business suffered in Europe and unemployment rose in countries like France and Germany. If interest rates don't decline later in 1982 in America, the world could begin to slide into a global business slump reminiscent of the Great Oil Price recession of 1974.

THE NEW TAX POLICY

While nobody wants a deep recession, it may prove to be a blessing in disguise to Reagan's new tax policy on savings. The savings incentives in Reagan's tax bill presented consumers with a maze of new options for their money, most of them designed to get people to stop borrowing and spending and put their money into longer-term investments. By depressing short-term interest rates, a recession would pull cash out of money markets, mutual funds and other short-term savings vehicles and into long-term investments. What's more, the specter of rising unemployment is sure to prompt consumers to repay debts and think about setting aside more money for the rainy days ahead. Nagging new doubts about the social security system may also persuade people to think more about financing their own retirement, something we will talk about later.

There is a dark side to any recession, beyond the grief it causes people. A recession increases the federal deficit because it reduces its tax revenues and raises outlays for unemployment and welfare compensation. It also raises the government's need to borrow, which is already tapping half of the net savings stream in our money supply. This could keep interest rates higher than they otherwise need to be, a condition that nobody wants in the months ahead. Here is where Reagan's new tax policy on savings could help. Though it offers almost too many options, the Great Reagan Experiment to turn America from a nation of spenders into a nation of savers appears to be working. Later in 1982, when Congress scrutinizes the Reagan savings policy, we think the nation's lawmakers will extend the tax deadline for all-saver certificates beyond December of 1982. If Congress votes to extend the plan, then it will have worked even better than Reagan hoped it would. In fact, Reagan might fight a deadline extension of his own plan because the more people who are saving in a tax-free plan, the less the U.S. Treasury would get in taxes. The less the U.S. Treasury receives in taxes in 1983, the less likely it is that Reagan can fulfill his campaign pledge to balance the budget by 1984. But the more people save, the less of the savings supply will be bled off by the government and the less pressure there will be to maintain high interest rates.

SAVINGS AND LOANS LOST MONEY

Let's talk about the savings revolution and the Reagan experiment to turn America into a savings machine. Once upon a time, people kept their money in mattresses and shoeboxes. It was close at hand, usually safe and ready cash. The disadvantage was that the money in the mattress lost at least 10 percent of its value every year as inflation took it away. People who didn't keep their money in mattresses kept it in savings banks, which paid them as much as seven percent interest and occasionally covered half what they lost to inflation. The monster that inflation became led banks to issue savings certificates, which cost at least $1,000 apiece and had to be kept for at least six months. They paid a higher rate than a savings account, they were still insured by the federal government, but they barely kept up with inflation. You also paid a penalty for early withdrawal. Nowhere was the impact of inflation more noticeable than on savings and loans banks. Fully 90 percent of the savings and loans institutions in this country were losing money in the last few years. In 1979, there were 72 savings and loans mergers, in 1980 there were 142, and in 1981 more than 150 merged to avoid going out of business. In the last five years, $43 billion left American savings accounts for more hallowed ground. Was it any wonder? A person in the 50 percent tax bracket had to make 24 percent on his money to break even in double-digit inflation. The last two places he was going to keep his money were at home and in a savings account.

A little more background before discussing the Great Reagan Experiment. While savers were pulling their money out of the banks, no new savers were coming along to take their place. In 1980, Americans saved 5.6 percent of their incomes while West Germans saved 11.1 percent, Canadians 12.7 percent and Japanese 14.2 percent. The American tax system has long been stacked against savers and in favor of spenders. For instance, the United States is the only major industrialized country that allows its people to deduct from their taxes the interest they pay on consumer-installment debts and mortgages. What did it mean? It meant that Americans were smarter to buy on borrowed money than to save for later on. The real after-tax cost of a mortgage between 1973 and 1979 was negative—the inflation rate was higher than the interest rate on the mortgage.

At the same time, the annual after-tax return on a Treasury savings bill was minus five percent. Money saved was money lost in purchasing power. Americans became "dis-savers," spending as much as they earned.

ALL-SAVERS CERTIFICATES

The Reagan experiment is an attempt to turn that around in two ways—by encouraging people to save and by cutting the federal deficit, thereby reducing the government's need to borrow and making that money available to business and consumers. The all-savers certificates that quickly came to life after the Reagan tax plan was unrolled were a part of that process. The certificates can be bought for $100 until the end of 1982, with a good chance Congress will extend the deadline at least another year. The first $1,000 of interest is tax-free, the first $2,000 if it's a shared certificate. At least 17 states have said they will go along with the feds and not tax the interest. Despite their name, the certificates are not for all savers. They pay interest equal to 70 percent of whatever the current rate is on one-year Treasury bills. That varies but no matter how it varies it means you must be in the 30 percent tax bracket for the deal to make sense. If you expect your 1982 tax bracket to be 30 percent or more, in other words if your gross income will be between $35,000 and $45,000 if you're married, and $25,000 to $30,000 if you're single, then the all-saver certificate is a good investment. The new deal isn't perfect. To get the maximum tax-free $2,000, a couple has to put up $15,860 and a single person $7,930—a large sum to tie up for a whole year. Pulling out early also earns a stiff penalty: automatic forfeiture of three months' interest and the loss of any tax break on whatever interest remains.

For people in lower than 30 percent tax brackets, it still makes more sense to put their cash in a money-market fund earning as much as 17 percent interest even though they must share the proceeds with the Internal Revenue Service. In fact, the lower tax brackets get more yield from six-month savings certificates, two-and-one-half-year savings certificates or even one-year Treasury bills, which pay taxable interest up to 18 percent. If the tax-free interest rate on all-savers certificates was 12.6 percent, it would be just about equivalent to a taxable 18 percent return for somebody in the 30 percent bracket. There is another way to profit from the Great Reagan Experiment. If any part of your investment plan is keyed toward retirement, even if you are already enrolled in a pension plan where you work, you can now put up to $2,000 a year into what's called an Individual Retirement Account. Your payments are tax deductible and you pay no taxes on the earnings until you begin withdrawing the money upon retirement. If you're self-employed, the Keogh retirement accounts now offer those eligible the chance to set aside up to $15,000 a year tax-free—double what was previously allowed.

RETIREMENT PLANS

The retirement accounts themselves are doubly tempting. Somebody earning $34,000 a year can save $667 in taxes by putting $2,000 into an IRA account. The principal plus whatever it earns can accumulate free of taxes until the person retires if he or she retires between the ages of 59½ and 70½. At compound interest rates, even modest contributions to IRAs and Keoghs can grow into substantial sums. IRAs and Keoghs give the saver flexibility. He can put his money into a savings account, a money-market fund, an annuity, mutual funds, stocks or bonds and switch around as he sees fit. The IRA offers a second flexibility. Even people who work for somebody else can set up their own retirement plan under the Reagan rule. It gives workers a new mobility, a new

freedom to change jobs they might not have felt before. One
Wall Street estimate is that the new rules open up IRAs for
as many as 40 million Americans who might have felt they
didn't have the option before.

Outside of all-savers certificates and retirement plans,
the savings answer to inflation is the money market, that
busy but nameless exchange where investors can buy
six-month certificates for a minimum of $10,000 and earn
15 percent interest on it. Or $10,000 Treasury notes that
mature in three months and bring 15 percent interest.
There is also the uninsured liquid asset fund sold by
stockbrokers that earns almost 17 percent. Commercial
paper and certificates of deposit pay the highest rates, only
about one to one and a half points below the prime rate. The
best deal of all is the two-and-one-half year certificate. If
you can tie up your money for that long, you can get 18
percent a year with compounding. The minimum investment can be as low as $100. The trouble with money-
market accounts is that many of them require a high
minimum deposit. An old story. You've got to have money
to make money. "The first guinea," Jean Jacques Rousseau
said long ago, "is sometimes more difficult to acquire than
the second million."

TAX BRACKET CREEP

Are there other ways to
cope with inflation? How do we cope with the yearly
insults to our currency that not only lower our buying power
but raise our earnings and push us into a higher tax bracket?
They've even got a name for it: tax bracket creep. That's
how insidious inflation is. "There is no subtler, so surer
means of overturning the basis of society than to debauch
the currency," said John Maynard Keynes. "The process
engages all the hidden forces of economic law . . . and does
it in a manner which not one man in a million is able to

diagnose." There is nothing easy about living with inflation but we must at least try to diagnose trends in ways that make it a little easier. Having enough money will be one major preoccupation of Americans until the turn of the century, when the successful demonstration of fusion power begins to drive energy prices down. Having enough money will always be important to Americans. As Frank McKinney Hubbard once said: "It's no disgrace t'be poor but it might as well be."

Once inflation is brought down to eight percent, we believe it will stay near eight percent out to the year 2000. Don't be frightened by depression talk. The United States has become depression-proof, in part because of the ongoing computer revolution that exercises such tight controls on money management. Once the same controls get a good grip on what causes the inflation rate to spiral, they will clamp down on inflation and maintain it at eight percent. Once inflation stabilizes, interest rates will also stabilize . . . at somewhere between 10 and 11 percent. That will make home ownership harder for most people but still within reach. We think that variable interest rates will catch on. Instead of rising with inflation, interest rates will be adjusted every three years based on the consumer price index.

HOUSING WILL
APPRECIATE

Even though there will be fewer millionaires as tax loops are being closed and fewer very poor, for those with long-term money to spare, the best return will still be in real estate and housing. You could do worse than follow Mark Twain's advice: "Buy land. God doesn't make it any more." Tight money will create a pent-up demand for housing that won't begin to be relieved until 1990 when new forms of prefabricated housing appear on the market and begin to lower housing costs. Housing will continue to appreciate rapidly, as much as 25 percent a year in major real estate markets like San Francisco, Los Angeles, Washington and New York. In that kind of a fast-moving market, a home can be treated like cash flow. Buying your own home is one hedge against inflation but it's not the only one. Purchasing real estate investment trusts is another, especially if interest rates stabilize and then start to come down. The largest real estate investment trusts are all survivors of the mortgage wars of the last few years and are making a strong comeback. We're thinking of REITs like Wells Fargo, Mortgage Equity, Bank America Realty, General Growth Properties and Connecticut General Mortgage and Realty.

There is an even better way to get on board the real estate boom. Look around to buy your own rental property and manage it yourself. Not only can you write the management expense off your income tax, you collect rental money along the way from your tenants. When you start looking, remember the old maxim: "Buy the least expensive home in the most expensive area." If not *in* the most expensive neighborhood, then at least *near* the most expensive neighborhood. We checked the records of one town house builder in suburban Washington and here's what we found. He built "luxury compacts" (three bedrooms, central air conditioning) in 1975 and sold them for $41,000, in an area where comparable houses were selling for $85,000. In 1980 he was able to sell these houses for $84,000. His money had appreciated 26 percent a year. Before he sold them, the builder rented the town houses, which meant that he wrote them off on his taxes as homes over 25 years and double-depreciated them as rental units the first few years. His capital gain was roughly 39 percent.

Remember, however, if you rent your own houses, you must be prepared for negative cash flows for each month if you have a large mortgage. Even if Uncle Sam pays half your taxes, you still don't get it back until the end of the year. You should also count on your house being unrented one month out of the year. Incidentally, with the new Reagan budget you can write off your rental house in 15 years, not 25, and take 175 percent off each year. This means that you are *depreciating* 11 percent of the value of the house each year rather than 8 percent even though your house is *appreciating* at a rate of 15 to 25 percent annually.

COLLECT YOUR RENTS

For those who don't want the headaches of managing their own rental properties, a Washington building firm named Miller and Smith has an intriguing investment proposal. Miller and Smith builds a house, sells it to an investor, then takes over the rental management with the provision that it can buy back the house at the end of one year. During the first year, Miller and Smith collect all rents and forward them to the investor, who pays the mortgage, taxes and insurance premiums. At the end of one year, the investor has two options. He can sell the house back to Miller and Smith for 110 percent of what he paid for it or he can hold onto the house and Miller and Smith will continue to manage it for an annual charge of one month's rent. The depreciation alone allows the investor enough of a write-off on his taxes to offset the difference between what he might make on rents and pay out in mortgage and taxes. If he sells at the end of a year, he makes 10 percent on his investment. If he holds onto the house, he watches it appreciate in value while he continues to collect his rents.

Investing money in business ventures that aren't your own is always a risky business but money can still be made doing it, especially if you look for investments that promise to help solve some of the world's most pressing economic problems. What are the world's most pressing economic problems? Its chronic shortage of oil and natural gas is one.

Another is its growing shortage of food, especially corn and wheat. World food reserves are the lowest they've ever been. We have no more than a 35- to 37-day food reserve on hand. One could always invest in the stocks of the companies that help the farmer do his work. Caterpillar, John Deere, J. I. Case, etc. If you want to be more speculative, learn how to buy grain futures on the commodity exchange.

ONLY 15 PERCENT MAKE MONEY

Before we tell you to jump into commodity futures with both feet, we should first warn you that only 15 percent of the people who play the commodity markets make money. The other 85 percent *lose* money. Clearly, these are rough waters for new swimmers but those who can ride out the waves stand to make money. There are at least two tricks to it. The first is to get a good broker, an analyst who watches commodity futures every day. The second is to keep your own eye on the weather and its effect on crop size. Most of the world's corn is grown in Iowa, Illinois, Nebraska, Indiana, Minnesota, Ohio, Michigan, Missouri and Kansas. Most of its wheat grows in Kansas, North Dakota, Oklahoma, Texas, Washington, Montana and Nebraska. You may want to consider putting your money in farmland. It has tripled in value in the last three years and has almost doubled every year in the last 10. Foreign investors with cash learned this a long time ago.

The risks of investing in oil and gas ventures are almost as high. There is always an enormous tax advantage because oil and gas ventures provide enormous tax shelters for people looking for them. As incomes rise with the cost of living and more people are pushed into higher tax brackets, then the tax shelters become worthwhile.

Drilling for oil and gas can be productive but it can also

be little more than a tax shelter. Nine out of ten holes drilled in the U.S. are dry and the costs are enormous. Do your homework. Find out what holes in new fields and what extensions of old fields run the greatest risk and present the most potential. The biggest payoff comes in the new fields where the prices are highest. Put your faith in the skill of the driller's general partner and his geological advisers. Ask to see the financial results of previous runs, ask how the partners located and bought the land they're drilling on. Don't forget—investors pay all the expenses.

There is always the stock market, not such a bad choice when you consider that so many cash-rich corporations are out buying up smaller companies. Some of America's smartest managers think the values of many companies are greater than their depressed stock prices would suggest. When adjusted for inflation, the Dow Jones average of 30 industrial blue chips was as much as 50 percent lower last year than it was in 1970. Any move toward lower inflation should benefit most stocks, though a good drop in interest rates will be needed before a real market rally can begin. Falling interest rates should help the stocks of companies that must raise large amounts of money, like banks and utilities. The best bets are banks with something else going for them, like banks located in the thriving regions of the Sun Belt.

CHANGING STOCK STRATEGY

What industries have the best investment potential in the years ahead? The highest growth industries, of course. Which industries offer the best hedge against inflation? The highest growth industries, of course. Which industries will show the greatest growth in the years ahead? Let's start out by discussing the industries that will show the least growth. These are the electric power companies, the tobacco companies, and the automobile makers. The electric companies will have a tough time in the next decade trying to get the public to use less energy while developing new energy supplies that live up to state and federal pollution laws. The tobacco industry faces the loss of much of its market because people will continue to stop smoking, in part in response to health warnings, and in part as a response to social pressures from their peers. Auto makers are playing catch-up with the Europeans and Japanese, praying and hoping that their traditional customers will buy Detroit's small cars instead of the Datsuns and Toyotas they have been buying. The steel industry figures to suffer as long as the auto industry does. One-third of the steel produced in the United States goes into American automobiles.

DELPHI POLL

The moderate growth industries will be electronic appliances, and those companies in the pharmaceutical and chemical industries that can take the greatest advantage of the gains to be made in genetic engineering, the art of gene splicing. Genetic engineering, of course, will be a major growth industry of the future. So will the industrial robot business, and so will the telecommunications business, an industry that covers everything from communications satellites to cable television to machines that talk and listen to the hardware and software makers for the office of the future. About a year ago, the now defunct magazine of the future called *Next* conducted a delphi poll of 77 Wall Street security analysts as to what stocks they thought would be the stocks to buy in the eighties. (Forget the nineties, it's too far off for even the best crystal balls.) What's the delphi poll? It's named jokingly for the Oracle at Delphi. In its poll of experts, it goes for at least two rounds. On the first go-round, the experts give their opinions and then are shown what the other experts said the first time around. Then the experts are polled a second time. The theory behind the delphi poll that the experts will get more serious and try a little harder the second time around, having seen what their peers have said the first time.

The surprising thing about the delphi poll is that it works. It was first used secretly by the Rand Corporation in the fifties. (The question: How many Soviet atomic bombs will it take to destroy America's munitions industry? The answer: 225.) The delphi poll has since been used to seek answers to the following: the number of traffic deaths on the Labor Day weekends; how famous statesmen of the past like Bismarck, Machiavelli, and Napoleon would regard current world events; the future of Connecticut; what politicians in San Mateo County in northern California say and what they really believe. How good is the delphi poll? In tests in which people are asked for the answers to impossible questions, the delphi poll provides the closest answer time after time. Sample: How many women marines were there on duty at the end of World War II? The answer is 23,145, of course. Anyway, this delphi poll came up with 28 stocks most likely to succeed in the stock market in the eighties. Stocks like IBM and Schlumberger were on the list, of course. But be careful. Stocks like IBM and Schlumberger tend to be high priced. They are like the odds-on favorite in a horse race. Even if they do as well as everybody thinks they will, they won't return as much of a profit as a dark horse would. The others on the delphi list were Intel, Digital Equipment, Dome Petroleum, Hewlett-Packard, Merck, M/A-COM, Warner Communications, Fluor, Northern Telecom, Scientific Atlanta, WANG, Harris, Raytheon, Texas Instruments, Advanced Micro Devices, Atlantic Richfield, Boeing, Perkin-Elmer, Tektronix, Xerox, Mesa Petroleum, Standard Oil of Indiana, AMAX, Baker International, Lilly and MCA. We have added a few like Tandem and Geosource in electronics and oil exploration respectively. We're also not sure about Boeing and Harris, which are subject to the swings of business fortunes more than most world stocks. The coming deep recession could damage these two companies badly.

Should people change their stock strategy in light of Reagan's Great New Experiment? Absolutely. Before, a taxpayer in a high-income bracket wasn't interested in stocks paying good dividends. Instead, he was always looking for the "great opportunity" stocks that promised rapid growth while paying small dividends. Now, with lower tax rates on corporations as well as people, investors have to take another look at stocks whose dividends are likely to rise under the new rules. In fact, some companies will *have* to pay higher dividends just to attract new stockholders. Meanwhile, there are always stocks with the potential for growth. Which are they? Clearly, aerospace and military hardware manufacturers are in for periods of good growth. The companies that will benefit the most will be Boeing, Lockheed, Pratt & Whitney, General Dynamics, Litton and the Newport News Shipbuilding Company.

Again, look for the stocks of companies that may help to solve the world's economic problems. Pore over the oil and gas producers, the companies that help them drill for the energy and pump it out of the ground. Mobil, Atlantic Richfield, Exxon, Mesa Petroleum, Schlumberger stand out in the energy industries. The world is short of natural resources. AMAX stands out. A good growth business is still electronics, especially that part of the business that will put together the office of the future. Tektronix, Xerox, Wang, Intel, Digital Equipment, Texas Instruments, IBM, AT&T and National Semiconductor stand tall. Robotics and genetic engineering are the two standout industries of the future. Cincinnati Millicron and Unimation, Texas Instruments, IBM, Westinghouse, Machine Intelligence Corp., Automatix, Inc., and Octex are exceptional in the robotic field. Cetus, Genetech, Johnson & Johnson, Merck and Eli Lilly are standouts in genetics. One could do worse than invest in the right kind of technology and one way to do that safely is through new mutual funds like Medical Technology Fund, NOVA and Nautilus, which was formed in 1978 and in 1980 showed a per-share increase in net value of 125 percent.

GOLD AND SILVER

Should inflation drop off to single digit numbers very quickly, there are always the high-grade municipal and utility bonds on which investors pay *no* state or federal tax. At last look, triple-A utility bonds were paying 11 percent interest. Families planning to pay college costs may be drawn to discounted bond issues. A recent example: You could get an AT&T 2⅞ percent bond due in 1987 for $610. If you bought $6,100 worth of these bonds for a 12-year-old who wants to go to college, they could be redeemed for $10,000 when he or she is 18. By putting the bond in the kid's name, you'd pay almost no tax. If inflation doesn't drop off, if for some unexplained reason it gets worse, then gold and silver and diamonds are worth another look. Trouble is, you get no interest when you invest in gold and the price movements of all the precious metals and stones are too volatile to attract prudent investment. Generally, people who invest in gold, silver, and diamonds don't have confidence in the American dollar. This was the case in 1976 and the years just after when the dollar took a nose dive. The dollar is back and we believe it will remain one of the strongest currencies in the world.

The Reagan tax cut voted in 1981 by Congress will help people decide how to cope with inflation in the years just ahead since it will give them more purchasing power to make the right decisions. We generally agree with the tax cut, especially that part of it that raised the estate tax limit from $100,000 to $600,000. After all, a $100,000 inheritance these days is not all that much. How many farmers' widows have had to sell the farms to pay the estate taxes? How many widows of small businessmen had to sell their dead husbands' furniture stores to stay afloat? We'd like to hand out a piece of advice to people who don't want that to happen to their families when they die. Buy a big insurance policy when you reach 45, but have a trustworthy family member (wife or older child) be the owner and beneficiary to keep the proceeds out of the taxable estate. Of course, under Reagan's Great New Experiment, you can leave everything to your spouse tax free. However, Reagan even increased the annual gift tax exclusion to $10,000, so you should give serious consideration to splitting the estate and/or insurance among all heirs.

If you're 45 years old or over and in reasonably good health, here's how to go about getting that big insurance policy. First, go to your own doctor and find out the kinds of questions they'll ask you. Ask about the exercises you should do and the performance tests they'll give you for stress. Find out from your doctor the kinds of questions you'll be asked on the insurance form. Make sure you take the examination when you want to, not when you're tired, run down or nervous. Be sure you know all the names of the clinics, doctors' offices or hospitals where you've undergone treatment and surgery. Write out your personal medical history, the prescriptions you've taken, the names of your family doctors. The more information you've written down, the better it will be. Tell the insurance doctor about all the exercises you do. Make sure you limit your intake of alcohol and coffee, especially if you don't smoke, and if you do smoke, don't do so before the examination. Finally, insist that you give them your urine specimen before they take your blood pressure so you can get rid of any excess salt in your body that might tend to raise your blood pressure. Believe us, it's good advice. Remember to look at inflation and get a policy that is adjusted by the consumer price index or realize that your face value will be less in the future.

THE TELE-
COMMUNICATIONS
REVOLUTION

▼▼▼▼▼▼▼

*"I believe that by the end
of the century the use of words
will have changed so much that
one will speak of machines that think
without expecting to be contradicted."*

—British computer pioneer
A. M. Turing in 1950

▲▲▲▲▲▲▲

The Sumerians invented the number system based on zeroes and tens about 4,000 years ago and the Chinese used an abacus to count numbers at least 2,500 years ago. For some still unknown reason, the time-counting machine called the clock didn't come along until 996, the slide rule didn't appear until 1621 and a mechanical calculator that could add and subtract wasn't invented by Pascal until 1642.

Things picked up after that. The first digital machine was a 1725 loom that wove a pattern controlled by holes punched in a moving belt, an invention improved upon in 1801 by a loom that was programmed by punched cards. In 1822, the first calculator arrived that could multiply and divide and in 1833 Charles Babbage began work on the Analytical Engine, a machine designed to store and manipulate numbers through a punched-card program to solve the most difficult mathematical formula. Though not a phraseologist, Lord Byron's daughter foresaw the future as long ago as 1842. The Engine, the Countess Ada Lovelace said then, "can do whatever we know how to order it to perform."

The Engine that Babbage devised was the forerunner of today's electric computers, the first of which ran on more than 18,000 vacuum tubes and filled the large room at the University of Pennsylvania where it was built in 1943. That was ENIAC, whose brainchild UNIVAC was delivered eight years later to the U.S. Census Bureau. Events have moved at such dizzying speed since then it is almost impossible to chronicle them. The first transistorized computer that shrank the machine's size and increased its speed came out in 1958, the first printed circuit in which hundreds of transistors were wired onto a single semiconducting circuit appeared in 1965 and the first calculator wired to a printed circuit that could fit in your pocket was on the market in 1969. That was the year Neil Armstrong landed on the moon, a feat made possible only by the speed and number-crunching power of his navigating computers.

How far have we come since 1969? We have a pocket computer whose electronic memory is greater than the ENIAC that filled a large room in 1943. We have a desk-top computer whose memory can store what 16,000 human brains can remember. Since electrons travel at the speed of light, the only limitation on an electronic computer's processing speed is the speed of light, 186,000 miles a second. Today's state-of-the-art computer processes five million operations a second and there is a classified computer at the supersecret National Security Agency whose classified speed is more than 100 million operations a second. Classified or not, computers will reach unheard-of speeds in the next 20 years. The average computer in 1990 will do 200 million operations a second and the machines coming out in 2000 will do eight billion operations a second. In a computer no bigger than a filing cabinet, those speeds will approach the speed of light.

Whatever else it's done, the awesome growth in computer power has spawned a worldwide telecommunications industry whose 1980 sales ran to $40 billion, whose 1990 sales are expected to be more than $80 billion and whose turn-of-the-century sales will climb to more than $160 billion. Sometime in the decade that ends in 1990, the business of the telecommunications industry in the United States alone will exceed the gross national product achieved by the United States in as recent a year as 1940. Telecommunications has been the fastest-growing industry in the world every year for the last 10 years and shows every promise of sustaining that kind of growth every year for at least the next 10 years. Only the robotics and genetic engineering industries pose serious growth challenges to telecommunications all the way out to 2000. We predict telecommunications will be the largest industry in the world and will have touched and changed the lives of most of the people living when the century ends.

Telecommunications will change the way people work, the way they learn, teach, shop, travel, the way they are entertained, and the way they get social and legal services, medical treatment and health care, and even the way they grow old. The machines of the future that will be spawned by the telecommunications revolution will include machines that speak and listen, recognize a voice, machines that can translate the words of somebody speaking English into the words of somebody who hears only in French. Machines are already in existence that recognize the sounds and meanings of more than 6,000 words. It will only be a matter of a few years before machines match and even surpass the average human vocabulary. What's more, they'll master vocabularies in every language from English to Chinese and Hebrew to Arabic. The machines will have the toughest time with Finnish. By the accounts of most linguists, there is no more difficult language anywhere than that spoken by the Finns.

VOICE RECOGNITION

Dictationists will be relics of the past in the office of the future. By the year 2000, there will be no stenographers' pool. In place of the steno pool will be computerized voice machines into which office personnel dictate their letters. When they're finished dictating, they'll push a button that instructs the machine to type the letter. No ordinary machine, it rattles off a page a

213

minute. As it's typing, the machine talks the letter through to the person who dictated it to make sure it caught all the words in the letter. How do we know this? Because there's a precursor machine already in existence. The way it works, a person assigned to use the machine reads a programmed list of 3,000 to 6,000 words into the machine so the machine can recognize the person's voice. Then, the same person reads into the machine a long text (it takes eight hours to read) that makes use of the same words. This is done so the machine can recognize the words in context. So far, these machines have proven 92 percent accurate and their eight percent inaccuracy really isn't the fault of the machines. Usually, the machine gets a word wrong or misses a word because the person who's doing the dictating has slurred the word or coughed or sneezed when saying the word. The secretaries of the future will have the job of making up for the eight percent inaccuracies. Needless to say, there won't be a big demand for secretaries in the office of the future.

Getting these machines to do language translations will be more difficult but it will be done in the next 20 years. The translation machines developed so far have had difficulty with idiomatic expressions and colloqualisms. Things like "the spirit is willing but the flesh is weak" come out in another language reading "the wine is fine but the meat is rancid." What starts out as "kiss mama good-bye" in English ends up as "throw mama from the train a kiss goodbye" in German. "You're cool" in English has been translated by machines into "you're freezing" in French. The fact is, classified translation machines do exist and will make their declassified appearance in the next 10 years. The White House uses a translation machine that's plugged into the hot line between Washington and Moscow. The Central Intelligence Agency and the National Security Agency make use of translation machines in monitoring radio broadcasts from foreign capitals. There are even machines in development today that, when they translate from English to Chinese or Japanese, will type out the translations up and down so the people receiving the translations can read them.

Machines that recognize voices will be the first on the market. In fact, one research firm in New Jersey has designed a microprocessor chip that costs less than $10 that can recognize up to 16 words of a person's voice. That's enough to identify a person through his or her unique voiceprint and has begun to be used to control employee access to security areas. Still another New Jersey firm has developed an inexpensive system that can recognize up to 400 words if speakers repeat the words until it recognizes their voices. This system has begun to be used by some government agencies to allow workers with top-secret clearances access to top-secret files. Voice recognition is the key to machines that will write out spoken words when they hear them. The time for this to happen isn't far off. The New York Telephone Company has already begun to do away with live information operators, substituting voice-operated computers that hand out a number when you give a name and address. Do you think that's a real operator's recorded voice passing on the time over the telephone? That's a computerized voice giving us the telephone time signal. Eventually, voice-operated machines will do more than listen, talk and type. Eventually, they'll carry out whatever commands are spoken to them. "Get Bill on the phone," an executive will say to this machine. Seconds later, Bill will be on the phone.

The telephone of the future will work great changes on the office of the future. The first annoyance to be wiped out by the telephone of the future will be "telephone tag," where a caller tries repeatedly to reach somebody whose line is busy. Computerized telephones available today let callers program their phones automatically to redial a busy number until it comes open. Phones of the future will include the storage and transmission of messages. Voice "store-and-forward" systems will allow an office worker to place a call at any time, leave a message and tell the telephone when to deliver the stored message. This system will also let callers carry a single message like the postponement of a meeting to everybody asked to come to the meeting by speaking the message once into the telephone. The way that business people meet is about to undergo remarkable changes because of the telephone. Computerizing the telephone and linking it to other phones by satellite will allow economical "teleconferencing" for the first time in the next few years, the first step in cutting down the $290-billion bill U.S. businesses get every year for business travel. This technology lets people in Los Angeles and New York talk to each other, see each other, and share the same viewgraphs, slides and charts as if they were in the same room. Not only does teleconferencing encourage people to be better prepared for business meetings, it tends to produce shorter, more organized and productive meetings. We predict computerized teleconferencing will reduce the wasteful practice of business travel by 25 percent in the next 20 years.

LIKE CAR RADIOS

The phones of the future will put the office of the future on the move where it belongs. Take the mobile phone, otherwise known as the car phone. In the past, mobile phone service has been hard to get and erratic after you get it. Voice quality has been marginal and the number of users and calls that could be made in any city at one time was limited. A new system will permit unlimited frequencies on car-telephone channels. This will be done by breaking up a large region of a city handled by a single transmitter and receiver into a honeycomb of smaller coverage cells, each with its own transmitter and receiver. A microcomputer in the trunk of the car will compare signal strength from several cells and pick the most powerful signal to serve the phone. Voila!

Make as many calls from your car as you want and expect to hear and be heard as well as you are in your office. We think car telephones will become almost as abundant as car radios and when that happens, the office of the future will really be on the move. The next step after the car phone will be the pocket phone, which will have no cords and wires and will let some people work even while they're walking to work.

THE CABLE

The future will find many office workers working at home. That will happen when the computerized telephone and the home computer move into the home at the same time that two-way cable television takes over the home. The timing for these events is not far off. By the end of the decade, 25 percent of all American households will own their own computers. Already, 21 million American homes have cable television, most of them two-way cable that link the home with at least one outside terminal. The cable called Qube that was installed in 4,000 homes in Cincinnati last year lets cable users vote "Yes or No" on local municipal issues, lets them give their opinions on the plots being followed on daytime television (should Mac and Rachel of NBC's "Another World" get back together?) and lets them plug into as many as 60 different channels that devote their time exclusively to special programming to cover news, women, children, blacks, Jews, the elderly, Hispanics, Christians and even physical fitness.

Besides Cincinnati, the cities of Indianapolis, Los Angeles, Miami, Omaha and Boston opened their doors to the cable last year. Signed up but not plugged in were Pittsburgh, Dallas, Houston and the suburbs of St. Louis. Meanwhile, Chicago, Cleveland, Detroit, Milwaukee, Philadelphia and Washington were studying to see which cable network they will sign up. With new subscribers signing onto existing cable franchises at the rate of 250,000 a month, cable penetration should reach the 30 percent level it takes to become an economic member of the mass media sometime in 1982. By the end of the decade, 60 percent of U.S. households will be wired into the cable.

Before we reach the year 2000, 90 percent of America's households will be on the cable and more than half of those will be plugged into the two-way cable that will let people work at home. This is not an idle thought. Already, most of the 600 employees of a British computer software firm work at home using computer terminals. Control Data in Minneapolis has enrolled 60 employees in a voluntary work-at-home project and Continental Illinois National Bank & Trust Co. has four stay-at-home employees transcribing recorded dictation for nighttime transmission to the bank's central computer. Walgreen, McDonald's and Mountain States Telephone are installing computer terminals in the homes of handicapped persons so they can be employed to help write new computer programs for the three companies.

The promoters of cable television fully expect their wires to become the keystone in a computer-linked home information center. Simply by sitting down in front of a video keyboard, home cable users will be able to book airline reservations, order theater tickets, make restaurant reservations, place off-track bets, play video games with opponents down the block or even with friends and relatives in other cities and tap into huge computer banks for information on everything from astronomy to zoology. People will be able to shop by cable television. You spell out on your keyboard the word of something you want to buy, say curtains, and up on the screen will come the descriptions and prices of the curtains being sold by the stores that subscribe to the cable's merchandise service. A few years from then, you won't have to type in the word "curtains." You'll just have to say the word to the terminal and in seconds you'll be shown what curtains you can buy, where you can buy them, what price you'll have to pay. Then you can order from the machine and bill the order to the machine.

Beyond the issue of the cable's impact on the work-at-home concept lies a larger question. What will be the cable's impact on American domestic life? The more people stay at home to work, the more they will get on each other's nerves. As the number of male and female room-mates and husbands and wives working at home goes up, so will the number of breakups, separations and divorces. We think the work-at-home concept will take hold in about 1993. We predict the divorce rate among the people who work at home will quadruple before the end of the century. There are more domestic issues than divorce involved in the widening use of the cable. As *Newsweek* magazine pointed out last year, the "cable ride may involve more dangers than its promoters would have the passengers believe."

Take the potential threat the cable poses to our privacy. Whenever subscribers order a program by punching a two-day console button, their choices along with their home addresses go into the cable's computer memory banks. While the cable networks (like Qube) have pledged to keep their customers' records confidential, some civil libertarians worry that some cable firms might peddle personal information to the highest bidder or form subsidiaries whose income is based on the market surveys they make of their own customers. Advertisers might want to tap into the buying tastes of the cable families. Politicians might like to tailor campaigns to their political tastes. Though banks and credit bureaus fall under federal privacy laws, no such restrictions have been applied to cable operators. Cable's instant polling capability is also a cause of concern. Theoretically, electronic polling should advance the cause of grass-roots democracy but political scholars point out that instant polls oversimplify complicated issues and permit no time for any kind of thoughtful deliberation. Former Federal Communications Commission chairman Charles D. Ferris has said that cable's two-way technology may someday replace "reflection with whimsy in national affairs."

A NATION OF VIDIOTS

Sociologists worry most about the cable's impact on family life. The average family member already spends more than seven hours a day tied to the tube and that's still the network tube, not the cable that's offering a choice of 60 channels, movies that are less than a year old, blue movies, live sporting events and live entertainment not carried by the networks. Studies done of the cable's impact on viewing time since the cable came on in 1973 confirm the worst of the sociologists' fears. Cable subscribers watch more television than their neighbors who don't have cable. Futurists fear we will become a nation of self-imprisoned "vidiots," cooped up in front of the cable all day long, passively dependent on the cable for our news, our work, our school and our entertainment. While we recognize the threat, we don't think this will happen. We think people will get stir crazy spending too much time in front of the cable. Even if the cable replaces the schoolroom so children can be taught at home, the kids will have to go to school two or three days a week just for the social contact. Even if the cable spawns more stay-at-homes, domestic life could be strengthened in the long run. "When Qube presented an exclusive live showing of the first fight between Sugar Ray Leonard and Roberto Duran, studies reported an average of nine people in each living room," Gustave Hauser, chairman of Warner Amex and owners of the Qube cable, told *Newsweek*. "People will use these facilities together. Keeping the family at home may help to re-create the family."

While we think the telecommunications revolution will be good news for most Americans, we think it will be bad news for the poor, the uneducated and the dwellers in the inner cities. As technological training and higher education become more and more important to the use of things like the two-way cable, as life grows more abstract for the middle-class people enjoying the benefits of the computer, the division between the haves and the have-nots will deepen. The cost alone of buying a pay-cable package (as much as $40 a month) may deepen this division. "Those who can afford cable will have their opportunities increase, particularly with the educational and cultural programming," said George Gerbner, dean of the University of Pennsylvania's Annenberg School of Communications. "The rich will become intellectually enriched, the poor will remain educationally impoverished." The two-way cable will even cost the poor some of the jobs they now hold. Retail salesclerks, for instance. They will disappear from some department stores where computers will do the selling. Even today, computers are taking over the jobs done by inventory clerks in supermarkets and department stores. By the year 2000 we think the demand for sales personnel will be reduced by 25 percent in the nation's department stores.

The elderly will be losers in the telecommunications revolution. Twenty-five percent of the elderly in the United States have incomes below the poverty line. How can they afford to invest money in computer terminals and monthly cable charges? Ironically, telecommunications could raise the quality of life more dramatically for the nation's senior citizens than for any other group in America. In survey after survey, older people rate as the services they most need a neighborhood supermarket, a public transportation stop, easy access to a doctor and clinic, a drug store, a bank and a department store. A cable channel dedicated to their interests would be a boon to the old. Will it happen? The gray channel would have to be subsidized by the government.

Programs about shopping, health, exercise, how to live on a low budget, what to expect from the aging process could all be made readily available if the money comes forth to provide a cleared channel. We think it will but we think it will take at least another 10 years to happen.

The first American institution to be impacted by the cable and its companion computer will be the U.S. Postal Service. Great change lies ahead for the post office, not all of it the kind of change it wants. Technologically obsolete and involved in jurisdictional disputes it could easily lose over the transmission of information, the post office is steadily losing to the telecommunications revolution its only source of profit, the first-class mails. The post office has seen its share of the private message market decline from 90 percent in 1950 to 80 percent in 1972 and to a little more than 50 percent in 1980. Electronic mail carried by Ma Bell and the other common carriers represented 20 percent of the nation's business mail in 1980. By 1985, we think about 25 percent of the financial transactions carried out in the U.S. will be done electronically. The Kappel Commission on Postal Reorganization has said that electronic funds transfer alone will reduce first class mail volume by 10.7 percent by 1985. People are already losing jobs as the sorting and handling of mail goes electronic. The sooner the post office faces the fact that it is not a communicator like the telephone company but a handler like a delivery service, the better its chances for the future will be. We can see the post office taking care of packages and large envelopes but the first-class mail business is going electronic.

LIFE AND LOOK OF THE FUTURE

Needless to say, the computerized cable will have an enormous impact on the over-the-air broadcasters, the NBC, CBS, and ABC television networks. In the last four years, the networks' combined share of the prime-time audience has fallen from 93 percent to 89 percent, a decline that most analysts attribute to cable competition. By 1990, some analysts predict the network share of the television audience will be down to 76 percent. The Ogilvy & Mather advertising agency predicts the networks will have less than 70 percent of the prime-time audience by 1990. "ABC, CBS and NBC," says John Naisbitt, senior vice president of the public opinion researchers Yankelovich, Skelly and White, "will be the *Life, Look* and *Saturday Evening Post* of the future." Predictably, the networks expect their total number of viewing households will go up, in part because the number of households in America is expected to climb from 75 million to 88.4 million in the next five years.

We think that cable's impact on network television will be stronger than the networks think. Network television is locked into its showtime format of afternoon soap operas and nighttime sitcoms, its sports diet of the National Football League and the National Basketball Association. Typically, cable subscribers get all that plus news tickers, sports tickers, stock tickers, bulletin boards and a 24-hour sports channel. Cable users plug in live to the House of Representatives, the Christian Broadcasting Network and the Black Entertainment Network. There is Warner Amex's Nickelodeon for children and there are independent superstations like Ted Turner's WTBS in Atlanta, WGN in Chicago and KTVU in Oakland, which have their signals beamed to a satellite that relays them to earth stations for transfer to local cables. The networks can't match it.

ED ASNER TO AGENT ORANGE

There are three networks but there are over 1,000 public access cable channels, the "free" part of cable television that is mandated by terms of the local franchise. Local franchises can get access to cable networks serving ethnic groups, the elderly or just the plain curious. More than four million cable subscribers reach into Ted Turner's Cable News Network, 24 hours a day of news gathered by six bureaus and sprinkled with commentaries by the likes of Ralph Nader and Phyllis Schlafly, a prime-time call-in talk show that's featured the Iranian ambassador during the hostage crisis, Ed Asner in the midst of the actors' strike and a veteran of Vietnam on the Agent Orange controversy about the effects of defoliants on our combat troops in Vietnam. Who watches all this stuff? Ted Turner says he doesn't know except that the call-in phones ring all day long from Long Island to Los Angeles. Then there's pay cable. More than one-third (17.2 million) of the cabled homes pay extra to pipe in year-old movies and made-for-cable variety shows. Time, Inc.'s Home Box Office and Viacom/Teleprompter's Showtime are the big operators, with over three-quarters of the pay-cable market between them. Buoyed by its success in Cincinnati, Warner Amex is taking its Qube system to Houston, Dallas, Pittsburgh and St. Louis where it will offer school courses, town meetings, department store sales and talk shows. Only big operators like Qube can do this. Warner Amex estimates that wiring a city like Dallas for Qube will cost upwards of $100 million.

RADIO

If cable television is going to leave its mark on network television, will it have any future shocks for radio? Unlikely. Having survived the onslaught of television in the fifties and sixties, radio entered the eighties in a reborn state that seems to have left it immune to future shocks of any kind. "Radio's golden age may well be over," said the now defunct magazine called *Next*, "but something like a silver age beckons."

Listeners and advertisers alike have discovered that radio does many things better than television (network or cable) and does it all for a cheaper price. Since 1967, reports *Adweek* magazine, radio's cost-per-million in reaching its audience has gone up less than television, magazines or newspapers. The result is that radio led all media in national advertising revenue increases in the seventies. Advertising revenues for 1980 were $3.6 billion, twice what they were a decade ago. Radio's audience is universal. There are almost 500 million radios in the U.S., six for every household. Radios are in alarm clocks, joggers' headphones, cars, boats, teenagers' rooms, in tiny transistorized models on the beach and in the Boom Boxes slung over the shoulders of big city blacks and Hispanics. At last count, there were 8,800 radio stations in the U.S. We think there will be more than 10,000 radio stations in America before the end of the century. The Federal Communications Commission has given its approval to 125 new AM stations and talks about licensing 700 more. The market will open up even more when the FCC ends the "clear channel" rights of stations powered by 50,000-watt signals. These stations were given "supersignals" back in 1928 to reach remote areas but since radio now reaches every corner of the country, there isn't any need for clear channels anymore.

Even radio benefits from the computer revolution that has spawned the communications satellites hovering above the earth, since radio can now offer stations multiple feeds at low cost and with what can only be called stunning sound quality. More than any other medium, radio is accessible, flexible and immediate. There is no faster or cheaper way to relay news to the world as it's happening. "If there's a coup or an earthquake," says Morley Safer of the CBS "Sixty Minutes" news team, "radio does it best. All you need is a reporter and a telephone." Another of radio's strengths is its emergence as an opinion forum, with the talk shows that are more like the town meetings of our forefathers than anything else on the air. The listener response is instant. Radio can teach television a lot about conversation. More and more Americans are becoming news junkies and the way they express it is in calling up their talk show hosts. People want to keep company with these talk shows. That's why we think all-news radio and conversation radio will continue to grow by leaps and bounds. Radio is immune to future shock.

What about newspapers? Are they immune to future shock? Not the way radio is but we believe newspapers will endure the computer revolution that has spawned cable television and given new life to radio. Cost is one reason newspapers will endure. Most of the 62 million newspapers delivered daily into American homes cost 25 cents or less. The current cost to pipe electronic news into the home is about $2.50 a day. Cost isn't the only reason newspapers will endure. There is the rapid computerization of the newspaper that's letting publishers reduce costs. Right now, there is no greater bargain anywhere than the American newspaper. There is also something as basic as the relationship that exists between the eye and the brain as they scan and ponder the printed page. "Television terminals will never replace newspapers," is the way it's put by Benjamin Crowninshield Bradlee, executive editor of the *Washington Post.* "I think newspapers are a better way of getting the news. It's something you hold, something you read again, something you go back to see what you missed —the ads, the local news, the foreign news, the national news, the whole schmear."

NEWSPAPERS

The computer will do almost as much to preserve newspapers as it has done to give birth to cable television. Reporters now type their stories at computer terminals, which send them on to other comput-

226

er terminals to be edited. Final versions of edited stories go on to computers that set the stories in type and lay out the pages of the next day's paper as the stories come along. Not far along will be computerized presses. The satellite is already an integral part of daily newspaper operation. For instance, the *Washington Post* beams signals from its plant in downtown Washington to a satellite and back to its satellite plant in suburban Virginia. On the signals are the printed pages of the next day's paper. More than 90 percent of the nation's newspapers are computerized and in the years ahead the figure will rise to almost 100 percent. Newspapers cannot survive without computers but with them they will survive very nicely indeed.

Not all newspapers will survive. Only the fittest, the strongest and the leanest. Those that don't survive in the years ahead will owe their demise to the electronic newspaper. England has had electronic newspapers since 1975. Teletext is the generic name for three of them, Ceefax, Oracle and Viewdata. Ceefax is owned by the Crown and the British Broadcasting Co., carries no advertising and pipes a format into home television sets that includes headlines, people in the news, bulletins, sports, weather, travel and reviews of movies, books and concerts. Oracle is owned by the Independent Television Authority and carries advertising along with local news that Ceefax doesn't trifle with. Viewdata was developed by the British post office, connects to the television set through the telephone and works something like two-way cable. Viewdata lets viewers ask for anything in the post office memory bank. News, sports, holiday and travel guides, education, quizzes, games, business facts and figures, even jokes. Not only England is into electronic newspapers. Australia, West Germany, Sweden, Denmark and Holland are deep into development of electronic papers.

COMPUTERS AS TEACHERS

More than the media will feel the impact of the computer revolution out to the end of the century. Together with the cable, the computer will change the face of education. Cable operators will soon offer educational programs tailored to specific interest groups, such as preschoolers, the elderly and poor in need of legal, medical and financial aid. Formal education services will solve the software difficulties that were largely responsible for the failure in the sixties of classroom television instruction. Cables will be wired between universities so the students at one school can learn from a professor in another. Two-way systems will be used for drill and practice. There will be regional and national education banks that can be reached by using toll-free push-button telephones. Holography will be introduced in some schools as a teaching tool. One estimate of computerized holography is that the entire contents of 26 miles of bookshelves can be holographed and stored in eight file cabinets. Computers have begun to make educational breakthroughs. An IBM 1620 at Stanford is being used to teach singing. The computer prints out a series of notes which the student then sings. The computer can even compare the student's pitch to the true pitch to see where the student needs to exercise his voice. At Texas A&M, a computer selects questions for tests and then grades the results. Medical students at Ohio State use a computer instead of a patient for some of their training. The students ask the computer for symptoms, then prescribe treatment. What held back educational institutions from barging into computers whole hog has been their expense. "I'm convinced that within five years computers are going to be so cheap that leading colleges will require students to own them, just like books," predicts Richard M. Cyert, president of Carnegie-Mellon University in Pittsburgh. "In ten years, no one will even think twice about it."

228

Nowhere in the next ten years will computers force more change than in the delivery of health care. Parahospitals staffed by paramedics will emerge, courtesy of computers that will diagnose what's wrong with a patient and instruct the paramedics how to handle treatment. The use of remote physiological sensors in patient's homes will also emerge, though they'll be limited for a while to patients under regular treatment for certain ailments and for patients recovering from surgery. Even today, computers are regarded as critical diagnostic tools in more than 20 percent of America's general hospitals. Closed-circuit television hooked into the diagnostic computers will let doctors in group practice monitor a patient's condition, conduct a voice-to-voice examination, diagnose what it is that's wrong and prescribe treatment. Already, computers at some medical centers linked up to X-ray machines can create diagrams of the patient's anatomy to help doctors detect cancers that might otherwise go unnoticed. In the computer memory banks at the National Library of Medicine outside Washington right now are the most current articles from more than 2,200 medical journals published around the world. They are instantly available to any doctor in the U.S. who has a compatible computer terminal.

Not everything the computer will trigger in the next 20 years will be of benefit to mankind. The fastest-growing crime in America today is not violent crime, it's white-collar crime. The embezzlement of banks by illegal computer programming practices, tax frauds, the theft and sale of confidential computerized information, illegal electronic surveillance and wiretapping will increase and be increasingly difficult to catch. Cable tapping, criminal electronic monitoring, theft of proprietary information from computer banks will mushroom in the years ahead as more and more thieves become computer experts. A year ago, a computer worker with the Social Security Administration was sentenced to 10 years in prison for manipulating a national computer to pay herself and two accomplices more than $100,000 in disability benefits. She was accused of processing disability checks under at least 10 aliases using real social security numbers, then of erasing all the computer's records of the payments when the checks were cashed. One estimate of computer crime in the U.S. is that it costs more than $500 million a year. We predict it will reach $1 billion a year by 1990 and soar beyond $3 billion a year by 2000.

9

▲▲▲▲▲▲▲

ROBOTICS–
THE NEXT WAVE

▼▼▼▼▼▼▼

*"The human machine was
terribly imperfect. Sooner
or later, it had to be removed."*

—*From the 1920 play* Rossum's
Universal Robots *by Karel Capek*

▲▲▲▲▲▲▲

*I*n the visionary drama that made him a worldwide celebrity, Czech playwright Karel Capek forecast a future in which men and women did almost nothing and robots did almost everything. Capek coined the word which came from "robota," the Czech noun for "work." In the world he foresaw, the factories of the future were run by robots who never ate, were never paid, never felt pain and never stopped working until they heard the factory whistle telling them to stop. One of Capek's robots did the work of two and a half people. Robots swept the streets, laid the bricks and manned the machines. Capek even had female robots as servants, saleswomen and stenographers. "There's a certain demand for them, you see," Capek explained. "People are used to it." Said one of the few humans to inhabit Capek's play: "All work will be done by machines. Everybody will be free from worry and liberated from the degradation of labor. The servitude of man to man and the enslavement of man to matter will cease."

More than sixty years after Capek wrote his stinging fantasy, the robots he predicted would liberate men from labor have begun to appear in the world's factories. Make no mistake about it, the robots are coming. Robots are already on the job in Sweden, France, Germany, the United States and Japan. They don't look exactly like the robots Capek envisioned in 1920, but they'll pass nicely for robots. These robots have television cameras for eyes, hydraulic and pneumatic manipulators for arms, viselike gripping devices for hands and small high-speed computers for brains. Rudimentary as they are, these robots do the jobs strong men once did. They paint, they weld, they grind, they mill, they cut, they lathe, they run drill presses and they operate machine tools. They work in sheet metal factories, automobile plants and aircraft production lines. They make cars, they make appliances and they make their employers a lot of money. At the end of 1981, there were an estimated 14,000 robots around the world on the job in factories where men had once worked. By 1990, we predict there will be as many as 200,000 robots on the job in the United States alone.

THE KING KONG ROBOT

The robot revolution is under way. A robot at the Charles Stark Draper Laboratory at MIT takes less than three minutes to put together a 17-piece automobile alternator and tighten all its screws. A Japanese robot called King Kong picks up a hospital patient, puts him in a bathtub and picks him back up again to return him to bed. A California rehabilitation center has rigged a robot to feed quadraplegics in response to the patient's voice commands. Robots of the past have always lacked the kinds of arms and hands that only people possess but even that is changing. The University of Utah has developed an artificial arm that moves like a real arm in response to an armless person's reflexes. The Japanese have an arm of aluminum and carbon fiber powered by 11 tiny electric motors that can duplicate almost any function of the human arm. Even more nimble electric arms are emerging. Carnegie-Mellon University in Pittsburgh is developing a robot arm that weighs less than what the human arm weighs. Engineers at Carnegie-Mellon are also at work on a robot hand that's so flexible it can insert tiny resistors, capacitors and transistors into printed-circuit boards for computers, the kind of work that women with dainty fingers do today in electronics factories. There is a robot finger at MIT that contains 256 pressure-sensitive switches that give the finger a sense of touch. Even now, it can discriminate between six different objects, including screws, washers and cotter pins. The University of Rhode Island has developed a bin-picking robot that can reach down and pick a rod or a box out of a bin and hand it to another robot in the right order. A robot hand that has three fingers and three joints, just like the human finger, is being worked on by Stanford University and the Jet Propulsion Laboratory. The fingers are run by cable tendons attached to the motors on the robot's forearm, meaning there's no need to mount the motors on the fingers and make the hand heavy and clumsy.

Robots are already in die-casting, spray-painting, forging, plastic molding, machine loading, spot welding, conveyor loading and materials handling. General Dynamics uses robots to fabricate wing panels for airplanes. Lockheed has put in a painting and processing line almost as long as a city block that's operated by robots and controlled by computers. General Electric has a crew of 47 robots who do nothing else but spray the enamel coatings on refrigerators. At GE's Hotpoint factory in Milwaukee, robots paint the dishwashers as they come off the production line. General Electric wants to increase productivity six percent a year and plans to swell its robot force from 120 in 1981 to 1800 by 1984. GE expects the robot market in the United States alone to grow from $65 million in 1980 to $1.5 billion by 1990. Chrysler has put robot welders in two of its K-car plants where they weld stamped steel panels into K-car bodies. At Chrysler's new plant in Newark, Delaware, no less than 98 percent of the welding is done by robots. Nobody uses robots as extensively as General Motors, which has welding, painting and assembly robots on the line at six of its plants in Michigan and Ohio. At its

Cadillac plant in Livonia, Michigan, two robots who look for all the world like mechanical praying mantises pluck engine blocks from a conveyor and hold them at just the right angles for other machines to prepare the blocks for the next step on the assembly line. GM is counting on robots to reduce its reliance on its human labor force, whose absentee rate of more than 5 percent costs $750 million to $1 billion annually. Clearly, the steel-collared robots are on their way.

NO COFFEE BREAK

The robots are on their way for a very simple reason. Robots raise productivity and reduce labor costs. Capek put it succinctly back in 1920 when he described the reasons the world wanted his robots. "The best sort of worker is the cheapest," he said, "the one whose requirements are the smallest." Robots don't eat, don't rest, don't sleep and don't take coffee breaks. Besides, robots don't tire in the heat or refuse to work in the cold. They're not annoyed by factory noise, they're not bothered by toxic fumes and they don't complain to their unions about working conditions. A skilled machine tool operator costs his employer $16 an hour. Your average robot costs about $4 an hour. Let's face it, robots produce more goods for less money. There is a *New Yorker* cartoon that sums it up. The cartoon shows two business executives smiling to each other as they walk between two rows of robots. "Just listen to all that whirring and buzzing and clicking," one executive says. "Not a single demand for a raise."

The rise of the robots represents what some economists call jobless growth. We've seen jobless growth before in the farming industry where rapid mechanization has reduced the number of farm workers dramatically in the last 20 years. Robotization is about to do the same thing in heavy industry. The time is coming when entire assembly line shifts won't include a single human being. The Germans have an expression for what lies ahead. It's called "Die Geisterschict." It means "ghost shift" and it aptly describes the production lines of the future. The impact of robotization on society will be enormous. Said the National Academy of Sciences not long ago: "The modern era of electronics has ushered in a second industrial revolution . . . its impact on society could be even greater than that of the original industrial revolution." Karel Capek said it even better in 1920. Said Capek: "Factories will pop like chestnuts if they don't buy robots to lower the cost of production."

WARRANTY AND REPAIR COSTS

Lowering the cost of production is what the rise of the robots is all about. Robots let factory managers reduce lead time and increase productivity. Inventories can be reduced if you've got robot production workers because you can produce goods in smaller lot sizes because you can produce goods faster. Chrysler says the main reason it installed robot welders on its K-car assembly line is that the robots improved the quality of the welding so much they cut the rejection rate of cars coming off the assembly line in half. Chrysler's hope is that more consistent high-quality welds will cut the warranty and repair costs of its cars when they're sold. General Electric says one of its robot painters saves the company $19,000 in paint every year, mostly because the robots don't waste paint. One auto company that installed robots to handle windshields says its worker accident rate plummeted because robots don't bleed when the glass breaks. One die-casting company reported that its robots increased output so much that it could afford to keep them going even in a business slowdown. The same company closed down its nonrobot machinery in a slowdown.

Ten years ago, the robot painters, welders and handlers

didn't exist because the machinery to make them go didn't exist. Cheap electronic memories and the smart kinds of software needed to give robots their computer intelligence didn't exist. What's more, the arms to give robots the flexibility and dexterity they need on the assembly line didn't exist. Ten years ago, robot arms were more like steam shovels than human arms. Robot hands had such a clumsy sense of touch no manufacturer would trust them to handle anything breakable, like glass. Some of today's robots are so careful and graceful they go months without dropping or breaking a thing. Not only have today's robots a developed sense of touch, they can see what they're touching through the powerful and sensitive binocular optics that serve as their eyes. New two- and three-dimensional vision systems for robots enable them to recognize objects by their silhouettes, something humans are often unable to do. New microcomputers give robots more than just an infant artificial intelligence. One robot built in a Palo Alto research laboratory to use a set of six tools selects the tool it plans to use next on the basis of how close within reach the tool is and how easy the tool is to grasp during each successive step in its task.

NEGATIVE PRODUCTIVITY

At the same time that the robots were developing their brains and a more finely honed set of senses, labor costs were rising round the world at such a rapid rate that they were pushing the world's factory managers closer and closer to robotization. About five years ago, labor and production costs began to have a serious impact on manufacturing productivity, especially in the United States. The productivity growth rate in the U.S., which had always been high enough to outdistance inflation and raise our standard of living, fell to 3.4 percent in 1978, to six-tenths of one percent in 1979 and then to a negative rate of 1.9 percent in 1980. Even in the years 1970 through 1977, our productivity growth rate compared unfavorably with the other industrial leaders of the Western world. The accumulated productivity gains for the U.S. in those years were 24 percent, less than half what France had accumulated, a little more than one-third what Germany had built up and less than one-fourth what the Japanese had piled up. Not surprisingly, capital investment by U.S. industry per American worker fell rapidly at the same time that capital invested per worker in competitor nations was on the increase. For example, West Germany's investment per worker rose from $298 in 1967 to $693 in 1973, while Japan's increased from $191 to $324. U.S. investment per worker fell from $258 in 1967 to $220 in 1973. Since the Tax Reform Act of 1976, capital investment per worker has fallen even further in the U.S. Something had to be done to raise productivity.

An enduring irony is that the lead to raise productivity by turning to robots was taken by the Japanese, who had the highest accumulated productivity growth rate in the world in the last 10 years. There's a reason for Japan's taking the lead. In the next 10 years, fully 25 percent of the Japanese work force will reach an age where they will retire at pensions equal to 80 percent of their base pay. Japan is pulling out the stops to pay for those pensions, including freezing the wages of those still in the work force who've reached the age of 40. One thing Japan decided to do to afford its coming tide of pensioners is to go robotic in every heavy industry where it can. Automaking, steelmaking, shipbuilding, appliance manufacturing, even the electronics industry where miniaturization of the parts discourages the use of robots. Japan now has more than 8,000 robots in use on assembly lines in its factories, more than all the other industrialized countries of the world have together. Japan is now producing 100 industrial robots a month for export. Japan has even built a plant that Karel Capek would marvel at. It is the world's first factory where robots are used to assemble other robots.

239

MECHATRONIC ROBOTS

Japan got an early start in going robotic. As far back as the mid-sixties, a Japanese scientist named Hiroyasu Funakubo of Japan's Medical Precision Engineering Institute began to develop an artificial arm for the armless infants born to mothers who had taken thalidomide during their pregnancies. By the early seventies, Funakubo had produced a lightweight arm whose eleven micromotors could match most of the human arm's functions. The arm's principle is proving to be the keystone of an emerging generation of mechatronic robots that promise to stake Japan's claim as the world leader in the robot business for at least the next five years. The mechatronic arm is far more precise and responsive than the heavy-handed pneumatic and hydraulic arms given to most robots. The Japanese are using the arm as the model for a snakelike robot that can crawl through pipes and narrow openings to inspect and even do repair work in inaccessible places. It is also the prototype for a watchman robot that can wash and wax floors while sending out radio signals that warn of either fires or intruders.

Funakubo's arm has already been mounted in pairs on a hospital bed and matched up with a robot electric cart that moves back and forth between the patient in bed and a storage cabinet at the end of the room. The cart and arms can be started up by the patient sending instructions through a keyboard or by voice command through an overhead microphone. Even whistles and gasps from patients unable to speak are enough to get the cart to bring nourishment or medicine to the arms, which then pass it on to the patient. So far, the arms can't peel the fruit they might have plucked off the cart but the time is not too distant when bananas might turn up on the patient menus. One outgrowth of all this research is a 25-fingered device developed by the Japanese National Cancer Institute to detect breast cancer in women. Equipped with a supersensitive strain gauge linked to a computer, the 25 fingers run along a breast looking for the smallest of lumps that might trip the strain gauges a different way. Not only could this robot device cut down the number of X-rays needed to probe a breast for cancer, it might prove more acceptable to women embarrassed by the probing of doctors and technicians.

ROBOTIZING THE WORLD

This kind of research illustrates the jump Japan has on the rest of the world in robot development. In fact, the new robot plant run by Fujitsu has the capacity to manufacture more robots in a year than are on the job throughout the United States. Japan has over 8,000 installed robots welding, painting, handling, tooling and assembling in steel mills, automobile factories and electronic assembly lines, and has plans to move into shipyards, textile mills and appliance factories and increase the number of its robots to 20,000 by 1985. The Japanese have even begun to lease their robots to smaller firms who get low-interest loans from the Bank of Japan to install them. Together with Fujitsu, Japanese robot makers like Hitachi, Mitsubishi, Toshiba and Kawasaki produced $180 million worth of robots in 1979 and plan to increase that to $1 billion by 1985. Japan has already moved into the export market, now supplying roughly 70 percent of the Western world's working robots, and produces 100 robots a month for export to the United States and Western Europe. The Japanese even export robots to themselves. Nissan Motors' new light truck plant in Smyrna, Tennessee, will use 200 Japanese robots to paint and weld the Datsun trucks coming off the Smyrna assembly line. If left to its own devices, Japan will robotize the world.

Spurred on in part by Japan's competitive edge, the United States (3,700 robots) is not far behind Nippon's lead.

One reason the U.S. is close behind Japan is that the U.S. is still the world's recognized leader in what's called CAD and CAM, which stand for computer-aided design and computer-aided manufacturing. These are the high-speed and inexpensive memories and software that let manufacturers program a robot so it can do more than just pick things up and put them somewhere else. These are the tricks that let you program a robot to handle a part and put it together with another part and put them together with a third part, all in the same motion. The U.S. is still so far ahead of the rest of the world in computer-aided design that even the Japanese get 90 percent of their CAD systems from the United States. The same thing is true of the microprocessors that are becoming an essential part of the new robots coming on the market. The U.S. owns at least three-fourths of the world's microprocessor market, which is now the fastest-growing business in the world.

THE PERFECT PUMA

American robot makers are concentrating their efforts on the development of the "smart" robot, the machine that will be able to use sight, touch, hearing and an advanced form of artificial intelligence to do more jobs and do them better than today's robots can. Take the example of the PUMA robot under development at a Palo Alto firm named Machine Intelligence Corp. One of the more simple tasks this robot can do is to return four wrenches scattered on a workbench to a wall rack. Simple as it sounds, it couldn't be done by today's working robot because today's working robot couldn't pick them up in order and place them back on the rack in order. But PUMA can. Instantly, PUMA chooses the wrench it can most easily grip at each step along the way and puts each wrench back in its right spot. The first wrench it gripped was separated from the others on the workbench and was thus the simplest to grasp. Robots like PUMA are the robots of the future. They are able to see, touch, hear and make the kinds of spatial reasoning decisions that can be made by the humans the robots are going to replace.

DUMB AND SMART ROBOTS

As painful as it is to contemplate, this new generation of robots will replace millions of humans in the next 20 years. Right now, the rule of thumb in the robotics industry is that today's robot replaces three production workers. That's if the robot works two shifts. If the robot works three shifts, he replaces at least four and sometimes as many as five people. The "smart" robot replaces five people, even if he works only one shift. We believe there will be 200,000 robots at work on American assembly lines by the year 1990, a mix of smart and dumb robots. By 2000, there will be as many as one million installed robots working in American factories, most of them smart robots. What will that mean? That will mean by the turn of the century that robots will have replaced 4.4 million workers. Most of them will have lost their jobs to the smart robots, who will have moved in on 3.2 million workers by 2000. It won't be an embarrassment to have lost your job to a smart robot. The smart robots will be so smart by the end of the century they will be inspecting goods as they come off the assembly line, checking weights, even checking tolerances in matching parts.

But even as the robots move in on production and assembly-line workers, they'll be creating thousands of *new* jobs. The robot business itself will be one of the three largest new industries to be born (the others are telecommunications and genetic engineering) in the next 20 years. One estimate we have seen by the Robot Institute of

America in Dearborn, Michigan, and with which we agree is that robot makers will employ almost one million people by 2000 to develop, produce and test the new smart robots coming on the line. There will also be a need for robot supervisors and robot maintenance men in the factories where robots will work. Robots are a lot like people. They'll make mistakes on occasion and they'll break down on occasion. The factories of the future will need human supervisors to check on the robots' work and they'll need human technicians to repair or rewire the robots when they break down. Can't you see it? There will be a wing of the factory of the future that will look like a robot emergency room, where technicians are replacing hands, arms and eyes on the robots who've lost the use of their senses. One estimate we've seen is that by 1990 American industry will employ 1.5 million robot technicians—call them robot application specialists. It will be a highly skilled job and pay $23,000 a year for only two years' experience in 1990. Not bad for starters.

PAINTERS, GRINDERS, MILLERS

Most of the displaced workers will come from the industries where robots are best suited to work. That means auto workers, metal workers and machinists. Some people think that robots are a threat to the entire blue-collar work force of 32 million people but we think that's absurd. At most, we think there are about eight million workers whose jobs could be done by robots. The dumb robots can replace welders, painters, grinders, lathe operators, millers, planers and machine tool and drill press operators. The smart ones can do the jobs now done by heat treaters, packagers, electroplaters, inspectors, filers, buffers and assemblers. Skilled workers in the tool and die industry are the safest. Their skills are beyond the abilities of most robots. There are some factory jobs robots will not be able to do until the 1990s. Robots are not able to match colors precisely so they cannot do paint-matching jobs. However, we expect that the further development of spectral analysis in the 1990s will make paint-matching jobs possible for robots. Similarly, future developments in holography should bring work requiring three-dimensional vision, such as detecting burrs on automobiles, into the domain of robot jobs. Finally, robots will probably not be able to work with fluids, soft goods and some textiles until the 1990s.

Auto workers will be hit hardest by robots because the auto industry will make the greatest use of robots. Not only is the auto industry already making the most use of robots, the assembly-line style of production is geared for robots. It is an old but true story in the auto industry that the best cars are built on Wednesdays and the worst cars are built on Mondays and Fridays. Monday's cars are built by people who are angry at having to go to work on Monday, are exhausted by the pace of the weekend and may even be hung over from weekend overindulgence. Friday's cars are built by people who are in a rush to leave work and start their weekend. The best cars have always been built on Wednesdays. How do the robots stack up as automakers? Of course, they build the same car every day because they don't play on weekends and aren't in a hurry to get anywhere. Early auto-maker experience suggests that the cars built by robots suffer a three times lesser failure rate than Wednesday's cars.

BIG BROTHER'S EXAMPLE

General Motors already employs 300 robots for painting and welding and will spend $1 billion before the end of the decade installing no fewer than 14,000 robots in its factories. So sold is General

Motors on the robots it plans to employ that the giant auto maker will build its new plants around the robots. In other words, General Motors is designing its new production lines to fit the robots rather than having the robots work their way into the assembly lines. As they always do, Chrysler and Ford will follow Big Brother's example and spend as much as they can robotizing their new plants. Nowhere in American industry will the robots rise as they do in the auto industry. The impact of all this? Our data tell us that the impact will be enormous on the auto workers, on their union and on the American blue-collar worker. Unless the United Auto Workers get together early on with General Motors, Chrysler and Ford and mutually plan how to bring the robots along and how to phase out and compensate their own production workers, there will be massive and painful dislocations in the states where the auto industry is concentrated. That means the Great Lakes states, California and New York. That means the cities of Detroit, Cleveland, Milwaukee and Chicago, where more than half the nation's auto workers live.

BLUE COLLAR WORKERS

We predict that a generous amount of assistance must be given to the displaced workers to find new jobs or ease into retirement. The auto industry must not follow the example of the coal-mining industry, which gave little help to the thousands of coal miners displaced in the sixties by mechanized mining machinery. A better example to follow are the nation's newspapers, which looked for ways to keep their printers and typesetters and engravers when 90 percent of the papers introduced computerized typesetting. If they couldn't retrain their experienced workers, they gave them early retirement or kept them on in other jobs and let attrition eat away the jobs lost to the machines. The auto workers must be given advance notice of their displacement if they're about to be displaced. The unions should also get a fair share of the benefits that build up from the productivity gains the robots will bring. Transition allowances of the kind that some firms pay workers they transfer should be considered. So should retraining allowances and generous severance plans if workers cannot be retrained or choose not to be retrained. There is a wrong way to do everything. The auto industry should plan ahead with the auto workers to make sure they move the robots into their factories the right way. At stake is the future of American heavy industry.

No matter what is done to ease the entry of the robots into heavy industry, the nation's blue-collar unions will come out as losers. In a sense, the blue-collar unions are already losing. Heavy industry is in the midst of a move to the Sun Belt, where unions are weak. Most of the Sun Belt states are right-to-work states, meaning their laws allow workers the right not to belong to unions if they don't want to join them. More and more, the younger blue-collar workers in the country are choosing not to belong to unions. The average age of the American union worker in 1981 was 53 years old. If present trends continue and younger workers stay out of the unions, the average age of the American union worker in 1990 will be 61. You don't need a crystal ball to see what could happen to the nation's unions if they don't do something about it. We predict that the blue-collar unions will get themselves deeply involved in heavy industry's transition to robots, making sure the robots displace their members as gently as possible. Involvement will let the unions get in on the ground floor of the transition to robots. The unions can't enroll the robots but they can sure unionize the thousands of technicians who will have to be hired to supervise, maintain and repair the robots. It's the only hope the blue-collar unions have for the future.

ATTENTION TO DETAIL

The big winners in the rush to robotize the nation's factories will be the nation's women. The rise of the robots means that factory jobs will no longer require brawn, strength and the ability to tolerate noise and dirt on the job. What robotizing will require are people who can sit down at keyboards all day long, shift after shift, and punch out the programs that start the robots, keep them going, change their direction when they have to and tell them when to stop. The experience for this kind of job may come from the stenographers' pool. We predict that by the year 1990 women will comprise one third of the nation's blue-collar work force. We predict that by the year 2000 women will make up half the blue-collar force. Do women want to work in factories? One unpublished study of the kinds of people who work on the high-paying automobile assembly lines to be built in the Tidewater region of Virginia found that women make the best assembly-line workers. When Tidewater women were given a description of the jobs they'd do on the assembly line, the vast majority of the women interviewed said they wanted to do the work. Most of the women who tested best for these jobs were PTA mothers in their thirties, just the right age bracket for people who would be handling the robots.

Hard on the heels of the factory robot will come the robot assigned to hazardous duty, the kinds of jobs that men and women can't do or don't want to do because they are not safe. We see five categories of hazardous jobs opening up for robots in the next 20 years. There will be the nuclear robot, the mining robot, the genetic robot, the underwater robot and the space robot.

The first one to make an appearance will be the nuclear robot. In a sense, this robot is already on the scene as the remotely controlled manipulator arms that handle radioactive materials behind thick glass walls. But we mean something that looks like the popular image of a robot which can do the jobs people do today, like the workers who dressed up in shielded suits to clean up Three Mile Island after that celebrated accident. The nuclear robot will do more than clean up after radioactive spills. It'll handle nuclear fuel, the radioactive fuel when it's spent, the spent fuel when it's reprocessed and the radioactive waste that's the result of the reprocessing. The nuclear robot will make the nuclear power industry a lot more acceptable to a skeptical public.

Next will be the mining robot with one hand like a shovel and the other like a drill. Let's face it, mining is a dangerous and unwanted job that sickens, maims and kills people every year. We predict the first mining robot will be a gold-mining robot. Why? Because the price of gold will keep rising and robots don't steal. A cousin of the same robot will be used in gold refining. He won't steal either. The gold-mining robot will be followed by the coal-mining robot, who won't get the black lung disease that afflicts so many coal miners.

Once the gold-mining robot appears, it won't be long before we see the genetic robot. That's going to be the robot that handles a lot of the new forms of life that are going to be created in the nation's laboratories by gene-splicing genetic engineers. Since nobody wants to have to account for a test tube spill that lets a lot of new and different germs loose in a laboratory filled with live technicians, we think there will be a genetic robot on the job before too long.

After the genetic robot comes the underwater robot, which may become the busiest of all the new robots. With exploration companies diving deeper and deeper into the seven seas to find oil, there is going to have to be an underwater robot to help out with the diving and the drilling that follows the diving. Mining the sea for its manganese, cobalt and copper only makes the need more urgent. The truth is, there already is an underwater robot. It's run by the U.S. Navy and it's called CURV, which stands for Controlled Underwater Remote Vehicle. Built with a television eye, powerful spotlights and clawlike hand, this robot has been used for years by the navy to pick spent torpedoes and Polaris missiles from the bottom of the ocean after they've been test-fired at sea. Fact is, the robot has been picking up spent Russian missiles after they've been test-fired into the ocean, too.

The last of these robots will be the space robot, who will do the tough parts of the job when we reexplore the moon and begin to explore Mars and the asteroids around the end of the century. If astronauts go along on these rides, they'll stay comfortably inside their spaceships while the space robot goes outside.

We'd like to make a few other forecasts about robots. No longer will robots be just heroes or villains. In the next 20 years, you'll see robots become teachers and playmates, both at home and in the classroom. Robots can instruct and entertain children as well as match wits with adults. What we envision are small, almost toylike robots that talk and test peoples' thinking, learning and creating skills. Or a computerized talking robot that can help people make decisions in the home. What recipe should I use for the dinner party I'm planning next week? What kind of carpet should I buy for the living room? We also can see an advanced robot teaching aid who talks to students by name, teaches them at their own speed and whose memory bank handles everything in their seven standard textbooks. In this robot's memory bank could also be answers to children's favorite questions. Like the first words spoken on the moon, great moments from history, interviews with people in the *Guinness Book of Records* and all the trivia that's crowded into the *Baseball Encyclopedia.*

The robot knows when a child gives the right or wrong answer to a question and will follow a wrong answer with an easier question and the right answer with a harder question. The robot laughs, cries and makes sarcastic comments when it thinks a child isn't serious enough. If the child misses an easy question, the robot might call the child "an inferior biological unit." Correct answers might prompt the robot to say: "IBM would be proud of you," or "Pretty good work for a nine-year-old."

There will be one robot that may not make an appearance in the next 20 years. Which one is that? The domestic robot, that's which. The household robot that always makes an appearance in comic strips and movies about the future may not make any appearance at all before we reach the turn of the century. Though it has the largest potential market (20 million households in the U.S.) and presents the fewest social adjustment problems, the domestic robot simply won't be able to do enough meaningful chores around the house to be cost effective. Who's going to pay $25,000 for a robot that dusts, mops and vacuums but can't do windows? Even renting a robot for $200 to $500 a month makes little sense. Suppose the robot makes a mistake and seriously injures a guest. Who would want that responsibility just for the novelty of having a robot around the house. Besides, your home is your castle. Who wants to turn over his castle to a robot?

But if for some indecipherable reason you have to have a domestic robot, you can buy one from Nieman-Marcus for $15,000. Who else but Nieman-Marcus would sell such a Christmas gift "for the person who has everything." Nieman-Marcus says the four-and-one-half-foot-tall robot dusts, vacuums, opens doors, serves guests, brings in the paper, picks up after the kids and walks the dog. There is also a $650 pet for the robot called Wires, a mouselike creature who lights up, blinks, squeaks, shakes its head and wags its tail. What's the robot's name? It should have been called Stanley or maybe Robotnik, the Czech word for servant. Instead, Nieman-Marcus has given it the prosaic name of ComRo 1. It never sold.

10
▲▲▲▲▲▲▲

JOBS
FOR TOMORROW

▼▼▼▼▼▼▼

"Hear how the hearse horse snickers
Hauling the lawyer away . . ."

—Carl Sandburg

▲▲▲▲▲▲▲

*T*here will always be law-
yers but there won't be as many lawyers in the year 2000 as
there are today. The hearse horse won't be hauling them
away. The lawyers will be hauled away because the demand
for lawyers won't be as great as it is now. There won't be as
many doctors 20 years hence either, in part because there
won't be the demand for doctors in 2000 that there is today.
In fact, to turn a phrase on an old nursery rhyme, there
won't be as many rich men, poor men, beggarmen and
thieves as there are today because the world's job markets
will change dramatically in the next 20 years.

Well, maybe there will be just as many thieves in 2000
as there are today. But there won't be as many textile
workers, there won't be as many automotive workers and
steel workers at the turn of the century as there are today.
The robotizing of the assembly line will see to that. There
won't be as many clerical workers either. Or as many
salesgirls and stock clerks. The computer will see to that.
Only one thing is sure about tomorrow's job markets: There
will be major shifts in employment patterns—though it
doesn't mean there will be major changes in the numbers of
people employed anywhere inside the job market.

Take yourself ahead to the 1990s and imagine the help-
wanted ads appearing in the *Boston Globe, The New York
Times* and the *Los Angeles Times*. This is what we anticipate for the classified pages of the *Washington Post* in the
nineties:

HELP WANTED

GERIATRIC SOCIAL WORKER: Inner-city private nursing home, immediate opening for capable, reliable person. Must be L.P.N. or have equivalent education. Salary $15,000 thru $22,000 depending on experience. References required. Equal Opportunity Employer.

LASER PROCESS TECHNICIAN: Near Prince William County heliport and the metro rapid transit system. Northern Virginia high-technology firm needs dependable, experienced laser technician. Should have two years related laser cutting machine experience or will train. Flex time and day care available. Job sharing and shared dividends. Salary $15,000 to $25,000 negotiable. E.O.E.

GENETIC ENGINEERING: Positions available for both process technicians and engineering technicians. Relocation. New plant in Wyoming. Must have two years technical education and training. Additional education paid by company. Moving expenses paid by firm. Company will buy your present home. Right to work. $20,000 to $29,000. E.O.E.

BATTERY TECHNICIANS: Near Route 66 and Manassas. Large oil firm needs five technicians with previous experience in fuel cells or high-energy batteries. High-school diploma or equivalent. Shift work, O.T. available, dressing rooms and private locker, discount on all corporate products. Education and managerial training available. $12,000 to $18,000. E.O.E.

These four ads will typify the shifts that are coming in the nation's job market, changes that are bound to impact the work force of the future.

300 MILLION
UNEMPLOYED

The key question facing us in the 20 years ahead is, Can the six billion people who will be alive in the year 2000 find work when so many of today's four billion are unemployed? Put it another way: Where will the new jobs come from in the next 20 years if we start to lose the old jobs to robots and computers? There's little question many of the old jobs will disappear, not just because of robots and computers. Take textiles, an industry that has had wanderlust since the spinning wheel that started it all in the north of England. Pity the poor Hong Kong shirtmaker. The business he stole from the United States and Western Europe is already migrating to Mexico and Thailand where the labor is cheaper than it is in Hong Kong. It won't be long before the Thais and the Mexicans lose their shirts to Egypt and Bangladesh. The same kind of thing is happening in steelmaking and ship-building. The business migrated out of the U.S. and Western Europe to Japan, where labor was cheaper. Now, it's moving to Korea and Taiwan where labor comes cheaper than it does in Japan.

Concerns and worries about unemployment are hardly new to our society. After all, nineteenth-century steel barons thought their businesses would die when all the railroads were built. The railroad barons thought their businesses would die when cars and trucks and airplanes came along. One of their contemporaries talked about the "growing armies of the unemployed." Who was that? His name was Karl Marx. Well, the 1930s justified many of his fears but the fifties and sixties should have buried them. Now, it's time to rejustify the fears of Karl Marx. At a rough guess, there are now 300 million unemployed people in the world. Almost eight million of this army of the unemployed are in the United States, with another nine million in the industrialized countries of Western Europe.

257

ONE OF 30 WORKS THE LAND

There's little question that employment patterns are shifting and will continue to shift throughout the world. Take agriculture. When Ronald Reagan was born, almost one-third of America worked down on the farm. Now, barely one out of 30 works the land in the U.S. The same trend is true in Europe and Japan, where one out of 20 work on a farm. The mechanization of the American farm led the American worker to heavy industry in World War II, then to the service industry after the postwar period. Nowadays, one out of three American blue-collar workers are in services, meaning they don't manufacture anything. They simply service the machines and people who do the manufacturing in the blue-collar industry and the machines and people who grind out the paperwork in the white-collar industry. This shifting trend will continue as robots take more of the jobs in manufacturing and computers take more of the jobs in the office.

We think one of the major jobs of the future will be the robot technician, whose numbers could run to more than two million by 2000. We say that because the robotizing of America (and all other industrial countries) will be the only way to raise industrial productivity. General Motors has already said it will spend $1 billion installing 14,000 robots on its assembly lines by 1990. Chrysler and Ford plan to follow suit. In fact, Chrysler put robots into its welding operation at its Jefferson plant outside Detroit and increased productivity 20 percent with 200 fewer workers. But robots aren't perfect. They have to be cared for. They have to be programmed before they go to work, maintained so they don't break down and fixed when they do break down. If they break down, they have to be replaced by other robots ready to go to work. Who's going to see that the backup robots are ready? The robot technicians, that's who.

ROBOT TECHNICIANS

The next generation of robots will be able to see, touch, hear, smell and even speak. They'll need tender loving care, which means lots of service jobs for the robot technicians. We predict there will be as many as 1.5 million robot technicians on the job in the U.S. alone by 1990, making a starting salary of $15,000 a year and a midrange salary of $24,000 a year. Unless you are the kind of pessimist who thinks robots will build robots to repair robots, you can count on a robot technician's job to be a ticket into the 21st century. Of course, if there are robot technicians, there will have to be robot engineers. We think you can count on a robot engineer's degree to be a first-class ticket into the 21st century, to a job that pays $28,000 a year to start. The robot engineers of the next century will design the third generation of robots who will replace the next generation.

COMPUTER PROGRAMMERS

The robots of the future will only be as smart and dexterous as the computer software that programs them, which spotlights another major job of the future. Nobody will be in demand in the next 20 years like computer programmers. Harvard University now insists that all of its undergraduates be able to write a simple, two-step computer program before graduating. That is a sign of the times to come. Another sign of the times to come is the microprocessing chip, which has inspired new electronic products like pocket computers and talking toys. The chip has also transformed old products into new ones, like washing machines programmed to use cooler water for gentler washing and telephone switchboards that will take and store messages. Some estimates suggest that in the U.S. alone, the demand for computer programmers already outstrips the supply by anywhere from 50,000 to 100,000. We think those estimates are conservative. We think that by 2000 there will be almost 1 million new jobs generated for computer programmers in the U.S., with starting salaries of $13,000 and midrange salaries of $25,000 a year.

LASER TECHNICIANS

It is often difficult to predict what new jobs will be created by new technologies. Often, we identify new technologies with job elimination instead of job creation. But when the invention of the transistor was announced in 1948, few technologists predicted the mushroom cloud that would follow it. Few people realized that this tiny electronic gate was the foundation of what soon will be the world's biggest business. Why should they have? After all, the transistor was conceived to be a replacement for the vacuum tube and no more. Even a few years after it was invented, one transistor still cost $15 and its use was restricted to things like hearing aids. The developments had not come along that cut its cost to a fraction of a cent and increased its use to thousands of new products. So it is with the laser, which came along 15 years after the transistor and which promises so many new uses we predict it will be the transistor of the next 20 years. The laser will replace machine and foundry tools in every tool and die shop in the world. The tool- and die-makers of the future will be laser technicians, whose numbers will mount so rapidly in the next 10 years they will reach 2.5 million by 1990 and whose salaries will match those of the robot technicians.

ENERGY CONSERVATION
TECHNICIAN

Two industries that will spawn numerous new jobs are energy and hazardous wastes. The snags with energy jobs are the numerous energy projects, cyclical and almost always influenced by politics and forecasts of energy demand and prices. Typical of the uncertainty of the energy future is synthetic fuels. Will the Reagan administration pursue Carter's goal of producing two million barrels a day of synfuels by 1992? If Reagan decides on even half that goal, there will be a synfuels jobs bonanza that will create as many as 100,000 jobs for synfuels engineers alone by 1990 with midrange salaries of $30,000 a year. But if oil prices stay the same or even rise just a little, the jobs bonanza could just as quickly disappear because synfuels development will no longer be so urgent. We predict one energy jobs bonanza will not be influenced by politics. We predict that by 1990 there will be as many as 1.5 million new jobs for energy conservation engineers and technicians. We think demand for energy technicians, making midcareer salaries of $26,000 a year, will exceed the supply for years to come in nuclear power plants, in coal, shale oil and tar sands extraction plants, even in solar engineering plants. Why? Reaganomics dictate a move to supply-side energy production that can only result in thousands of new jobs. Even if the Democrats replace Reagan in 1984, they can only make moves in energy that will create jobs.

WASTE TECHNICIANS

We're not as certain about the hazardous wastes industry but we'll go out on what we think is a short limb and predict 1.5 million new jobs for hazardous waste technicians, whose most experienced practitioners will earn $28,000 a year by the year 2000. While it's true that robots will be used to clean up the worst of our industrial wastes, there won't be enough robots in the world to clean it all up. Environmentalists estimate that decades, and billions of dollars, will be needed to clean up the nation's industrial mess. When the requirements for collection, transportation, disposal and monitoring of radiological, biological and chemical wastes are included, the number of workers needed will exceed 1.5 million. The cleanup of Three Mile Island alone will take an estimated 10,000 workers 10 more years to complete. It doesn't seem futuristic to us to predict they'll be joined by an army of more than one million to clean up the rest of America.

THE GENE MACHINE

No new industry will make more of an impact on America and the industrial world in the next 20 years than the gene-splicing business, whose ranks of high-technology firms staffed by Ph.D. biologists and chemists will explode far beyond the turn of the century. Who can predict what the world of genetic engineering will bring? Already, gene splicing has been hailed as one of man's most awesome accomplishments, as splitting the atom was half a century ago. The "Gene Machine" is with us, whether we like it or not. Behind us are the laboratory synthesis of insulin, interferon, human growth hormone, new antibiotics to treat bacterial infections and new anticoagulants to break up blood clots in the arteries. Ahead of us are things like genetically altered corn and wheat that will suck nitrogen right out of the air and eliminate the need for ammonia fertilizers. Genetic engineering will produce fuels from wastes, plastics from sugar, sweeteners from cheese. It will even leach metals from ores and clean up oil spills. Says Britain's *Economist* magazine: "It is one of the biggest industrial opportunities of the next

20 years." Our prediction? It's a modest one. We predict there will be at least 150,000 new jobs by 1990 for genetic engineering technicians alone, whose salaries will top $30,000 a year to start.

PARAMEDICS

There will be major new job breakthroughs in the delivery of health care in the next 20 years. If the demand for doctors goes down as we expect it will, the demand for paramedics to do the jobs once done by nurses and doctors will explode. One reason is the tools that medicine will have to diagnose what's wrong with people. These tools will eliminate the jobs of doctors at the same time they create jobs for paramedics. The increase in population and in the numbers of elderly people can only accelerate the demand for paramedics, whose numbers we think will increase by 1.3 million by 1990 and whose salaries will reach $29,000 a year by midcareer. Another explosive medical field will be the geriatric social technician, who will be essential to the mental and social care of the nation's aging. We forecast a need for one million workers, starting out at $15,000 a year, by 1990. Finally, we think that a distinctive job of the future will be a job we'll call bionic technician. He and she won't be bionic themselves, they'll range from mechanics who make the bionic arms, legs, hands and feet of the future to those who are involved in letting the blind see and the deaf hear with new bionic instruments. We think there will be at least 200,000 new jobs for bionic technicians in the next 10 years. They'll be paid well—$32,000 a year after a few years' experience.

It's coming, all of it. Robots are coming that will eliminate jobs and create jobs in the factories, and computers are coming that will do the same things in the office. The U.S. Department of Labor now identifies 28,000 job titles in the American economy, many of them obsolete, like a tea taster, or on their way to obsolescence, like a linotype operator. By the time the Labor Department gets around to revising its list (it changes it every 10 years), most of the jobs on the list will have changed. That is one of the prices we pay to keep up with technological change.

Artists who can create something original will be more richly rewarded than they are today. So will entertainers and professional athletes, who will be made America's richest people by cable television in the years ahead. Imagine the way cable television will bid to broadcast professional baseball's playoff and World Series games. The cable will offer baseball at $1 per seat for each first-round playoff game, $2.50 for each second-round game and $5.00 a seat for each World Series game. Assuming 35 million cable television sets and seven World Series games, that comes to a potential gross for the World Series alone of more than $1 billion. Now, imagine what the players will ask for as their rightful share of those receipts. If you want to grow up to be rich, be a baseball player.

Let's consider the future of the labor movement, which celebrated its one-hundredth birthday in 1981. Trouble is, organized labor celebrated its centennial in turmoil. We believe the turmoil will persist. Sustained unemployment and changing job roles and patterns are eating away at labor's ranks. Persistent inflation and growing public opposition to large wage increases are threats to labor unions' promises to deliver a better living standard to their members. Once the most powerful force outside the White House, labor's political machinery is still struggling to stay afloat in the wake of the Republican tidal wave of 1980. It is possible that labor unions have sunk to their lowest ebb since the Great Depression years of the 1930s. "What we face is not a passing period of acute crisis," AFL-CIO President Lane Kirkland has said. "Rather, we face a permanent challenge to our basic role in American life."

While America's population rises, labor's ranks dwindle. Union membership in the United States is now somewhere between 21 million and 22 million workers, the lowest it's been in six years. That's less than 20 percent of the work force, labor's smallest share since the end of World War II. Much of the decline has come in industries where labor has always been strongest—automobiles, rubber, steel. The United Auto Workers have lost almost $400,000 from dues-paying members since 1979 because of automobile industry layoffs. Hard times in the trucking business have put more than 100,000 teamsters out of work in the last four years. At the same time, unions are finding it harder to enlist new members. Young women moving into the blue-collar work force are reluctant to join unions because they think they're dominated by men. Many young men find it just as hard to join unions because they think unions favor older workers. Factories are moving to the Sun Belt, where right-to-work laws are stronger than they are in the traditional industrial states of the Northeast and Great Lakes. It all adds up to a less potent labor movement. The fact is, unions now win about 45 percent of the representation elections held by the National Labor Relations Board, down from a 60 percent win rate less than 20 years ago.

Just as bad, labor has lost its political clout. Union leaders accustomed to easy access to Washington are straining to adapt to an outsider's role. The White House took away the welcome mat the moment Reagan was inaugurated. That more than disturbed labor's leaders because every Republican president since Dwight David Eisenhower has at least sought their counsel when the political pots were boiling. As of January 1982, AFL-CIO President Kirkland had seen Reagan just twice. Kirkland's union is not even welcome at the Labor Department, which has consulted the AFL-CIO on rare occasions when the Reagan administration has pushed through new regulatory changes that impacted the workplace. Things are no better on Capitol Hill. The AFL-CIO long ago put its own political agenda on hold while it struggled to defend itself against a wave of antilabor proposals. There is no question that the Republican tsunami that swept Reagan into the White House carried labor's political base out to sea. Unions have become almost ignorable, politically, a condition we think will persist for years to come.

What labor must watch most in the years ahead is technology, which in the past has often been one of labor's benefactors in the ways technology has improved working conditions. We think this is a condition that is changing. Take the celebrated strike in 1981 of the Professional Air Traffic Controllers Organization. When PATCO rejected a tentative contract in July of 1981, the union threatened to strike unless its demands for higher pay and more time off were met. The Reagan administration refused and the union went on strike. Everybody remembers what happened. More than 12,000 union members were fired. Interestingly enough, the American public supported the Reagan administration against the union. What lies ahead for air traffic controllers? No matter what happens politically, their jobs are doomed and the reason their jobs are doomed is the technology that's coming along to put them out of work. The Reagan administration had an ace in the hole during its eleventh-hour negotiations with the controllers. It was called AWACS, which everybody knows stands for Aircraft Warning and Control System. Forget the *warning* part and concentrate on the *control*. One airborne AWACS can control the departures and arrivals of more than 150 airplanes around a major metropolitan airport. Look for a different kind of AWACS taking over for the air traffic controllers in the 1990s. It will be a satellite hovering over the United States, watching, tracking and controlling airline flights in every major city of the country.

Just as technology can take jobs away from people, it can also give people jobs. In the long run, we think technology will give us more jobs than it takes away. While the Reagan administration was making it harder for air traffic controllers, it was making it easier for nuclear power plant operators by easing the regulations for the licensing of nuclear power plants. We believe that more nuclear power plants will be started up in the mid- and late eighties, which will result in thousands of new jobs for nuclear power plant operators in the 1990s. There is another new technology aborning that will create new jobs. It's called synthetic materials. Synthetics are not new. We've had synthetic rubber since World War II, when the Japanese cut off our natural rubber supply from Indonesia and Java and forced us to invent a substitute. The same situation faces us in the years ahead, when metals like chronium, titanium, manganese, cobalt and nickel will grow increasingly scarce. Technology is already at work inventing the synthetic ceramics, fibers, composites, polymers and glasses that will take their place. Production of these synthetics will be done by thousands of new technicians working in laboratorylike plants bearing little resemblance to the steel mills and open hearth furnaces of today. As worrisome as it might seem, new technology should not be viewed as a threat to labor. General Motors forecasts that by the year 2000 more than half its work force will be skilled tradesmen trained for their jobs by new technology.

NEW HARDSHIPS ALONG THE WAY

Expressed one way, the worker who accepts technology and is willing to retrain for the jobs of the future is far more likely to be employed than the worker who fights it. Says United Auto Workers economist Daniel Luria: "Resisting automation is probably a lower route to employment than accepting it." There will be hardships along the way. More and more workers will have to change old habits, learn new skills and move to new locations. Working patterns of the future will not be easy on 40-year-olds. If you're 40 or over, you like to think that you've mastered whatever you've been doing. Suddenly, what you've mastered is no longer needed. It will put awful strains on people over 40. But they must steel themselves for the day ahead and retrain for the future. The forest is fast filling up with the dead wood who refuse to retrain. The director of one West Coast engineering firm says that when his librarian of 15 years refused to computerize the library he had no choice but to replace her with a librarian who would. A Booz Allen study of 300 executives at 15 companies concluded that 10 percent of the managers would refuse to accept electronic work stations (at video consoles). Booz Allen predicted the 10 percent would lose their jobs without ever understanding why they lost them.

What we've talked about mostly is employment for the future. What about unemployment in the future? Unemployment has always been with us and there's no reason to expect it won't be with us in the years ahead. Of course, the conditions of the unemployed have changed dramatically in the last 50 years. A furloughed auto worker in 1930 had no unemployment compensation or government benefits at all, while the same auto worker today collects up to 90 percent of his after-tax pay for at least six months while he looks for another job or waits for his old job to open up again. Still, the stigma of unemployment has become just that, a stigma. Employment is now like a talisman to modern man. In societies from the Greece of Socrates to the Britain of Oscar Wilde, hard work was left to the lower classes. No longer. In our society, labor is more of a blessing than a burden. In contemporary times, hard work is looked on as something that can give new meaning to life. While we have eased the plight of the unemployed by compensating them for their trouble, we have made it harder for them to overcome the stigma of being unemployed by making it too easy for them to get by.

PEOPLE LOOK TO
GOVERNMENT

In the past generation alone, Americans have come to view joblessness as a failure of the economic system instead of the individual. More and more, people look to government to solve the problem of idle workers. As a result, the cost of unemployment to government has become staggering. For every percentage point the jobless rate rises, the cost to the federal government goes up $25 billion from the combination of lost tax revenue and paid-out unemployment benefits. Payments under the umbrella of federal programs set up to return laid-off workers to the labor force and to train unskilled workers to enter the labor force were $11 billion in 1980 and almost $12 billion in 1981. Since the federal government launched its all-out war on unemployment almost 20 years ago, almost $100 billion has been spent on programs to help the unemployed. Whom have they helped? The jobless now range between eight and nine million, up from less than four million in 1962 when a lot of the aid-to-jobless programs began.

We think there should be a new approach to joblessness. We think the federal government and private industry and the labor movement together must look ahead more to the future, do a better job of forecasting the kinds of jobs that will be available and set about training the nation's work force to fill those jobs. Even in recessions, there are thousands of jobs that go begging. In part, they are service jobs that many people don't want to fill. But for the most part, they are jobs that call for skills that the unemployed don't have because there were no retraining programs available to teach them the skills. The U.S. Department of Labor's Bureau of Labor Statistics has identified 60 jobs that it describes as the fastest-growing occupations in America. Few of them require four-year college degrees; some have no educational requisites beyond high school. All of these 60 fast-growing occupations offer starting salaries in excess of the national norm, rapid salary increases and open doors to promotions. Most importantly, many of these jobs are stepping-stones to business ownership where personal earnings take off.

SOLAR TECHNICIANS IN
THE SUN BELT

Some well-known trades and some brand new trades will flourish in the coming years. Among the old trades whose futures are bright are opportunities for what we might call operating engineers, people who can run cranes, bulldozers; automobile mechanics; heating, cooling and refrigeration mechanics and appliance servicemen. The most promising new trades are in the energy fields. Solar technicians in the Sun Belt, for instance. Energy conservation technicians in the Northeast. Reagan's deregulation of oil and natural gas will surely be followed by stepped-up drilling for both so it's not hard to predict there will be a rising demand for oil-field technicians of every stripe. These jobs involve long hours and hard work but the compensations are enormous. Oil-field workers often earn as much as $60,000 a year. Drilling for oil and gas at sea will trigger a new demand for an unusual job, that of professional diver. The risks of jobs like divers have come way down in the past 10 years. There is little risk at all to the divers staffing professional diving companies, most of which are located in Houston and New Orleans. Remember, jobs are concentrated in locations. You can't expect to graduate from a technical school in your hometown and right away find work as an aircraft mechanic if your hometown is in Maine and you don't live near an airport. For example, jobs in the electronics industry are mostly in California, Arizona, Massachusetts, Texas and New York. If you want to work in electronics, move to those states and you'll have a better chance.

We'll forecast three new jobs for the future that the Bureau of Labor Statistics leaves out. One of these jobs we'll call housing rehabilitation technician, a catchall word for somebody who's expert at making a new house out of an old house or making a new house out of brand new materials. World population will double in the next 35 years and that will intensify demand for housing so strongly that we think as many as 1.75 million new housing technicians will be needed by 1990. Our second new job is holographic specialist, a cousin of the robot technician, who will work in the robotized factory of the future specializing in servicing the optical computers that compare the inputs they're getting from the factory floors to the three-dimensional holographic data stored in other computers. We forecast a demand for 200,000 holographic specialists by 1990. Finally, there is the battery technician, the person who will service the next generation of fuel cells and batteries that will be used to power the cars and homes of the future. We think the demand for battery technicians will be 250,000 by 1990. In short, we do not believe there will be a shortage of jobs in the next 20 years. Only a shortage of creative, imaginative people to fill them.

All the future jobs we've mentioned so far are jobs we are predicting for the next 20 years. Are there other occupations that might take off out to the end of the century? Let's speculate for just a moment. Restaurant chefs could be in enormous demand, due to the increase in leisure time and the dual careers of husbands and wives. The rapid increase in the quality and quantity of frozen foods will cause a demand for more chefs and nutritionists by food packaging companies. There may be more city managers because there will be more satellite cities in need of them. The boom in leisure time will create vast numbers of new jobs for hotel managers and for public relations and advertising specialists, whose job it will be to promote new uses for leisure time. Rental assistants will proliferate because people will want help in finding vacation spots and summer rentals as well as homes. The same will hold true with dieticians who will be consulted frequently as people become more conscious of their appearances. Geriatric foods consultants will also be in demand, as well as licensed practical nurses for the elderly. The number of pharmacists will double in the next 20 years. After all, if the people of the future are going to live longer, they will need their corner druggists more than ever.

THE
SPACE PROGRAM:
WILL IT FLY?

▼▼▼▼▼▼▼

*"I believe that all
that is possible is
striving to come into being."*

—*André Gide*

▲▲▲▲▲▲▲

$\mathcal{N}$owhere are developments moving more rapidly than they are in space technology. Not even thirty years old, the use of machines in space to forecast our weather, survey the entire earth, communicate over it and explore beyond it has achieved a promise that not even Jules Verne could have expected in such a short time. Twenty years ago, these machines couldn't even hit the moon. The last fifteen years have seen them explore Mercury, Venus, Mars, Jupiter and Saturn. One of these machines is already on its way out of the solar system. Another will reach Uranus in 1986 and Neptune in 1989. By the year 2000, the only planet in our solar system that man's machines will not have visited will be the distant planet Pluto.

Look ahead to 1989, look ahead to spring of that year when the Milky Way is most dazzling, when the moon appears fuller and the planets brighter than at any other time of year. Half a billion miles from earth, a silvery spacecraft shaped like a round-bottomed bucket and named for the 17th-century Italian who revolutionized astronomy descends into the seething ammonia clouds of the giant planet Jupiter. Hanging at the end of a parachute to slow itself down, the Galileo spacecraft built by California's Jet Propulsion Laboratory will be the first man-made object to fall into the atmosphere of the planet that dominates our solar system. A planet so large that it almost became a second sun, a planet so massive that a storm in its clouds called the Giant Red Spot is larger than the earth, a planet so big that it is bigger than all the other planets put together.

RADIO NOISE

While the 335-kilogram probe plows through the Jovian clouds, a 1,100-kilogram spacecraft flies overhead to receive the radio signals the probe sends back as it descends deeper into Jupiter's atmosphere. Back from six instruments aboard the Galileo probe comes information about Jupiter never gleaned before. Back comes the size of the ammonia particles that make up the clouds, the abundance of hydrogen and helium below the clouds, a measure of the internal heat produced by the planet's enormous pressures, the size of the lightning strikes that are the source of the mysterious radio noise transmitted by Jupiter. In the one hour before it's crushed and burned up by the planet's dense atmosphere, the Galileo probe will tell us more about Jupiter than all the telescopes on earth told us in the last 400 years.

The Galileo mission to Jupiter won't end with one hour of radio transmission. At the same time that the probe is being crushed by Jupiter's atmosphere, the overhead spacecraft that has served as the probe's radio relay to earth is flying inside the orbit of the strange moon of Jupiter called Io to slow itself down just enough to be caught by Jupiter's gravity. Now in an egg-shaped orbit around the giant planet, the overhead spacecraft begins a photographic mission of the planet and its four giant moons that promises to be the most sophisticated and productive mission ever flown to the planets.

NINE VOLCANOES

Eleven times in the ensuing 20 months, the Galileo spacecraft will fly around Jupiter and its four large moons, Io, Ganymede, Callisto and Europa. It will fly 1,000 kilometers from Io, photographing its nine active volcanoes from so close in that the television broadcast back to earth could be the most spectacular live event of the century. The spacecraft will come a scant 300 kilometers from Ganymede, the largest of the four large moons (Jupiter has 12 altogether) and one that is believed to be half ice and half rock. At no time will any of Galileo's encounters with Io, Ganymede, Callisto and Europa be any farther away than 2,000 kilometers (1,200 miles) and it will be its close calls that prove its undoing. At the end of 20 months, the spacecraft will have accumulated so much radiation on its passages around Jupiter that it will die of radiation poisoning. Its instruments will short-circuit, its optics fog over and its radios go dead. No matter. In the 20 months they are expected to function, the instruments, optics and radios will transform our knowledge of Jupiter the same way Galileo transformed the science of astronomy almost 400 years ago.

While it might be the most dramatic mission planned for the planets, Galileo will not be the most productive in space in the next 20 years. That role goes to the Large Space Telescope, four tons of world-class optics that will be carried by the space shuttle into earth orbit two years before Galileo reaches Jupiter. There are not enough superlatives to describe the Space Telescope, whose perch above the shroud that is the earth's atmosphere will let it peer 10 times deeper into the heavens than the largest telescope on earth. That puts it almost to the edge of the expanding universe, back through 14 billion years and 90 percent of the time it's taken the universe to evolve.

MYSTERY LIGHT

Astronomers fully expect to use the Space Telescope to witness what galaxies of stars went through after the Big Bang explosion created the universe 16 billion years ago. The Space Telescope may tell us for the first time the precise age of the universe, the exact distance from the Milky Way to other galaxies and the precise speeds at which other galaxies are flying away from us. Do invisible black holes really exist? The Space Telescope should tell us. What are those mystery points of light called quasars near the edge of the observable universe that appear to be 100,000 times stronger than our sun? The Space Telescope should tell us. Will the cosmos go on expanding forever or will it contract at some future time and explode again to recreate itself in another Big Bang? The Space Telescope should tell us.

Before it even begins to look far into the cosmos, the Space Telescope will survey all the planets in our solar system. It will study the spring storms on Mars, the 300-mile-an-hour winds that whip up the sulfuric acid clouds on Venus and the giant permanent hurricanes that stand out in the cloud tops of Jupiter. One of the first things it will observe will be the rings of Saturn, especially the mysterious spokes that seem to join the rings and that scientists believe are the results of colossal lightning strikes that generate as much electricity as a nuclear power plant does on earth. After that, the Space Telescope will be trained on the nine active volcanoes of the moon of Jupiter called Io, so that when Galileo passes that exploding moon in August of 1987 it will know just where to look to get the best glimpse of a celestial body in volcanic turmoil.

WOBBLING STARS

Once it has surveyed the solar system and been calibrated for a deeper look into the heavens, the Space Telescope will survey the 200 stars nearest to our own sun to see if there is any evidence that they have planets in their orbit the way our own sun does. At nearby stars, large planets might show up in the Space Telescope as tiny pinpoints of light. Or the stars themselves may wobble a bit as they move through space, suggesting that planets in orbit are pulling at them and forcing them off a straight and narrow path. By 1990, we think we will know if our own solar system is unique or if other stars are the centers of solar systems like our own. The consequences of the discovery of another solar system are obvious. It will be the strongest evidence yet that we may not be alone in the universe.

Exciting as they are to contemplate, Galileo and the Space Telescope are not the only ambitious space missions planned for the next 20 years. The Soviet Union, the European Space Agency and Japan plan missions to pursue Halley's Comet when it flies round the sun in 1986 as it has every 76 years since at least the time of Christ. Will the United States take up the pursuit? Or will the world's leading spacefaring nation take a back seat to one of the greatest shows on earth? In the years ahead, the United States and the Soviet Union will no longer have space to themselves. The European Ariane rocket booster will be carrying its own booster by 1985. Japan will make louder noises about getting into space in a bigger way. Already, the Japanese National Space Development Agency, which is planning projects to be carried into space aboard the American shuttlecraft, is toying with plans for a Japanese shuttle. If President Reagan forgoes a flight to Halley for budgetary reasons, he will be urged to plan a mission to a comet like Bennett, Encke or West, which return to the earth's environs more often than Halley and generate the same scientific interest as Halley does. At stake is more than the $300 million needed to reach a comet with a spacecraft that could return to earth with a sample of the comet on board. At stake is the future of the United States as the standard-bearing nation in deep space. The return of a cometary sample could be just as important as the first rocks brought back from the moon. After all, scientists believe that the stuff comets are made of is the oldest cosmic matter in the solar system, primordial dust whose origins go back further in time than any of the planets or moons in the solar system. The importance of a mission to Halley has not been lost on the Russians. Flying a French camera, the Soviets will meet Halley's Comet with a spacecraft that is far superior to the Japanese and European entries. Still, the Soviets are not the space navigators the Americans are. Their Halley probe will pass no closer to the comet than 6,000 miles. An American spacecraft was designed to fly right through the tail of the comet less than 500 miles from its head.

A WORLDWIDE CALAMITY

If the United States decides to go on bearing the standard, the next 20 years have boundless possibilities in deep space for America. On the drawing boards are missions to orbit a giant radar antenna around Venus to peer through its hundred-mile-thick clouds for a picture of its fiery surface. There is a plan to land robot instrument capsules on the so-called earth-approaching asteroids like Icarus and Anteros, especially Anteros since it's easier to reach than any of the others. Why land on an asteroid? To find out what it's made of, naturally. There's another reason for landing on an earth-approaching asteroid. Some scientists think the earth is in danger of colliding someday with one of the earth-approaching asteroids, a collision that could trigger a worldwide calamity the equal of a nuclear war. After all, scientists now believe that the extinction of the dinosaurs 65 million years ago came about because a meteor no larger than six miles across burned up and put so much dust into the atmosphere that it blocked the sun's light for years, killing off all the green plants on which the dinosaurs lived. Landing on an asteroid would teach us how to land on a moving asteroid. Later on, if we discovered an asteroid on a collision course with earth, we could land another robot carrying an atomic bomb on the asteroid. Blowing it up would steer it off its collision course with earth.

There are other serious missions on the planning boards. There is a plan to fly a prospecting mission over the north and south poles of the moon where scientists believe there is an abundance of methane and water frozen in the permanent shadows of the polar craters blocked out from the sun. If we ever want to establish an exploration base on the moon, we must put it near a source of water and energy. The discovery of frozen methane and permafrosted water in the shadowed craters at the poles would radically change the way space planners think about a future manned base on the moon. There is a similar plan for a prospecting mission over the north and south poles of Mars where water is believed to be locked up in the giant polar caps on Mars. If we should ever want to send men to Mars, we would once again want to put them near a source of water. Finding the water would be a necessary first step in landing men on Mars.

Beyond the moon and Mars, there are plans to send a Galileo-type mission to Saturn, which is half a billion miles beyond Jupiter and almost one billion miles from earth. This mission would involve sending a probe into the atmosphere of the moon of Saturn called Titan. Once again, a sister spacecraft would orbit the rings of Saturn while it acted as radio messenger for the two probes. Why probe a moon called Titan? There are some space scientists who view Titan as the most bewitching body in the solar system. With a nitrogen atmosphere twice as dense as our own earth's, Titan probably resembles a primitive earth more than any other body in the solar system. Though locked in deep freeze more than one billion miles from the sun, Titan literally looks like the earth did 3.5 billion years ago before life began on earth.

While there are many scientists who devoutly wish to land on a body like Titan, which may be a precursor of life, there are just as many who want to sample the surface of Mars and return the sample to earth. Their point is that if life exists today anywhere else in the solar system it exists on Mars. The two Viking spacecraft that landed on Mars in 1976 found no signs of life in the red soil of Mars but that doesn't mean life doesn't exist on Mars. The same Viking spacecraft sent back photographic proof that canyons deeper, wider and longer than the Grand Canyon run all across Mars, evidence that water once ran on Mars with the same abundance that water runs on earth. After all, the canyons could only have been carved into Mars by rushing rivers of water. Life probably cannot exist without water.

MARTIAN GERMS

The question is, Did life exist on Mars when Mars had plenty of water and would life have survived the Ice Age that froze the planet aeons ago? If life existed but did not survive, evidence of it would still be present in fossils in the Martian soil, which is enough of a reason to mount a sample return mission. Trouble is, the cost of such a mission is between $2 and $3 billion, almost too much even for a spendthrift nation to pour into one mission. Since it may be contaminated with germs that could devastate the human population, a Martian soil sample could never be returned directly to earth. It would have to be examined in earth orbit in superclean conditions aboard the space shuttle by trained scientists willing to volunteer for the assignment.

282

It will be 50 years before a manned mission to Mars is undertaken, a voyage that could take two years and expose the astronauts making the trip to more radiation than industrial workers are allowed in their entire lives. The psychological difficulties of a two-year space odyssey might be even tougher to overcome. How will a three-man crew deal with the tension and anxiety of being alone together on a hazardous flight for two years? Should there be a woman aboard to ease some of the tension? Should two women and one man make the flight? Should there be two men and two women aboard? These are not idle questions. The crew on one long sea voyage threw a $2 million experiment overboard to make room in the ship's refrigerator for their Coca-Cola. In the Antarctic, there have been numerous mental breakdowns and three murders. Soviet cosmonauts have sulked at the opposite ends of their Salyut space station. Once, they turned off their radio for two days because they were tired of the ground's nitpicking suggestions. The lack of privacy, discomfort from the oxygenated atmosphere, the fluid shifts below the skin, the constant distorted conversation with the ground, the tedious exercise routine and the uncomfortable clothing are all stresses in space. "Even the monotonous light and sound levels can drive them nuts," California State University social scientist B. J. Bluth said. "They become sense-deprived."

There are other missions that can be done for far less money than it takes to obtain a sample of Mars for earth. There is a mission afoot called the Tenth Planet Explorer that would send 20 radio beacons in all directions beyond the orbit of Pluto so they would fan out like flower petals in search of a tenth planet in the solar system. If one of the beacons encountered this undiscovered tenth planet, it would be pulled off course by the planet's gravity and radio this event back to earth. There is also a plan to put a probe on the same Explorer that would descend into the icebox atmosphere of Pluto to see what has kept the ninth planet away from the sun in deep freeze for so long. Some people think there shouldn't be a Pluto, that conditions that far from the sun are so inhospitably cold that even a planet like Pluto should never have formed there to begin with. Finally, there are plans to explore the most extreme heat of the solar system as well as its most extreme cold. Scientists want to fly into the atmosphere of the sun with something called the Star Probe which, as it nears the sun, would be cooled off with big reflective mirrors that work the opposite way a greenhouse works. Though a kamikaze mission, the Star Probe in its short lifetime would give us more information about the sun than all the telescopes on earth have given us through time. If the Star Probe flies, it will become the fastest-flying machine in history. So far, the fastest machine ever was Helios, a U.S. spacecraft that came within 27 million miles of the sun in 1976. Even at that distance, the enormous solar gravity whipped the craft around the sun at 153,000 miles an hour or 232 times the speed of sound. Flying that much closer to the sun, the Star Probe will easily break the all-time speed record for machines. There is no limit to what space can promise in the next 20 years.

Of course, the next 20 years belong to the space shuttle, the four spacecraft with wings the size of a DC-9 jetliner that are named Columbia, Challenger, Atlantis and Discovery. After all, they will have the job of carrying the Star Probes and the Tenth Planet Explorers away from earth to get them started on their missions. Think of the space shuttle the next time you drive down a highway. The space shuttle can carry 32 tons of cargo into earth orbit every time it flies and with four of them available one can fly every week. Think of that the next time you drive down a highway and pass a fully-loaded semi-trailer rig. The space shuttle can carry that whole rig into orbit around the earth and take along a couple of small passenger cars on the same trip. Not only can the space shuttle take up 32 tons, it can bring 16 tons back to earth. That means the space shuttle can haul a large satellite into orbit, then go back three years later and bring it home to earth to replace burned-out parts and carry it back to space again. The Large Space Telescope is a classic example of how the space shuttle will be used. Once it's in orbit, the Space Telescope will be visited every few years by the space shuttle, whose astronauts will replace whatever parts of the telescope need replacing to keep it operating. Scientists hope to use the Space Telescope for at least 15 years, which would be a new lifetime record for anything ever flown in space.

Over the years, hundreds of exotic uses have been drummed up for the shuttle. One was to have the shuttle carry away the earth's radioactive garbage and fire it out toward the sun. Another was to haul our most hardened criminals into space and leave them in some orbiting cell for the next 20 years.

The space shuttle has been talked of as an orbiting garbage truck, removing old spacecraft and rocket parts from orbits where they might pose a collision hazard to newer spacecraft. Orbiting junk from old missions does create what engineers call a debris rain. One NASA astrophysicist has said that one out of every 10 future spacecraft is likely to collide with this debris rain and since heavy and costly shielding would be needed to protect spacecraft against collision, the idea of using the shuttle to collect space garbage might not be bad. The shuttle has long been mentioned as the ultimate amusement park sensation to carry journalists, television anchormen, moviemakers, the celebrity rich, politicians and even presidents into space for the joy of the ride.

$1 BILLION BY 2000

Besides trucking satellite cargo back and forth, the shuttle will have many serious uses out to the year 2000. To begin with, the shuttle's cargo bay is big enough to install a compartment called Spacelab where small but specialized manufacturing can be carried

285

on, the kind of manufacturing that would take advantage of the weightless state in earth orbit. Cutting tools could be made harder and stronger in orbit than any ever made on earth, meaning their lifetimes and cutting speeds could be improved by orders of magnitude. Ball and roller bearings that might never wear out, magnetic materials of superconducting skill and electronic components of unheard-of speeds could be made in the shuttle. One study estimated the market for spacemade electronics at $1 billion by the year 2000. Manufacturing in space where heat doesn't rise and where heavier things don't settle to the bottom offers distinct advantages over earthbound manufacturing. For example, pure metal crystals could be grown and pure crystalline glass could be produced by melting and cooling them out of contact with molds or crucibles. The biggest users of the shuttle will be the private corporations and individual countries that will use the shuttle to carry their communications satellites into space, not the "switchboards-in-the-sky" that serve as alternatives to transoceanic telephone cables but multichanneled monsters five times the size of the communications satellites hovering over the earth today.

One of the first uses for a multichanneled monster would be to link up every library in the United States to a central data bank whose contents would be the Library of Congress. Right after that, put into geosynchronous orbit (meaning it hovers over one spot because it's moving at the same speed as the earth) a large satellite that has two powerful radio antennas sweeping the United States in north-south and east-west directions so they cover the whole country. The sole purpose of these two antennas is to track the tiny radio transmitters that customers have placed secretly in their packages, their trucks, their ships and even on themselves to keep a constant record of their movements. The first customer for this location service might be the Pentagon, which would want to know the whereabouts of its atomic arsenal as it's being moved. Next would be nuclear fuel users who'd want to make sure terrorists didn't steal their fuel. Gold and diamond shipments could be tracked this way. So could payrolls, large tankloads of gasoline, rare paintings, literally anything being shipped that might be the target of thieves. The same multichanneled monster could be used as a national search-and-rescue service. Every pleasure boat, every small aircraft in the country would have its own radio beacon that would constantly be monitored by Big Brother in the Sky.

LIVING IN SPACE

Skylab and Salyut have proven that people can tolerate long stays in space. There was some concern that long voyages in weightlessness would leach out too much calcium from the bones but the record-breaking stays of the Soviet cosmonauts in Salyut showed that the calcium loss stops at the end of three months. Plans are already being drawn up for the first space station, which has been called Spacehab by its NASA creators. Spacehab would be roomy enough for astronauts to grow some of their own vegetables, which would have to grow in revolving drums that would have centrifugal force to imitate gravity so that the roots of the plants would know which way to go. The way it's being designed, Spacehab will have eight inflatable, connectable pods where as many as 100 people will live and work. Ten space shuttle trips would be needed to construct Spacehab. Crew members would sleep in bags fixed to the walls, which would be built to be puncture-resistant. People will move about using anchors to do stationary tasks and wearing shoes with suction cup soles to avoid floating off the floor. Spacehab's central area will have toilets, a shower, a laundry, first-aid cabinets and vending machines. At one end will be the world's first electronic library of talking books.

We think the space shuttle will trigger a worldwide

communications revolution, largely because the shuttle can put the kinds of large, high-powered satellites into geosynchronous orbit (22,400 mile altitude) that permit the use of small, low-powered transmitters and receivers on the ground to communicate through space. By 1990, all the multinational corporations and all the major countries of the world outside the Soviet bloc will have used the shuttle to put their communications satellites into space. China will have its own satellite network, Indonesia will have a network, all the Islamic countries from Morocco in the west to Pakistan in the east will have a network. The biggest beneficiary of all these networks will be the telephone customer. We believe the shuttle will make communications through space so commonplace that a telephone call from the United States to Japan or to Western Europe will cost 50 cents by 1990 and 25 cents by the year 2000. What's more, you'll be able to receive the call or place it through a battery-powered wristwatch radio just the way Dick Tracy used to do it.

As important as the shuttle will be to space communications, it will be just as important to the surveillance of our planet from the vantage point of space. Peaceful surveillance as well as military surveillance. From where but space will we be able to spot forest fires just as they flare up? Or crop disease? Insect infestations? Icecap, sea ice and glacier movement? Wildlife activity? The most important surveys the shuttle will make will be military. Everybody has heard the stories that cameras can read the license plates of cars from space. As Henry Kissinger has said so often, things that are facts "have the added advantage of being true." The truth is that cameras in space can tell whether a person on the ground is a man or a woman. They can even tell if that man or woman is wearing a wristwatch. The time is coming when space cameras will be able to read a wristwatch and tell what time it is.

PARATROOPER
FLUNKOUTS

At no time did space pho-
tography prove itself more useful than when the Soviet
Union invaded Afghanistan in 1980. American satellite
cameras not only witnessed the invasion, they documented
it in such detail that the Central Intelligence Agency was
able to count the number of Russian tanks, trucks and even
troops who moved into Afghanistan. From its space photographs, the CIA was able to tell that the Soviets had moved
their regular Russian troops into Afghanistan and kept their
Turkistan troops in place along their borders with Turkey
and Iran. This told the CIA that the Soviet Union feared
such a worldwide reaction from its invasion of Afghanistan
that it was worrying about trouble along its southern borders.
The space photographs of the Soviet invasion of Afghanistan
were so good that they told American intelligence experts
that many of the invading troops were soldiers who had
flunked out of paratrooper school. It was the Russians' way of
telling the troopers to "shape up or ship out."

The Pentagon is banking its future on the space shuttle. It is building its own spaceport for the shuttle to take off
and land at California's Vandenberg Air Force Base. It will
operate a new military space center at Peterson Air Force
Base in Colorado Springs and will have its own version of
the Mission Control Center in Houston. The shuttle will
carry no fewer than 11 Pentagon payloads into space in the
next four years, starting in 1983 with a supersecret spy
satellite so big it would cost $150 million to put it into
space on a conventional rocket if one could be built to carry
it. This surveillance satellite is so big that the shuttle's
hydrogen engines will have to be throttled up to 109
percent of their normal operating capacity to lift it into
orbit.

STRUNG OUT

Nothing illustrates the usefulness of the shuttle like the six Navstar satellites the shuttle will carry into orbit for the navy in 1985, 1986 and 1987. To be put into a 12,000-mile-high orbit where they will join 12 other identical satellites, the Navstars will be strung out like beads around the earth to provide the quickest and most precise navigation service ever devised. The Navstar network will be so accurate that a ship, plane or even a foot soldier will be able to get a fix from Navstar in less than 15 seconds on where they are to less than 15 feet in any direction. Navstar will tell a jet fighter moving at 1,500 miles an hour its approach speed to a target within one-fifth of a mile an hour. Navstar will tell an aircraft moving blindly toward a refueling tanker in the dark down to one ten-millionth of a second when it can expect to encounter the tanker.

Before the turn of the century, we think the shuttle will be testing weapons in space such as laser weapons and pulsed-beam weapons, like those we saw in *Star Wars*. Pulsed-beam weapons have been tested in the laboratory for the last 10 years, can fire a beam of particles with the speed of light through clouds, rain or fog and are the ultimate weapon. Lasers have already been used by the air force to shoot down drone aircraft. They'll be tested in space against other satellites and they'll be positioned in space as a defense against missile attack, striking the missiles with a beam of high-powered light that burns right through the missiles while they're still on their upward flight away from earth. Next year, the shuttle will truck an experimental laser into orbit that will help guide the shuttle pilots to enemy satellites to cut their radio antennas or even pull them into the shuttle's cargo bay to sabotage them or return them to earth for inspection. The shuttle is such a sophisticated machine it can fly itself home to earth, which is something the air force's F-16 can already do. If an F-16 pilot is hurt in aerial combat, the plane's computer could take over and fly him home to safety. If the computer notices that the pilot hasn't touched the controls for a certain length of time, it would assume he's hurt and take over control of the plane.

Wars will be fought in space the way the air war was fought in the early years of World War I. Nobody shot the other side's warriors down. They limited themselves to aerial reconnaissance, photography and occasional bombing. That's the way space warriors will do it, limiting themselves to stealing their opponents satellites or silencing their radios. To begin with, space war will be a gentleman's war, the way airplane pilots waved at each other as they flew by in the early days of World War I.

SMART PHOENIX

The space technology of the next 20 years will leave a firm imprint on the weapons of war. In fact, space technology has already left its mark on warfare. Take the Phoenix, the air-to-air missile carried by the F-14, the F-15 and the F-16. The Phoenix is a better airborne weapon than the laser guns we saw in *Star Wars*. A pilot can fire the Phoenix at an unseen target 30 miles away. The Phoenix will first home in on the heat exhaust of the target's jet engine, then when it gets half a mile from the target will check it out optically and then will use its Doppler radar to blow itself up if it "thinks" it's not going to hit the target amidships. The Phoenix does more than think. It can track 12 different airborne targets at once, figure out if they're friend or foe and then fire 12 independent missiles if it decides they're foe. Not even the weapons in *Star Wars* were that smart.

The space technology of the next 20 years will make obsolete the most sophisticated weaponry we can think of today, like AWACS, the airborne radar and computer that can track 240 separate airplanes and ground targets at once. There will be satellites doing all that work 10 years from now. Besides pinpointing the whereabouts of planes in the air and tanks on the ground, the spaceborne AWACS will be able to control air traffic around half a dozen major airports at once. The air traffic controllers strike of 1981 will become but a dim memory. There won't be any need for air traffic controllers in the year 2000. It will all be done by machines.

The most exotic new weapon of the next 20 years will be the Stealth bomber, whose skin is invisible to radar because it absorbs the radar signal instead of letting it echo back to the transmitter. There will be more than Stealth bombers. There will be Stealth lighter-than-air vehicles that will be able to carry as many as 3,000 troops into combat behind enemy lines at night. The only better weapon than Stealth is a submarine but even the submarines may be made obsolete in the next 20 years. On the drawing boards is a laser that casts a blue-green light and penetrates the ocean. Not even submarines will be safe in the wars of the future.

EPILOGUE: TELESCOPING THE FUTURE

▼▼▼▼▼▼▼

*"Today's extravagance
becomes tomorrow's necessity."*

—Gloria Wasserman,
American educator

▲▲▲▲▲▲▲

*T*he majority of us will be better off in the year 2000 than we are today. We'll feel better, we'll look better and we'll live longer. Of course, there will be change but it won't be the kind of change that worsens our lot in life. There will be hardship but most of it will be the kind of hardship we can endure and overcome.

You can expect an eight percent per year inflation rate out to the year 2000, which is an acceptable rate of inflation. That means that interest rates in the world will stabilize at 11 percent, which is a livable rate of interest for people who want to own cars, appliances, and their own homes. There will be fewer billionaires but that will be the result of tax reform cuts, which after all are long overdue in the United States. There will also be fewer Americans living in poverty as jobs and welfare reforms are made through the years ahead. Do you want to be rich? The top entertainer's or professional athlete's already high salary will be tripled by cable television. You will retire later as you live longer. Taxes will go down as stock prices go up and as America reindustrializes robot factories to raise productivity. The energy crisis will be a crisis of the past when we begin to generate nuclear electricity with fusion power for the first time.

Cars will cost twice what they do today but they will be half their present weight and get twice the gasoline mileage. Automobile lifetimes will double in the next 20 years, in part because people will once more put a value on durability. Cars will be safer because they'll all be smaller.

In the United States, the future looks south. The only thing that will restrict mass migrations to the Sun Belt is a water shortage. Look for much of the world to suffer water shortages but look for much of the world to solve its water shortages. Look for the countries of the Middle East to build nuclear desalting plants and look for the United States to tow glaciers out of the Arctic to the East and West coasts to tap them for their water.

Women will be much better off by the year 2000. Almost 60 percent of all the adult women in the United States will be in the work force by the year 2000, holding down jobs held only by men in the fifties and sixties. More women will fulfill themselves professionally, socially and sexually in the years ahead. There will be a morning-after birth control pill for women. Fewer elderly women will live alone, choosing if they are widows to move in with single elderly men. Liberal attitudes about sex are here to stay. In 1989, the Equal Rights Amendment finally will be ratified. By 1990, American women will have achieved the same kind of sexual parity won long ago by the women of Scandinavia, where one-fourth of the members of the Finnish Parliament are women.

There will be medicines that improve and restore memory and stave off senility. There will be pills that cure fear of heights, fear of elevators, and fear of flying. Men will take drugs to grow hair, women will take drugs to keep their hair from turning gray. There will be a nutlike snack to keep teeth white, strong and free of cavities. There will be a hormone for weight control, another for growth control and a third for memory control. There will be a nonaddictive painkiller more powerful than morphine. There will be medicines that cure addictions to drugs and alcohol.

Ahead of us lie vaccines to prevent tuberculosis and immunize people against their own tumors, the kinds of cancer like breast cancer that appear to be caused by viruses and seem to run in families. The list of diseases that will be cured by gene splicing is staggering. Sickle-cell anemia and Tay-Sachs disease may be racial ailments of the past. People with genetic disease will undergo gene therapy, where the abnormal gene is removed and a healthy gene spliced in to take its place. There will be new drugs to dissolve blood clots and gallstones, new drugs to prevent the buildup of stomach acids that trigger ulcers and of cholesterol and glycerides that cause hardening of the arteries. There will be an artificial liver, an artificial spleen, and an artificial pancreas. There will be artificial blood that can be given to people with any blood type and that carries none of the risk of infection that human blood can.

We will soon enter a checkless and cashless society. Funds will be transferred by voiceprint and almost nobody will shop in person. Two-way home television will let you dial a store, check prices on your screen and order by credit card. You will still need cash but instead of carrying it around you'll stop at your neighborhood automated teller and withdraw it when you need it. Don't be frightened by depression talk. The United States is depression-proof, partly because of the ongoing computer revolution that exercises such tight controls on money supply. The variable interest rates will catch on. Instead of rising with inflation, interest rates will be adjusted every few years based on the consumer price index. For those with long-term money to spare, your best return will still be in housing and real estate.

If you're a Catholic, you can expect your church to slowly change its position on birth control and divorce. If you're Methodist, Lutheran or Presbyterian, you can expect more women ministers in pulpits on Sunday. And if you're a Reform Jew, you can expect more women rabbis in the temple on the Sabbath. Expect to find fewer members of cults and a weaker Moral Majority.

We can anticipate big things from the Large Space Telescope after it's put into orbit in 1985. The Space Telescope will tell us the precise age of the universe, whether black holes exist and what quasars are all about. The Space Telescope should also tell us if the cosmos will go on expanding forever or if it will explode again in another Big Bang. This will be a heavy cosmological answer to a heavy cosmological question and would alter religious thought for centuries to come.

The strongest, most stable country in the world will continue to be the United States. Second in turn will be Australia and Canada, mostly because they're so rich in raw resources. China will be more of a world power for the same reason Japanese influence will wane. China has its own coal, oil, and minerals. Japan has almost none of its own. The Soviet Union will have domestic trouble in the years ahead. In 1985 or 1986, the Russian race will be a minority in their own country and the Soviet Union will face the instability that comes with minority rule. Iran faces political chaos for years to come. By 1990, there may not even be enough oil wells in Iran to sustain the country. Libya faces serious trouble. Look for Egypt to occupy Libya without opposition from the Soviet Union or Libya's friends in Syria.

The biggest single change to expect in the next 20 years is the reunification of Germany. As bad as that might sound to some people, the merging of East and West Germany bodes well for the future. A reunited Germany means a neutral zone free of nuclear weapons between Western Europe and Eastern Europe, a condition that all of Europe has desired for years. It also takes East Germany out of the Soviet camp and puts more pressure on the Soviets to seek peaceful solutions to the Polish question. All this can only serve to ease the European tensions between the superpowers.

As troublesome as it is, the Middle East will make it through to the end of the century without seriously harming the rest of the world. The turning point for peace will come when Israel releases the West Bank and allows the Palestinians to establish a separate state. Expect Israel and Jordan to agree on the joint construction of a canal from the

Mediterranean to the Dead Sea, a technological achievement that will bring the two countries so close together that a new cooperative link will form between Israel and the Arab world. As the Middle East begins to prosper again at the end of the century, so will most of the rest of the world.

We expect wars to break out in the last part of the century but they will be border skirmishes compared with what the world has lived through in the first half of this century. There will be no nuclear wars between the super-powers. The years ahead may be difficult, but on the whole they are years of hope and promise.

INDEX

Abortion issue, 29, 173
Adweek magazine, 225
Africa, instability of, 121–126, 140, 143, 148–149
Aggression, drug treatment for, 56
Alcoholism, 23, 42
Alexander, Tom, 167
All-saver certificates, 194, 196–197
Angina pectoris, 65
Antiaging revolution, 69–71
Appendectomy, 67
Argentina, 107, 109, 110, 135, 140, 146–147
Arteries, drug treatment for, 64
Arthritis, 49, 62
Artificial body parts, 47, 67–69, 240, 263
Asner, Ed, 224
Asteroid exploration, 280–281
Athletes, professionals, 15, 264, 295
Australia, 111, 115, 127–128, 142–143, 144–146
Automation (*see* Robots, robotics)
Automobiles, automobile industry, 8, 13, 14, 31, 33, 82, 100, 235–236, 245–246, 258, 295–296
  new kinds of, 14, 31, 100, 101

Babbage, Charles, 211
Bacterial production, 62
Battery technicians, 271
Beta blocker, 65
Biomass energy source, 89–90
Bionic technicians, 263
Birth control, 17, 29, 40, 171
Birth rates, 26, 40–41
Blacks, 43, 44

Blindness, treatment of, 49–50, 64
Blood, artificial, 68
Blood clot treatment, 48, 64
Blood pressure treatment, 64
Bluth, B. J., 283
Bolivia, 135
Bond market, 207
Bradlee, Benjamin Crowinshield, 226
Brain research, 47, 52–60, 61
Brazil, 7, 91, 135, 140, 146–147
Breast cancer treatment, 60–61, 66, 240–241
Buddhism, 169, 181, 182–183
Business, 34, 35, 37
  forecasting by, 6, 7
  new technology and, 15, 213–216
Bypass surgery, 65–66

Cable News Network, 224
Cable television, 15, 29, 30–32, 38, 191, 217–224, 264, 295
  disadvantages of, 219–221, 226
  two-way, 29, 30, 32, 189, 217–219, 221, 228, 297
CAD, 242
Calcium blocker, 64
Canada, 94, 111, 124
Cancer vaccine, 60, 64
Capek, Karel, 231, 233, 236, 237
Carter, Jimmy, 22, 91
Cash, use of, 32, 189, 192, 297
Castro, Fidel, 140, 143, 151–153
Catholic Church, 10, 171–177, 180–181, 297
  clergy of, 14, 157–158, 173–177
Cavities, prevention of, 50
CDCA treatment, 65

301

Center for Futures Research of the University of California, 6
Central nervous system, repair of, 57–60
Cetron, Marvin J., 6
Chase Econometrics, 6
Childhood disease, elimination of, 69
Children, 43
  parents and, 9, 16, 24, 25
  sexual freedom of, 41–42
China, 41, 112, 114–115, 129–130, 131, 140, 182–183, 288
Churchill, Winston, 5, 137
Cigarettes, 8, 69
Cimetidine, 65–66
Cities, aging of, 35, 36–37
Civil rights, 22, 28
Clark, John G., Jr., 165, 166
Clough, Arthur Hugh, 185
Coal, 80, 81, 84, 92–93, 101, 124–125, 127, 128, 129, 130, 249
COMECON countries, 141
Commodity markets, 202–203
Common Market, 12, 120, 133
Computers, 211–212
  in education, 228
  in health care, 229
  news media and, 226–227
  programmers, 248, 259–260
  translating, 213, 214–215
  voice recognition and, 191, 215–216
  work-at-home and, 218–219
Confucianism, 15, 181–183
Confucius, 19
Congressional elections, 28–29
Conservatism, 7, 16, 22–24
  duration of, 23, 27–28
Consumerism, 8, 114, 117, 131
Council on Environmental Quality, 92
Crick, Francis, 61
Crime, 28, 36, 37, 41, 42–43, 44, 56, 128
  white-collar, 44, 229–230
Cuba, 140, 143, 151–153
Cuelho, Tony, 166
Cults, 165–166
Curran, Charles, 166, 171, 175–176, 177–178, 179
Cyert, Richard M., 228
Czechoslovakia, 159

Data Resources, Inc., 6
Deafness, treatment for, 49

Delphi poll, 204–207
Depression, treatment for, 52, 55
Desalinization, 121
Deuterium, 98–99
DeVries, William, 68–69
Diabetes, 48, 62, 67–68
Divorce, 7, 9, 16, 24, 38–39, 172–173, 219
DNA research, 61, 70
Dopamine, 54–56
Doty, Paul, 61
Down's syndrome, 63
Draft, military, 44
Drug abuse and addiction, 23, 52–55
Drunken driving, 9, 42
Dwarfism, 50–51, 62
Dynorphin, 53–54

Eastern Europe, instability of, 130–131, 157–160
Economic stability, 109
  capital investment and, 124, 126–127, 130
  consumerism and, 114, 117, 131
  energy sources and, 109, 110, 112, 113, 114, 116–119, 120, 121, 122, 123, 126, 127–128, 129, 130, 132, 133, 134
  export-import ratios and, 109, 120, 121, 124, 128, 132
  food resources and, 110, 114, 115, 122, 128, 129, 130, 134
  income gap and, 107, 117, 125, 133
  industrialization and, 111, 114, 118, 124, 126, 128–129, 132, 135
  inflation rate and, 109–110, 118, 120, 132, 133, 135
  labor force and, 111, 117, 122, 125, 127, 128–129, 131–132, 133, 134
  natural resources and, 109, 110–111, 112, 120, 121, 122, 123, 124–125, 126, 127–128, 129, 130, 134
  unemployment rate and, 107–108, 118, 123, 125, 129
Economist magazine, 262
Education, 8–9, 228, 250–251
Egypt, 119, 140
Eisenhower, Dwight D., 77
Electric power industry, 80, 81, 96, 100, 139

Electronic funds transfer, 189–192
Electronic newspapers (England), 227
Energy, 16, 24, 33, 139
    prices of, 13, 14, 31, 80, 82, 83–85,
        86–87, 89, 90, 91, 93, 95, 98,
        100
    renewable forms of, 33, 89–90
    technician, 261, 270
    (See also Economic stability; specif-
        ic forms of energy sources)
Energy Crisis, 79–101, 295
    causes of, 79–83
    fuels crisis vs., 79
    inflation caused by, 83
    Middle East crises and, 85–88
    remedies sought for, 83, 89–101
Enkephalin, 53–54
Entertainers, 15, 264, 295
Environmentalists, 79, 81, 262
Environmental Protection Agency, 92
Equal Rights Amendment, 22, 28, 44
Ethnic groups, 36, 37, 38, 43, 44
European Space Agency, 279
Evelyn, John, 161

Family patterns, 24, 25, 26, 31–32,
    38–41, 71
Fast breeder reactor, 97–98
Ferris, Charles D., 220
Fink, Arnold, 166, 178, 179, 180
Finland, 44
Food industry, 271
Foot-and-mouth disease, 64
Forecasting:
    accuracy of, 7–8
    basic concepts in, 6
    futurism vs., 12
    profession of, 4–13
    value of, 13–15
Forecasting International, 6–12
Foreign aid, 127, 135
Fourth World, 111, 112, 127
    as nations in jeopardy, 112, 121–
        122, 135
France, 100, 106, 112, 113, 119, 132, 233
Freeman, S. David, 92
Freud, Sigmund, 56
Funakubo, Hiroyasu, 240
Futures Group, 6, 71–72

Galileo space mission, 275–277, 278,
    279
Gallstone treatment, 64, 65

Gandhi, Indira, 11, 126
Gasohol, 90–91
Gasoline, 12, 13, 80, 82, 84, 89,
    90–91, 100, 101, 295
Gene splicing, 50–51, 62–64, 262
Genetic engineering, 50–51, 61–64,
    204, 243, 249, 262–263
Geothermal energy, 89–90
Gerbner, George, 221
Germany, 93, 106, 131–132, 233, 239
    reunification of, 112–113, 131, 140,
        154, 298
Gide, André, 273
Giscard d'Estaing, Valéry, 132
Glaciers, uses of, 34
Gold, 132, 188, 207, 249
Gray Panthers, 27–28, 29
Great Britain, 112, 124, 132–133, 227
Great European War, possibilities for,
    157–160
Greek and Russian Orthodox church-
    es, 177, 178, 180–181

Hair, drug treatment of, 50
Halley's Comet, 279–280
Hauling of commodities, 101
Hauser, Gustave, 220
Hazardous wastes, 96–98, 99, 261–
    262
Health care (see Medicine and health
    care)
Heart, artificial, 68–69
Heart attack treatment, 64–65
Heart surgery, 47, 65
Hemophilia, 63
Hepatitis, 64
HGH treatment, 50–51
Highways, electrified, 100
Hinduism, 169, 183
Hitti, Philip K., 166, 169
Holography, 228, 271
Homosexuality, 41, 43
    among clergy, 14, 174, 179
Housing, 13, 28, 29, 31–32, 199–201
Housing rehabilitation technicians,
    270–271
Hubbard, Frank McKinney, 199
Hudson Institute, 6
Huntington's disease, 62
Hydrocarbons, 84
Hypertension treatment, 70
Hysterectomies, 66

Income distribution, 15, 24, 31, 32–33, 107, 117, 125, 133, 221, 295
India, 7, 11, 112, 126–127, 140
Indochina, 112
Indonesia, 107, 140
Industry:
 geographical shifts in, 239, 257, 265, 270
 humans vs. robots in, 243–247
 robots in, 15, 33, 37–38, 49, 129, 205, 233–249, 295
 (See also Labor force; Unions)
Infectious hepatitis vaccine, 60
Inflation, 14, 27, 31, 35, 83, 109–110, 118, 120, 132, 133, 135, 192–193, 195, 198–199, 200, 207, 295
Insulation, building, 82–83
Insurance "as a hedge," 208
Interest rates, 31, 193, 194, 199, 203, 295
Interferon, 63–64
International tensions, 7, 11, 85–88, 298–299
 national vital signs and, 106–136
 war risk and, 139–160
Investments, 193–207
Iran, 5, 7, 11, 85, 87, 107–109, 110, 111, 118, 119, 141, 156–157, 164
IRA plans, 197–198
Iraq, 7, 11, 85, 86, 87, 113
Ireland, 164
Islam, 164, 168–170
Israel, 7, 11, 12, 34, 85, 86, 87, 109, 113, 116, 119, 120–121, 140, 298–299
Italy, 133

Jamaica, 111, 143, 151–152
Japan, 68, 82, 93, 106, 112, 128–129, 140, 182–183, 279
 labor force and robotics in, 35–36, 38, 233, 239–241
John Paul II, Pope, 10, 157, 175
Johnson, Lyndon, 21
Jordan, 34, 298–299
Judaism, 164, 165, 177, 178–180

Kahn, Herman, 6, 50
Kappel Commission on Postal Reorganization, 222
Kenya, 7

Keogh plans, 197–198
Keynes, John Maynard, 198
Khalid, king of Saudi Arabia, 85
Khomeini, Ayatollah, 118
King, Martin Luther, 22
Kirkland, Lane, 264, 265
Kissinger, Henry, 288
Korea, 140
Kuwait, 11, 86, 87, 88

Labor force, 9, 15–16, 35–36, 38, 111, 117, 122, 125, 127, 128–129, 131–132, 133, 134, 264
 changes due in, 255–271
 computers and, 189, 213–214, 215–216, 218, 221, 266, 271
 employment opportunities for, 243–248, 258–263, 266–267, 270–271
 retraining for, 246–247, 267–268, 269
 robotics and, 15, 33, 37–38, 49, 129, 205, 233–249, 258–259
 unemployment and, 36, 43, 107–108, 118, 123, 125, 129, 193, 246–247, 257, 268–269
Large Space Telescope, 15, 277–278, 285
Laser technology, 17, 49, 99, 260, 290, 292
Latin America, instability of, 134–135, 140, 146–147
Law, 8, 24, 42–43, 44
L-dopa, 55–56
Libya, 119, 140
Life span, 16, 17, 27, 47, 69–71, 129
 possible consequences in extension of, 71–75
Lincoln, Abraham, 103
Lovelace, Countess Ada, 211
Lumpectomies, 66
Luria, Daniel, 267

McCarthy, Eugene G., 66
Magnetic Fusion Engineering Act, 99
Magnetohydrodynamic energy source, 89–90
Malaria, 64
Mao Tse-tung, 130, 182
Marriage, 16, 39, 40, 71
Martian space mission, 282–283
Marx, Karl, 188, 257

Mass transit, 37
Mastectomies, 66
Maugham, William Somerset, 187
Mead, Margaret, 39
Medical insurance, 8, 25
Medicine and health care, 8, 14, 17,
    27, 47–75, 208, 229–230, 263,
    296–297
Memory improvement, 48, 51–52
Menopause, 66
Mental retardation, treatment of, 51
Mexico, 87, 134, 140, 143, 152–153
Microprocessor market, 242, 259–260
Middle class, 25, 109, 126
Middle East, 112
    instability of, 7, 11–12, 85, 116–
        121, 140, 149–150, 156–157,
        298–299
Military, 5–6, 15, 43–44
    international tensions and, 139–160
    national stability and, 108, 117,
        120, 125–126, 128
    space projects and, 286, 289, 290–292
Money, 13, 30–31, 187–192, 297
Mood modifying drugs, 48, 50, 52, 55,
    56
Moral Majority, 29, 164, 166
Mormon church, 166–168, 177
Mugabe, Robert, 123–124

Naisbitt, John, 223
Naloxone, 53
NAPTO (North Atlantic and Pacific
    Treaty Organization), 139, 141–
    142
National Academy of Sciences, 5
National Labor Relations Board, 265
National Library of Medicine, 229
National Sisters Vocation Conference,
    176
National Space Development Agency
    (Japan), 279
National stability, 5, 7, 11, 85, 87,
    106–136, 298
    corruption and, 108
    cultural conflict and, 110, 113, 114,
        116–121, 122, 123, 125, 126,
        131–132, 133, 134, 135
    expectations and, 108, 114, 123–
        124, 130
    geographic position and, 111, 112,
        116, 120, 126, 128

loyalty vs. strength and, 108, 119,
    125–126
middle class and, 109, 126
military and, 108, 117, 120, 125–
    126, 128
population levels and, 110, 115,
    120, 122, 126, 127, 129, 130,
    134, 155
ranking of countries in, 111–112,
    119, 131, 135–136
religion and, 108–109, 110, 111,
    113, 116, 118, 120, 127
technological levels and, 111, 112,
    113, 114–115, 121, 122, 124–
    125, 128
terrorism and, 119, 133, 143, 150,
    152–153
twenty-year forecast on, 135–136
urban growth and, 110, 123, 126,
    135
NATO (North Atlantic Treaty Organi-
    zation), 106, 112, 139–140, 141,
    157, 159–160
Natural gas, 80, 84, 94–95, 113, 127,
    129, 130, 133, 134
Natural Gas Policy Act, 94–95
Navstar space program, 290
Network television, 222–224
Newspapers, 226–227
Newsweek magazine, 219, 220
New York City, 35, 36–37
New Yorker magazine, 236
Next magazine, 204, 224
Nigeria, 122–123, 148
Nuclear energy, 16, 24, 33, 79, 81, 89,
    95–99, 113, 114, 121, 248–249,
    266–267, 295
    fusion vs. fission, 98–99
    hazards of, 95, 96, 97
Nuclear free zone, 153–155
Nuclear Regulatory Commission, 96
Nuclear weapons, risk of war and,
    140, 143, 145–148, 153–155, 160

OAS (Organization of American
    States), 147
Oil, 93–94, 101, 139
    Arabs and, 7, 11–12, 13–14, 82, 84,
        85–87, 88, 89, 112, 113, 116–
        119
    exploration costs and, 87–88, 95
    1973 price rise of, 85–87

Oil (*cont.*):
  political aspects of, 85–87
  profligate use of, 81–82, 92–93
  U.S. production of, 82, 84, 85,
      87–88, 94, 95
  world supply of, 84–85, 88, 94, 113,
      114, 122, 127, 129, 130, 133, 134
O'Leary, John, 86
Operating engineers, 270
Orwell, George, 50

Painkillers, nonaddictive, 48, 53–54
Palestinian issue, 121
Paralysis, treatment for, 57–60
Parkinson's disease, 54–55
Pascal, Blaise, 211
PATCO vs. AWACS, 266
Paternity leave, 25
Pharmaceuticals, 40, 48–57, 60–61,
    62, 64–65, 71
Phobias, drug treatment of, 49–50,
    56–57
Phoenix missile, 291
"Pleasure pill," 50
Plowshare program, 81
Plutonium, 97–98
Pneumonia vaccine, 60
Poland, 7, 9–10, 112, 131, 157–159
Political stability, 109
  administrative competence and,
      109, 122–123, 130, 131, 133,
      134, 135
  central authority and, 109, 118,
      122, 124, 125, 127, 134, 135
  dissidents and, 108, 118, 119, 120,
      125, 126
  transfer of power and, 109, 114,
      118, 120, 122, 131
Politics, 16, 21, 22–23, 24, 27–29,
    265, 296
Pollution, 33, 81, 92, 129
Population, 16, 26–27, 40–41, 139
  geographical shifts and, 13, 34,
      36–37
  national stability and, 110, 115, 120,
      122, 126, 127, 129, 130, 134
Postal service, 222
Prisons, 9, 43
Productivity, 233–239, 295
Project Forecast, 6
Protestant churches, 164, 166, 177, 181
PUMA robot, 242–243

Qaddafi, Mu'ammar al-, 119
Qube, 217, 219, 220, 224

Radio, 224–226
Radioactive waste, 96–98, 99
Railroad, electrified, 100
Raisman, Geoffrey, 57–60
Reagan, Ronald, 14, 22, 27–28, 97, 98,
    156, 193–197, 207–208, 265–266,
    279
Recessions, 86, 193, 194, 269
Recreation industry, 15, 30, 32, 222–
    224, 264, 271
Religion, 14–15, 40, 41, 163–183, 297
  ecumenical movement in, 180–181
  national stability and, 108–109,
      110, 111, 113, 116, 118, 120,
      127
  nontheistic, 181–183
Retirement, 16, 33, 35–36, 197–198,
    295
Ringwood, Ted, 96
Robots, robotics, 15, 33, 37–38, 49,
    129, 205, 233–251, 295
  advantages of, 236–243
  forecasts about, 248–251
  hands and arms of, 234–235, 238,
      240–241
  human dislocations and, 243–247
  as major new industry, 243–244
  range of activities by, 234–236,
      248–251
  "smart" and "dumb," 242–245
Rousseau, Jean-Jacques, 198

Safer, Morley, 225
Samuelson, Paul A., 187–188
Sandburg, Carl, 253
Saudi Arabia, 34, 85–87, 88, 107, 117
    –118, 140, 149–150
Savings, 193, 194–198
Scandinavia, 25, 115, 135
Schizophrenia, treatment of, 52,
    55–56
Schlesinger, James R., 96
Schmidt, Helmut, 112
Schoeenher, Richard, 166, 174
Scopolamine, 49
Scott, David, 166, 175, 178, 179
Senility, treatment of, 52, 55
Senior citizens, 7, 16, 26–28, 29,
    35–36, 37, 40, 221–222, 263, 271

Seventies, conservative trend in, 22
Sexual mores, 7, 8, 16–17, 21–22, 23, 38–42, 296
Sickle-cell anemia, 62
Sixties, change in, 21–22
Skin patch medical treatment, 49
Snyder, Solomon, 52–53
Social change, 16, 296
  extended life spans and, 70–75
  Hegelian swings in, 22, 23
  in sixties and seventies (summary), 21–23
  path in U.S. of, 8, 44
  in Sweden, 8–9, 16, 23–26, 33
Social Security program, 8, 33
Solar Electric Research Institute, 90
Solar energy, 33, 89–90
South Africa, Republic of, 122, 124–125, 140, 143, 148–149
Soviet Union, 91, 112, 113, 114, 127, 130–131, 135, 279, 280, 287, 289
  possible belligerent moves of, 140–143, 144–146, 150, 154, 157–160
  U.S. and, 139, 142, 154–155, 157–160
Space exploration and projects, 22, 114, 250, 275–292, 297–298
  medical advances and, 48–49
  military and, 286, 289, 290–292
  multichannel space satellites and, 286–287
  national interests and, 279–280
  prospecting missions in, 281
  Spacehab and, 287
  space shuttle and, 284–286, 287–288, 290
  surveillance flights and, 286–287, 288
Spain, 120, 133–134
Spinal cord, treatment of, 57–60
Stanford Research Institute, 6
Star Probe, 284
Star Wars, 290, 291
Stock market, 33, 37, 202–207, 295
Students, 21, 22, 23, 25, 30, 37
Sun Belt, 13, 34, 35, 247, 265, 296
Surgical techniques, 49, 67
Surrogate mothers, 17, 39
Sweden, 7, 107, 135, 233
  as bellwether nation, 8–9, 16, 23–26, 33, 39, 42, 43, 50

Synthetic fuels, 90, 93, 261
Synthetic materials, 262, 267
Syria, 87, 119

Taoism, 169, 182, 183
Taxes, 32–33, 193–194, 195, 196–197, 198–199, 201, 206, 207, 295
Tay-Sachs disease, 62
Telecommunications industry, 204, 211–230, 243, 286, 288
Telephones, 215–217, 288
Tenth Planet Explorer, 283–284
Thatcher, Margaret H., 132
Third World, 111, 122–126, 127, 154
Three Mile Island, 96, 262
Tidal energy, 89–90
Titan space mission, 281–282
Tonsillectomy, 67
Transplants, in brain and spinal cord, 59–60
Trial marriages, 40
Tuberculosis vaccine, 60
Turing, A. M., 209
Turkey, 7, 10–11, 141–142
Turner, Ted, 224

Udall, Morris K., 97
Ulcer, treatment of, 64, 65–66
Underwater industries, 249
Unions, 15, 27, 33, 36–37, 247, 264–266
United States, 106, 117, 124, 127, 135, 140, 164, 176–177, 233, 238–239, 241–242
  continued stability of, 111, 155–156, 297, 298
  possible conflicts faced by, 139, 142–153, 156–160
  space exploration by, 275–282, 285, 287, 289, 291–292
Uranium, 84, 95, 97–98, 125, 127, 128, 130

Vaccines, new, 60–61, 63–64
Valery, Paul, 1
Vasopressin, 51–52
Venezuela, 87, 94
Vietnam, 112, 140
Vietnam war, 21, 22
Volunteer army, 43–44
Von Karman, Theodore, 5

War gaming, 142–143
Wars, 15, 85, 86, 87, 91, 105, 116, 291, 299
  risk of, 139–160
Warsaw Pact countries, 131, 141
Washington Post, 226, 227
Wasserman, Gloria, 293
Watergate, 22
Water shortages, 33–34, 121, 296
Watson, James, 61
Watt, James, 101
Weight control, 51
Welfare programs and policies, 9, 15, 16, 25–26, 27, 29, 40
Western Europe, instability of, 131–134, 140, 154, 159–160
Wharton School, 6

Wind energy, 89–90
Women:
  feminist movement and, 8, 16, 21–22, 28, 38–41, 44
  medical procedures and, 60–61, 66
  in religion, 14–15, 21, 175–178
  working, 8, 23, 38, 39–40, 248, 265, 296
World Trade Center, 83

Yatow, Rosalyn S., 45
Yom Kippur War, 87, 120
Yugoslavia, 7, 141

Zimbabwe, 122, 123–124, 140, 148
Zimmer, Linda, 191